CASTRO'S SECRETS

THE CIA AND CUBA'S INTELLIGENCE MACHINE

BRIAN LATELL

palgrave
macmillan

CASTRO'S SECRETS
Copyright © Brian Latell, 2012.
All rights reserved.

First published in 2012 by PALGRAVE MACMILLAN® in the United States—a
division of St. Martin's Press LLC, 175 Fifth Avenue, New York, NY 10010.

Where this book is distributed in the UK, Europe and the rest of the world, this is
by Palgrave Macmillan, a division of Macmillan Publishers Limited, registered in
England, company number 785998, of Houndmills, Basingstoke, Hampshire RG21
6XS.

Palgrave Macmillan is the global academic imprint of the above companies and has
companies and representatives throughout the world.

Palgrave® and Macmillan® are registered trademarks in the United States, the
United Kingdom, Europe and other countries.

ISBN 978-0-230-62123-7

Library of Congress Cataloging-in-Publication Data
Latell, Brian.
    Castro's secrets : the CIA and Cuba's intelligence machine / Brian Latell.
      p.   cm.
    Includes index.
    ISBN 978-0-230-62123-7 (hardback)
    1. Intelligence service—Cuba—History—20th century. 2. United States. Central
Intelligence Agency—Cuba. 3. Castro, Fidel, 1926– I. Title.
JL1009.5.I6L37   2012
327.12730729109'046—dc23
                                                                          2011042920

A catalogue record of the book is available from the British Library.

Design by Letra Libre, Inc.

First edition: April 2012

10 9 8 7 6 5 4 3 2 1

Printed in the United States of America.

This book is also for Jill

and

for our sons

Jerome Simon "Jerry" Latell

and

John Wray Latell

I confess that many times I have meditated on the dramatic story of John F. Kennedy.

It was my fate to live through the era when he was the greatest and most dangerous adversary of the Revolution.

—Fidel Castro, April 24, 2009

CONTENTS

Four pages of photographs appear between pages 148 and 149.

ACKNOWLEDGMENTS

I OWE A SPECIAL DEBT OF GRATITUDE TO FLORENTINO ASPILLAGA Lombard, the most valuable defector ever to flee the Castro brothers' secret services. Other former Cuban intelligence and security officers also shared astonishing secrets with me. Among them, José Maragon, Francisco Compostela, Lazaro Betancourt, Miguel Mir, Roberto Hernández del Llano, and Juan Sanchez Crespo deserve special thanks.

I am grateful to the many CIA operations officers—nearly all of them anonymous—who shared valuable recollections and insights. Archivists and librarians at the National Archives in College Park, Maryland, the Cuban Heritage Collection at the University of Miami, and the Hoover Archives at Stanford University provided valuable assistance. I want to especially thank Jorge Machado and Bill Ratliff at Stanford and Steve Tilley, Mary Kay Schmidt, and Amy de Long at the National Archives.

All of my colleagues at the Institute for Cuban and Cuban American Studies at the University of Miami helped in important ways, especially Jaime Suchlicki and Pedro Roig, the latter when he was director of Radio and TV Marti. Clarisa Arguello at Miami's Richter Library and Karina Gutierrez helped me find obscure published works.

Intelligence historians Keith Melton and Hayden Peake were always available to provide counsel. Don Bohning, Dan Flores, Albert Hernández, Howard Jones, David Laux, Octavio Ramos, I. C. Smith, Sally Swenson Cascio, Juan Tamayo, and Joe Urban all helped in significant ways. My old colleagues Pat Maher and Marty Roeber commented helpfully on early draft language. Axel Gylden and Jean Daniel in Paris helped me, with grace and friendship, to shape portions of the story. And others who agreed to be interviewed and who helped in so many other critical ways know how much I appreciate their assistance and respect their wishes to remain anonymous.

My editor, Luba Ostashevsky, provided needed encouragement and counsel. My agent Sterling Lord, founder and chairman of Sterling Lord Literistics, and the best in the business for decades, has been my most intrepid ally. But no one has helped me more than my wife Jill, who patiently read every sentence in all of their versions along the way. As always, she has been my refuge and my fortress.

AUTHOR'S NOTE

MORE THAN A DOZEN DEFECTORS FROM CUBA'S ELITE INTELLI-
gence and security services speak in these pages. They worked during different
eras for the Castro brothers, with bare-knuckled dedication, dueling with the CIA
from the dawn of the Cuban revolution through the late 1990s, until each made
the dangerous decision to flee into the welcoming arms of American officials. A
few of these brave men must live obscurely with new identities assigned by federal
authorities because they are under Cuban government death sentences.

Florentino Aspillaga Lombard, the most knowledgeable Cuban defector ever
to change sides, appears here with his true name, although he has lived with a
new one since 1987, surviving two assassination attempts by Cuban operatives.
Aspillaga agreed to share his personal saga with me during about fifteen hours
of recorded interviews. He also gave me a copy of a revealing personal and professional memoir written soon after he arrived in the United States. Until now
scarcely any of his memories have appeared on the public record. He has asked
nothing of me in return for his remarkable story, has put no limits on how I tell
it, and has no stake in the publication of this book.

I have also interviewed other ranking defectors from the Castro brothers'
intelligence and counterintelligence agencies and their personal security and
commando squads. Some of these men speak in true name, others I have had to
disguise for their protection. (When names are changed, readers are told.) All of
the defectors knew that my purpose in meeting with them was to write this book
unveiling the mysteries and crimes of Cuban intelligence over the last half century. They too asked nothing of me other than a *cafecito* now and then, and that I
retell their stories accurately.

All of them knew of my own three-and-a-half decades of foreign intelligence work for the CIA and the National Intelligence Council. Most had read my earlier book, *After Fidel*, and were comfortable conferring with me, most of them on numerous occasions. I had never met any of them during my years in government, although I was familiar with much of their reporting and experiences. In almost every instance, I knew, for example, how highly they were regarded by American intelligence authorities, and how thoroughly their bona fides had been verified.

Nevertheless, in our meetings I applied most of the same debriefing rigors that are standard for intelligence and law enforcement officers. In some instances I was able to confirm what one defector told me by asking another who had not worked closely with him in Cuba. My knowledge as an historian of the Castro brothers and their revolution—as a CIA Cuba desk analyst, National Intelligence Officer for Latin America in the early 1990s, and a university lecturer for 30 years in Washington and Miami—permitted me to pose questions to them with authority. When recounting an especially interesting story in response to a question, one defector told me, "No one ever asked me that before."

Their recollections have also been checked against the memories of many former CIA officers I interviewed. Nearly all of them have requested anonymity, but they spoke to me candidly and in numerous meetings, phone conversations, and correspondence. I also had the good fortune to know many of the now-deceased senior CIA officials whose curious and controversial roles in the Cuba wars of the early 1960s are described here. I interviewed several of them before their deaths.

My research inevitably led me to the hundreds of thousands of pages of declassified CIA documents stored at the National Archives. There is no other trove of American intelligence history as brutally revealing of once highly sensitive operational secrets as these records related to the assassination of John F. Kennedy. Legislation passed by Congress, and signed into law by President Bill Clinton in 1992, created the Assassination Records Review Board. The members had the authority to require the declassification of all U.S. government documents considered relevant to the assassination in Dallas. In my last position at CIA, when I served as Director of the Center for the Study of Intelligence from 1994 to 1998, officers of the Center's Historical Review Group—mostly Agency retirees working on contract—were responsible for declassifying the CIA documents. The CIA History Staff was also part of the Center I managed.

Since my own retirement I have read thousands of those historical records—headquarters assessments by analysts and operatives, field cables, debriefing and polygraph reports, assessments of spies working for CIA, and revealing Agency histories—many of which were released to the Archives with the greatest reluctance and concern. Readers will learn for the first time the identities of secret CIA agents, successful deception operations run against Fidel Castro and his intelligence chieftains, the inner workings of Cuban intelligence, and previously unknown details of the Kennedy-era CIA assassination plotting against Castro.

It was an extraordinary revelation by Aspillaga during my first meeting with him that led me down the circuitous path this narrative pursues. He told me of the order he received early on the morning President Kennedy was shot that strongly suggests prior Cuban government knowledge of what Lee Harvey Oswald would do. Skeptical at first, my research over the last few years led me to declassified reporting from two other reliable American intelligence community sources—both deceased—whose stories about Oswald and Cuban intelligence officers lend significant weight to what Aspillaga told me.

But this is not just a book about the most notorious and documented crime of the twentieth century. It is the first penetrating look into the workings of one of the world's best and most aggressive intelligence services, now known to have been personally led for nearly fifty years by Fidel Castro, acting as Cuba's supreme spymaster. The defectors all agree that almost nothing of importance in Cuban intelligence operations against the United States happened without Castro's involvement. So this is really a many-layered story about him; his character, conspiratorial instincts, audacity, devious brilliance, and hatred of the United States. His many secrets exposed here for the first time reveal Fidel Castro in ways never before fully appreciated.

ONE

BETTER THAN US

WE SPOKE SOFTLY, SEATED AT A CORNER TABLE IN A RESTAURANT a few miles from CIA headquarters in the northern Virginia hamlet of Langley. My friend had retired several years earlier, but I still considered him the foremost Agency expert on Fidel Castro's remarkable intelligence services. I was seeking insights and anecdotes, stories of success and failure in the CIA's decades of jousting with Cuban spies. But my old colleague, a classically trained operations officer, was uncomfortable talking about his work. So, I wasn't prepared for what he eventually volunteered, sheepishly to be sure: "I believe the Cubans have the best intelligence service in the world."

Since then, I have heard variations of that judgment from other qualified intelligence veterans more times than I can remember. Many retired CIA officials stand in awe of how Cuba, a small island nation, could have built up such exceptional clandestine capabilities and run so many successful operations against American targets. As another CIA officer told me, "Boy, did they do a job on us!"

Current and former FBI officers agree. They share a grudging admiration for Cuban intelligence and the ease with which it burrowed spies and moles and agents of influence into significant American institutions. A former FBI officer who tracked Cuban intelligence told me, "They outperformed us by any objective measure." Indeed, for years they ran circles around both the Agency and the Bureau.

The Cubans were underestimated for more than a quarter of a century. From New Year's Day in 1959, when Castro won power, until the summer of 1987, they were viewed as bush-league amateurs, Latino lightweights in the conspiratorial sweepstakes of superpower espionage. And that was exactly the way the cunning Cubans wanted to be perceived. It allowed them to work clandestinely, in the shadows, largely beyond the sight and even the cognizance of their American adversaries.

Another American intelligence official who worked against the Cubans in the 1970s and 1980s admitted to me: "We just didn't think we needed to be that good against them, but we did. They were better than us. In truth, we lost during most of the Cold War to the Cubans."

They simply were not taken seriously. After all, as the thinking went at CIA, how could an impoverished third-world country—a Caribbean one at that, and in the grips of a chaotic revolution—possibly compete with the best intelligence service in the world? The fun-loving Cubans would not make good spies or spy-masters. They had no experience in espionage or international intrigue and, until Castro took power, Cuba had never run a foreign intelligence service. His neo-phyte spies had to learn the complex, rarefied world of intelligence tradecraft from scratch. Surely they would need many years to acquire real competence. Or so the Americans believed.

The reality was different. The General Directorate of Intelligence, or DGI, and other Cuban intelligence and security services got up and running in record time. Like besieged Israel following its independence in 1948, Castro and his com-munist revolution—under mortal threat from the United States during the early 1960s—developed a foreign intelligence service that quickly rose into the ranks of the half dozen best in the world. And in some covert specialties, particularly in the running of double agents and counterintelligence, my friend was right: For decades Cuba's achievements have been unparalleled. There, as in Israel, the government knew that perfecting undercover capabilities, for both offensive and defensive purposes, would be essential for survival.

Yet for about three decades Washington remained ignorant of Cuban ca-pabilities. A document prepared in the CIA in the 1960s and recently declassi-fied highlights the foolishly patronizing attitudes of an Agency officer involved in Cuba operations. "Cubans generally constitute very poor agent material," the anonymous author concluded. "They do not know the meaning of security. They do not take orders well, and the lonesome courage required for espionage is rarely part of their make-up. They make good fighters but poor spies."[1]

It would not be until June 1987 that the Agency finally came to rue such self-defeating nonsense. It was on the first Saturday of that month when Florentino Aspillaga Lombard, the most informed and highly decorated officer ever to defect from Cuban intelligence, thrust himself into CIA hands through the American embassy in Vienna.

In 1985 he had been honored by the Cuban leadership as "intelligence officer of the year." He was so consistently good that a year later he was runner-up for that award. He had also once received a handwritten commendation from Fidel, a rare honor few others experienced. He had to keep it locked in a safe, however, because the document was classified *Muy Secreto,* Top Secret. It singled him out for the crucial role he had played in July 1979 helping to ensure the military victory of the Marxist Sandinista guerrillas in Nicaragua. Fidel did not want the extent of Cuba's role in that intervention to be known beyond Cuban military and intelligence circles.

Aspillaga had spent much of his earlier career in the DGI's sister service in the Ministry of Interior, the even more obscure General Directorate of Counter-intelligence, the DGCI, known on the island as Contra Inteligencia. His last assignment was as the commanding DGI officer—the Center chief—in Bratislava, in what was then communist Czechoslovakia. He went there late in 1986 under light cover as a Cuban trading company official but was actually in charge of all intelligence and counterintelligence. He was the only DGI officer in that region, now the nation of Slovakia, handling all the Cuban agents operating from there and conducting counterintelligence operations across the border in Austria. He also had monitoring responsibility for the four thousand Cuban workers toiling in local factories as restitution for the economic subsidies Cuba received from Czechoslovakia.

Although no one in the DGI ever doubted Aspillaga's loyalty, he had been seriously contemplating defection intermittently since the late 1960s. He is not certain when those subversive thoughts of flight first developed or what provoked them. But as James Angleton, for decades the paranoiac head of the CIA's powerful Counterintelligence Staff (CI) and an expert on moles and defectors, once observed—long before anyone heard of computer viruses: "You never know when a worm goes into someone's head."[2]

None of the motives that typically move defectors seem to have applied in Aspillaga's case. He was at the top of his form, respected and honored. Barely forty when he switched sides, he already held the rank of major—*comandante*—and was all but assured of further promotions. He had been a member of the Communist Party and its Marxist predecessor organizations since he was twenty. He had suffered no personal humiliation, was not an alcoholic or seeking fame or fortune. He had not stolen from his service, and suffered from no financial problems. He does not speak of any bolt-from-the-blue realization that instantly turned him against Castro or communism. He loved Marta Plasencia, a beautiful young Cuban woman working in one of the Slovak factories, and he took her with him when he defected, but she was not why he decided to flee. He could have divorced his wife—also a DGI officer—and married Marta in Bratislava.

There were precipitating events, however, "push" and "pull" factors that motivated him to commit treason. A few weeks before Aspillaga's run across the Austrian border, Rafael del Pino, a two-star general and one of Cuba's most decorated military officers, defected by flying a military Cessna to Key West. He was the highest-ranking Cuban military officer ever to seek asylum in the United States. Aspillaga admired this aviator hero and was moved to emulate him.

And, to the CIA's enduring credit, Aspillaga told me of another reason for his decision. It may in fact have been the most compelling motive. He had greatly admired from a distance an Agency officer—handsome and dashing, and deeply involved in covert Cuba operations. Aspillaga told me that when he was in Havana running counterintelligence operations against the Agency, he had regularly observed this man, whose identity cannot be revealed here.

American intelligence officers played a similar role in unknowingly inducing at least one other high-level Cuban defection. A second former DGI officer I have interviewed extensively told me that he decided to leave communist Cuba because he also admired individual CIA officers. Another dozen defectors from Castro's intelligence and security services who are quoted or cited here fled for a variety of other reasons. For nearly all of them, however, a slowly nurtured hatred of the oppressive communist system, a coalescing fear and loathing of Fidel Castro, and admiration for American freedoms and opportunities were the "worms" wriggling in their heads. Two have settled in Paris, others in Latin America, but the United States—though not necessarily the Cuban exile mecca of South Florida—is the preferred destination for nearly all the rest.

For the complex and brooding Aspillaga, there were still more reasons for his defection. Slowly, during the many years he served Fidel, he was being alienated by his narcissistic commander in chief. A jolting experience occurred in 1977 in Angola, on the west coast of Africa. Aspillaga was present one night at a Cuban military base near Luanda, the Angolan capital, when Fidel arrived, strutting and preening like a conquering Roman legionnaire. It was in fact a triumphal moment worthy of celebration: Two years earlier, Cuban intelligence and military forces had played the decisive role in assuring the victory and rise to power there of an allied Marxist revolutionary movement. The Cubans had fought and defeated powerful South African military forces and put down a coup against the leader they had secured in power. The lengthy intervention had been a heroic and dangerous undertaking thousands of miles from home.

Castro delivered a speech late that night to hundreds of his military and intelligence officers, all standing before him in uniform and at attention. Aspillaga recalls being in the front echelon, no more than twenty or thirty feet from his commander in chief. Fidel was exhausted after traveling several thousand miles by air. Fatigue might explain why he said things he would never want on the public record.

He was euphoric, glorying in what *he* had accomplished in Angola and elsewhere in Africa and other Cold War conflict zones. The speech was all about his triumphs, his valor, his audacity, his exceptional leadership qualities. He said almost nothing about the contributions of the uniformed men arrayed before him or the sacrifices of the many Cuban dead. Aspillaga was repulsed; it was the first time he had been in Castro's presence. He told me Fidel compared himself to the Nazi propaganda chieftain Joseph Goebbels: "Castro said he could lead the multitudes better than Goebbels. That's how he said it . . . how to guide people to do what you want them to do." It was *fidelista* hubris in the most heinous extreme. "I knew he was evil," Aspillaga said. "I told myself, this man is crazy." It was the first staggering blow to the unqualified loyalty Aspillaga had felt for Fidel and the revolution since childhood.

Personality factors no doubt also influenced the decision to defect. Like so many of his former colleagues—indeed, like the best intelligence officers anywhere—he is strong spirited, adventurous, iconoclastic, and inclined to risk taking. So, perhaps, like not a few defectors, he was drawn to the danger of the act, the sheer excitement of switching sides and running the gauntlet to get there: a moth drawn to a flame. That morning when he made the fateful decision to seek out the CIA in Austria, he knew that a death sentence would be imposed on him in absentia. And because of the extraordinary and sensitive secrets he would share with his new American friends, he had no illusions that he would ever receive a reprieve from Fidel.

Aspillaga was in his early sixties when we sat down together on three different occasions in safe, out-of-the-way places, talking in extended recorded conversations. I was impressed with his intensity, religious convictions, and exceptionally good memory. He was always loquacious and cheerful, although, like most defectors uprooted from their countries, I knew he also suffered bouts of emotional turmoil.

He asked nothing of me in exchange for sharing his personal history and many remarkable insights into the inner workings of Cuban intelligence. During our first session he gave me an English-language copy of a nearly two hundred-page typed manuscript of analysis and recollections of his work. He had finished composing these untitled memoirs in 1990, three years after his arrival in the United States. In its pages, and in our conversations, he chose to put on the public record for the first time some of Fidel Castro's most closely guarded secrets.

Scarcely any of his spectacular revelations have been openly discussed before. He told me, for example, about the DGI's most valued acquisition, at least until the time of his defection: a penetration agent, or mole, in the upper reaches of the government in Washington. This man was so sensitive and influential an inside source that only Fidel and a single DGI case officer ever knew his identity.

The Cuban case officer had no other responsibilities but to meet with the American spy when he traveled abroad, where clandestine rendezvous could easily be arranged. This was before the introduction of sophisticated computer-based communications systems the DGI later would use with its top American agents. Back in Havana, the case officer brought the man's reports directly to Fidel, who then decided whether any information could be shared with others in the DGI, including its director, or in the political leadership. Aspillaga told me, having been told by the case officer, that even Ramiro Valdés, Fidel's trusted minister of interior who had oversight responsibilities for all Cuban intelligence and security agencies, was rarely if ever informed.

The American spy was Castro's personal supermole in the Washington establishment. Fidel made every decision about how to deal with him: where and how clandestine meetings would be conducted; what questions the DGI officer should put to him; how to use him in deception and influence operations. This was the ultimate in compartmentalization and source protection, rare in the intelligence practices of other countries but not in Castro's Cuba. It was probably because only Fidel and the Cuban case officer knew the American spy's name and position that he was never prosecuted in the United States. Aspillaga did not know his name or where he worked in Washington, but told me he suspected the man was burrowed in at either the CIA or the Pentagon.

Judging from the extreme care taken in handling the spy, he must have been an equally or even higher level penetration than Ana Belen Montes, Cuba's other star Washington mole. She spied for nearly sixteen years, most of them in the Pentagon's Defense Intelligence Agency, before being arrested in September 2001. By then she had achieved high rank, enjoyed top-secret and other special clearances, and worked in a position of considerable responsibility. If, as it seems, the earlier penetration was an even more treasured Cuban source, he must have occupied an important subcabinet or comparably sensitive position.

Fidel and the mysterious mole apparently developed a long-distance affinity. Castro may even have met secretly in Cuba with this traitor to congratulate and encourage him and to revel in their success at duping the American "imperialist" enemy. As his country's supreme spymaster for a few months short of forty-eight years, Fidel always delighted in personally meeting with his best foreign agents.

Three other American moles who ultimately were prosecuted and imprisoned are known to have basked in private audiences with the leader they adored. Montes, Walter Kendall Myers—who held a senior position in the intelligence branch of the State Department in Washington—and his wife, Gwendolyn Steingraber, all enjoyed congratulatory conclaves with Fidel. Put up at a Havana guesthouse in January 1995, the Myers couple spent about four hours with Castro one evening. Myers later enthused that the Cubans had given him "lots of medals" and that Fidel "was wonderful, just wonderful." It was the rapture of a true believer in Castro and his revolutionary causes.

According to Juan Antonio Rodríguez Menier, another important DGI defector, a still-unidentified English woman said to be working undercover for Cuba somewhere in the United States was also honored this way. Like the four Americans, she had allegedly spied for many years, and also, according to Rodríguez Menier, provided Cuba with unspecified but "priceless information."[3]

Aspillaga told me that the DGI had enlisted two productive spies inside the State Department. He said that sometime before his defection, two elected members of the US House of Representatives had been separately recruited and had visited Cuba by way of third countries, leaving no traces. It is difficult to imagine that Fidel was not personally involved in those triumphs, secretly meeting with the congressmen, charming and encouraging them to support Cuban causes. Gerardo Peraza, another defector from the DGI, told a Senate subcommittee in 1982 that Cuban intelligence had also made clandestine inroads within the US Senate, but the senator questioning him in open session interrupted him before he could provide details on the public record. Peraza did emphasize that the Senate was a major Cuban intelligence target. There can be no doubt that elected members and staffers of both houses of Congress still are.[4]

Aspillaga warned the Agency of a DGI operation that was planned against a CIA officer overseas just in time to defeat it. Information he provided compromised penetration agents seeking sensitive government positions.

He shared with me glimpses into Fidel's personal life, including the story of a previously unknown child, named Ramón, that Castro had with a young American woman not long after he won power. I also learned of a university professor in the United States who worked as a trusted DGI influence and access agent. She was American born but fluent in Spanish, and had spent time in Cuba as a volunteer in the sugarcane fields as a member of what the Cubans called the Venceremos—We Shall Triumph—Brigade. Aside from her subversive effectiveness in molding her students' thinking, her principal value to Cuban intelligence was as a talent scout and proxy recruiter. Notably, according to Aspillaga, she persuaded one of her most outstanding students, a young man of Latin American descent, to work for Cuban intelligence. Aspillaga described her as the student's *maestra guia,* a master or teacher guide.

When she thought her student was ready to be pitched, she traveled with him to a third country friendly to Cuba and handed him off to her own DGI case officer. By then, as a result of her influence, the young man was ready to serve Fidel. He was recruited and went clandestinely to Cuba for tradecraft training. One of the more important skills he acquired was the ability to beat the Agency's polygraph—the lie detector machine. The expectation was that he would gain employment at the CIA and begin working there as a Cuban mole. Indeed, Aspillaga recalls that the plan came alarmingly close to succeeding, and might have, had he not defected when he did. He told me that he never knew the identities of any of these Americans, or how many others in addition to that student were detected and neutralized by the FBI. But I am not aware of evidence on the public record that anyone meeting his descriptions was ever prosecuted.

Sadly, the same was true with respect to three turncoat CIA officers. Aspillaga shared recollections of two with me, and other DGI defectors I have interviewed provided additional details. All three of the CIA traitors seem to have begun working for Fidel after they had already left the Agency. That is small solace, however, because they inflicted grave damage and served their new masters for extended periods. Sharing sensitive secrets about CIA sources and methods, they exposed former colleagues and served as expert advisors after they switched sides. Two, Philip Agee and Frank Terpil, allegedly were used as spotters and bait in operations against Agency personnel. They—and perhaps the third American—worked at DGI headquarters in Havana as resident advisors to Cuban intelligence.

Agee, who died in a Havana hospital in January 2008, was the best known of the three. He did considerably more damage than the third defector, who I will not name. Suffice to say that this man was also an experienced Agency case officer, considered so valuable an acquisition by the DGI that he was housed in a luxurious Havana guest villa with a swimming pool. The facility was known, for obscure reasons, as La Lata (the can).

Russian spymaster and defector Oleg Kalugin wrote in his memoirs that Agee first approached Soviet intelligence in Mexico City in the early 1970s but was turned away. He then went to the Cubans, who, according to Kalugin, "welcomed him with open arms." Aspillaga insisted that Agee "always worked for Cuba" and never for the Soviets. Kalugin added that in the 1970s and 1980s, the DGI continued to go after current and retired CIA officers and, without elaborating, claimed they "enjoyed some success."[5]

Frank Terpil, code-named Curiel, or "guinea pig," by the Cubans, was for a number of years the most valuable operational asset of the three American turncoats. He traveled to Bratislava during the winter of 1987 on a forged Cuban passport with two DGI officers. Their objective was to recruit a supposedly disaffected CIA officer, a computer specialist. He was to be offered $500,000 for his services but did not appear at an arranged rendezvous. Terpil was also housed comfortably by his hosts, in a spacious home at the Hemingway Marina outside of Havana. I am told that the residence was liberally seeded with concealed bugs and cameras. By 1995, the surveillance had found him wanting; Terpil reportedly was arrested, accused of financial crimes.

MORE SHOCKING YET was Aspillaga's revelation that Cuban intelligence was running what was probably the largest and longest-lasting double-agent operation in the annals of modern spycraft. More than four dozen Cubans, recruited by the CIA as spies, were actually doubles working for the DGI. After Aspillaga had revealed their deceptions, the official Cuban media identified twenty-seven of them, men and women of various ages and from different walks of life. I. C. Smith, a senior FBI officer who worked Cuban issues in Miami at the time, wrote that with respect to Cuba, "the human intelligence capability of the CIA and the United States . . . was suddenly zilch."[6]

Incredibly, counterintelligence warnings or investigations do not seem to have come into play in the CIA. Even Angleton's large CI staff was never involved. Cuba was outside of its mandate. Nor had it been involved during the CIA's calamitous Bay of Pigs invasion in April 1961, an operation that also had been thoroughly penetrated by Cuban intelligence. The obsessive Angleton was focused on the Agency's main enemy, the Soviet KGB. No one on the CI staff, or anywhere in the CIA, thought that the Cubans were good enough to be running their own moles and double agents.

Yet there had been at least one earlier known case, perhaps forgotten in subsequent years. An official Agency history, now declassified and stored at the National Archives outside of Washington, acknowledges the existence of an exemplary Cuban double. Known in the Agency by his cryptonym, AMFOX–1, he had been recruited by CIA as a "stay-behind" agent before the American embassy in Havana was shut down in January 1961. He continued reporting covertly for a dozen years, until 1973, when he was finally detected and his duplicitous services were terminated by CIA.[7]

Most of the approximately four dozen Cubans who served as doubles against the CIA had been unreliable from the start. They were "dangles," attractive bait—carnada in Cuban terminology—that the DGI proffered to unsuspecting and eager CIA officers. They had been carefully selected by Cuban intelligence for their psychological and intellectual suitability and the positions they held, and then they were intensively trained in a special school. Once recruited by the CIA, some remained on the Agency's payroll for many years. In clandestine meetings with CIA case officers in cities all over the world, they were debriefed and given new assignments. Not all of them were Cuban; a few European sycophants of Castro's revolution also worked as doubles. Aspillaga told me of one he knew as "Spaghetti."

If the official Cuban media can be believed, one of the Cuban doubles—Eduardo Leal Estrada, an official in the Ministry of Communications—was actually feted by the CIA in a secret award ceremony "with drawn curtains and in total silence" in a hotel room. On the recommendation of CIA director William Casey, he was supposedly given a $10,000 bonus for his spurious spy work and a gold medal with appropriate Agency inscriptions. Known as Agent Alejandro to the DGI, he was considered an especially valuable source by the CIA because of his knowledge of Cuba's national communications systems, including the coaxial cable network then being installed across the island. "The enemy was very interested in trying to defeat that endeavor," he told the Cuban government press after being exposed.[8]

Antonio Garcia Urquiola was another typical case. Like more than a dozen of the double agents, he was regaled as a hero by the Cuban media soon after Aspillaga exposed him. A captain with Cuba's main shipping line, he had been trained in counterespionage in the mid-1960s and assigned the code name "Aurelio." He was therefore an ideal candidate for the DGI to dangle. He was offered up in Amsterdam in 1978, quickly recruited by the CIA, and assigned the code name "Alejandro." He began meeting with case officers during ports of call. The CIA provided Aurelio/Alejandro with secret writing equipment, and supposedly he sent hundreds of messages to his handlers using invisible ink. He was later given a sophisticated transmitter that beamed concentrated burst messages to an American satellite or, according to the Cuban government exposé, to a CIA office on the fifth floor of the American diplomatic mission that was established in Havana in 1977. The code name he was assigned when transmitting messages to the Agency was supposedly "Dadon."[9]

Garcia later claimed he had been paid $1,500 monthly in the latter years of his double service. By the time he was exposed, more than $120,000 had been deposited for him in secret American bank accounts. With DGI training, he says he was able to pass the Agency's polygraph test. Later he boasted to a Cuban government reporter that "the device is meaningless." (Another of the doubles claimed to have passed it three times; only one admitted to failing.) Garcia admired one of the CIA officers he dealt with frequently, describing him as "very experienced and professional." But overall, he claimed, they "underestimated us and viewed us with contempt . . . they really blundered."[10]

In some of the double-agent cases, the Cubans outsmarted the Agency by using clever psychological deception and performance techniques. One of their dangles—they called him "Robert"—presented himself as rebellious and eccentric. According to Cuban press accounts, he intentionally missed meetings with his CIA case officer and was cavalier when explaining why. It was a role scripted by the DGI to shake up the mix with the belief it might actually increase the CIA's interest and confidence in him. He would not come across as a trained intelligence officer. And perhaps too it was done just for the sport of it, following guidelines laid out by Fidel himself, to see how much they could get away with. Another Cuban artfully played the role of a naïf who could easily be satisfied and fooled.

The challenges of orchestrating this symphony of counterespionage deceptions would have strained the ingenuity and resources of even the largest spy services. The best-known earlier example—the double-cross system run by British intelligence—succeeded in completely controlling German espionage on the home front during World War II and, prior to the Normandy invasion, ingeniously deceiving the Nazi High Command in Berlin about where the Allied forces would land. Winston Churchill, intimately involved in those deception operations as prime minister, famously referred to them as his "bodyguard of lies."

J. C. Masterman was an Oxford don enlisted into a leadership role in running that complex operation. "Administrative problems were formidable," he wrote, "almost overwhelming." Copious records had to be kept on every double agent in order to avoid inconsistencies in reporting that might betray them. Every bit of information passed, the time it was done, and the likely implications of releasing it to the enemy had to be recorded. And there were fewer British doubles than in the Cuban operations.[11]

In wartime Britain, as in Castro's Cuba, double agents had to be quarantined from each other. Only a small number of staff officers could be aware of any one case, and in Cuba, there were just a few, including Aspillaga, who knew of them all. Nonetheless, the DGI's elaborate doubles structure was inherently precarious: If the CIA had uncovered any one of them, others might well have come under suspicion too as counterintelligence concerns were heightened. Any serious error could unravel the entire complex. The Cubans' skill at keeping their own double-cross system secure for so long was an unparalleled accomplishment. After Aspillaga's defection, CIA officers could only grudgingly marvel at how totally they had been duped.

The Cuban successes were a tribute to the country's supreme spymaster. Other men, handpicked by Castro and his brother, Raúl, held the top offices in the DGI and other security services, but it was Fidel himself who led and personified Cuban intelligence. He presided as the grand master of the Cuban double-cross system, just as he insisted on managing all the most important agents and moles. Each of the doubles was handled by a DGI case officer who had to be intimately familiar with every development in a case. But these officers were mainly record keepers, logisticians. Fidel made all the most critical decisions.

He conceived the strategy, playing the game of deception three or four moves ahead and always with a number of pieces simultaneously in motion. He decided who could be dangled and who could not; which ministries and government agencies should be shielded from the CIA; and what information—termed "feed" or "smoke" by American and British intelligence—could be passed to the enemy. I have not been able to determine whether Fidel personally screened candidates to be dangled, but chances are good that he did at least in some cases.

Often he permitted doubles to share surprisingly sensitive data with the CIA to enhance their credibility. Most of the disinformation was factual and truthful, so when it was passed, it would more likely be accepted as valid. The feeds would have to seem sufficiently important too—revealing Cuban government secrets—in order to keep the ruse from raising suspicions. The CIA, after all, measured the worth and reliability of its agents on the merits of their reporting. Still, obviously the doubles could not give away really sensitive information. This is why no one from Cuban intelligence or the military was ever dangled.

Fidel's commanding role stands in surprising contrast to how the British double-cross system was managed. The Twenty Committee was a collegial body of intelligence careerists and university dons, chaired by Masterman. It was represented by the Roman numerals XX—also, of course, signifying "double cross," the X being a close typewriter keyboard symbol to a cross. Members met weekly in near-total secrecy to weigh all important decisions. Together, they approved what feed could be given to the enemy and devised the deceptions to be inflicted on German intelligence and military planners.

Masterman wrote that the Twenty Committee acted "as a clearinghouse where the work of various agents could be compared and kept within a reasonable measure of consistency." Agents should neither contradict nor parrot each other when passing their feed; either course could raise suspicions on the receiving end. Keeping it all straight and in balance was a formidable challenge for Masterman's team.

Fidel was not tempted to create anything like a Cuban XX committee. He played that role himself, with the boundless self-confidence and audacity that are among his defining traits. He was not averse to incorporating some checks and balances into the running of the Cuban doubles, but there was never any doubt in the ranks that it was really his show. In short, Fidel was the singleton equivalent of Masterman's Twenty Committee, and he was just as flawlessly successful.

After Aspillaga's defection, the theory and practice of doubles and dangles tradecraft was enshrined in DGI instructional literature. One sophisticated study was drafted by Zayda Gutierrez Perez, a DGI major who studied at the communist East German Ministry for State Security, the infamous Stasi. Completed in 1987, it reveals in considerable detail many of the underlying principles Fidel dictated for running penetration agents. Originally published in German and stored in the Stasi archives in Berlin, the study came to light after the two Germanys were reunited. It is the only substantial internal DGI document that I know of that has found its way onto the public record.[12]

Gutierrez wrote about "intelligence offerings," the quaint Cuban term for "feed." Fidel's role in choosing the offerings is not explicitly acknowledged, though the major hinted at his involvement, writing that "the highest state officials . . . must take part." She made clear that the overriding objectives of the program were manipulating and disinforming the CIA. The DGI learned a great deal from the deceptions; "highly valuable knowledge was gained," she wrote. Cuban intelligence perfected its own tradecraft as it learned from CIA methods. According to the Cuban media, it acquired a bonanza of satellite and other advanced communications gear from the double agents.

But in fairness to the many CIA professionals at all levels who were taken in by the Cuban deceptions, it must be emphasized that, when carried out by a skilled intelligence service, doubles deceptions are exceedingly difficult to detect. Richard Helms, from 1962 to 1965 the CIA deputy director for plans, the top spymaster, and future director, testified under oath about this area of secret tradecraft during a Senate hearing in 1975. He said, "This is one of the most difficult and tricky aspects of secret intelligence work, and there isn't anybody who's been in it very long who hasn't been tricked once, twice, maybe many times. You just start each time afresh, taking the same chances and hazards . . . it is extraordinarily frustrating."[13]

AS ASPILLAGA WAS UNMASKING Cuban operations during the summer of 1987, Fidel was plotting his revenge. The DGI was instructed to put together an elaborate media campaign to expose still more Cuban successes against the American archenemy. These new revelations were also acutely embarrassing.

About two dozen of the doubles and some of their family members were rounded up in Havana and transformed briefly into media stars. Carefully scripted, they told similar tales of CIA perfidy, real and invented. Lengthy feature stories and photo spreads about their double lives soon began rolling out in the pages of *Granma*, the official Communist Party daily paper, and on state television.

More than thirty of the doubles were sent on a whistle-stop tour around the provinces, presented everywhere as intelligence heroes. Fidel took part, hosting an assembly in the defense ministry's main hall, the Sala Universal, with many of the double agents present. His brother, Defense Minister Raúl, and dozens of ranking intelligence officials were there. Incredibly, Fidel spoke for fourteen hours, reading many of the feeds he had helped draft that the double agents provided to the CIA. One of his bodyguards, a DGI officer who later defected in New York, shared his recollections of that event with me. He had to endure the entire spectacle, standing adjacent to Fidel. "My feet were swollen and sore," he told me. "I was standing near Castro the whole time, guarding him."[14]

Cuban television aired an eleven-part series, *The CIA's War Against Cuba*, claiming to show in shocking detail how Agency personnel and operations on the island had been compromised for about a decade. The programs were viewed with mounting alarm at CIA headquarters, each containing fresh new surprises.

Fidel was orchestrating the entire show. Aware of the historic tensions that marred relations between the CIA and FBI, he found a devious way to exacerbate them at the CIA's expense. He had the DGI prepare dubbed English-language versions of the programs and arranged for a set to be delivered to I. C. Smith, the FBI's Assistant Special Agent in Charge of the Miami field office.

Visiting CIA officials later asked Smith how he had acquired the dubbed tapes; they could find only Spanish-language versions. He was coy, indulging in a bit of harmless interservice gamesmanship. "I asked them for a set," he said in his syrupy North Louisiana drawl. Then he walked away from his annoyed Agency counterparts, providing no further explanation.[15]

The Cuban documentaries were professionally done. Aspillaga told me that a special production group he knew of must have done all the work. The series featured extensive filmed coverage of Americans from the diplomatic mission in Havana as they engaged in what appeared to be basic intelligence tradecraft in remote areas of the island. Smith has written that they were CIA officers surreptitiously filmed by Cuban counterintelligence "leaving and picking up packages containing radios, money, and instructions for Cubans ostensibly working for the CIA."[16]

The DGI surreptitiously recorded and filmed a few of the Americans during clandestine meetings with double agents in European capitals. The television series also featured documents supposedly written and photographs taken by CIA officers at various locations in Cuba. There was no explanation of how Cuban intelligence managed to acquire those materials, although clearly it had been through clandestine means. The exposé showed containers with bundled Cuban pesos, radios, and racks of seized communications gear. A hollow artificial rock was said to have been used in the countryside as a dead-drop device for the CIA to pass documents to a double agent.

One of the programs pictured a child's toy, batteries, and furniture and described them as CIA concealment devices. An elegant Italian Maltese named Mauro Casagrandi—Cuban code name "Mario"—claimed in an hour-long interview with Cuban security officers to have been recruited by the CIA in Madrid, where he also passed a polygraph exam. A longtime resident of Cuba, he chuckled as he explained in fluent Spanish that over time the Agency paid him a quarter of a million dollars while he worked under Cuban control as a double agent. He did not say whether he got to keep the money.[17]

Double agent Juan Luis Acosta, captain of the Cuban tuna fleet—"Mateo" to the DGI—was one of those featured in a starring role in the press and on the TV series. He was selected to send the final coded message to the Agency after it became clear in Havana that all the double-agent deceptions had been exposed. The Cuban press claimed it was sent via an RS–804 satellite transmission device provided by the CIA. "On behalf of the state security agents and our fighting people, I am sending this last message. Viva Fidel!"[18]

The televised series was meant, of course, to put the CIA in the worst possible light. An American was shown conducting an operation wearing a T-shirt with "SUPERMAN" imprinted in large block letters running across his back. As the camera panned to get a close-up, the narrator intoned about the CIA's arrogance and bullying belief that it is all-powerful.

Another American was seen near his car, searching for his keys supposedly lost when he placed a package in a wooded area, presumably for an agent to retrieve. In a similar rustic setting, the irate wife of another American is heard shouting "You idiot!" as he is seen outside his car concealing an object. A man is shown conspicuously leaving chalk marks on a park bench. Another is viewed perching on the tailgate of his vehicle in a wooded area testing what the Cuban media claimed was satellite communications gear intended for an agent.

All of the men caught on film, and the wives, are oblivious to the Cuban surveillance. Yet clearly multiple cameras were used in filming some of the incidents. Segments were shot from above, which probably means that small, sophisticated cameras with telescopic lenses were placed in tree limbs. They must have been remotely controlled because they panned left and right to follow the Americans as they moved about. Aspillaga believes the Cubans' surveillance skills—what they call *chequeo visual*—were "among the best in the world."

Targets were seen in close-ups and from various distances, so the cameras had zoom capability. Some of the sequences were filmed from eye level, dead straight ahead of the subjects. All of the footage shown on Cuban television was clear and in sharp definition. The programs demonstrated exceptionally sophisticated technical and surveillance skills. They also demonstrated that the DGI must have assigned a huge number of agents to monitor the Americans. All of the films were taken during daylight hours; it is not clear to what extent operations that may have been conducted at night went undetected.

Fidel and his intelligence bosses took considerable pleasure in taunting the Agency, hoping no doubt that the programs would ignite a firestorm of media and congressional criticism in the United States. It is interesting, nonetheless, that Castro and other top leaders stayed out of the show. To my knowledge, he never spoke on the record about his successes or the CIA's humiliations.

As it turned out, the programs and their implications received scant attention in the American media during the summer of 1987. Other major developments—especially the Iran-Contra scandal and questions about President Reagan's role in it—dominated the news that season. And, fortunately for the CIA, the two intelligence oversight committees in Congress cooperated either by suppressing the story or by never insisting on being fully apprised of it. Surprisingly, too, there were no leaks until years later. Perhaps in the summer of 1987 no one in Washington had a taste for another witch hunt.

There cannot be any doubt, however, that the CIA leadership was motivated to keep a lid on the story. So in the end, despite the Cubans' determined efforts, the Agency sailed through the crisis with only minimal damage to its reputation by the televised exposé and the fiasco of the Cuban double-cross operations. In contrast, the wounds to morale were devastating.

Yet a tantalizing question the exposé left open, groaning to be answered, was just how the Cubans knew in advance precisely where to position their cameras. The double agents could not have told counterintelligence where to install surveillance equipment to capture the Americans on film and audiotape. Agents would not be told in advance by the CIA where they would need to go, say, to retrieve money or communications gear. They would receive detailed instructions only *after* their handler had made the delivery. These fundamental practices are described in any beginner's manual about human intelligence or law enforcement tradecraft. The inescapable conclusion, therefore, was that, somehow, the CIA had been penetrated.

No matter how they had managed to do so—most likely it was in Havana, where they have overwhelming operational advantages—it was clear that the Cubans had been at it for a number of years and had attained extraordinary access to sensitive Agency secrets.

To my knowledge, these dreary conclusions have never been openly discussed before. I believe they would be indisputable, however, to anyone who viewed the Cuban television series and had even an amateur's understanding of clandestine tradecraft—say, from watching spy movies or reading good espionage fiction. It was, of course, the regime's intention to dramatize in the TV series that the CIA was deplorably inept and remained vulnerable to superior Cuban tradecraft.

Yet the most troubling question was never asked in public as far as I know. *How* had the CIA been penetrated?

I can only speculate. The Cubans may have had access to a CIA facility or, much less likely, were intercepting and decoding Agency communications. The worst of the possibilities—and one of the least likely—is that the suspicion Aspillaga shared with me was correct: Fidel's personal supermole in Washington was a CIA officer assigned to the Cuban affairs staff. Perhaps there was such an Agency traitor, who might eventually have come under suspicion and was then neutralized and removed but who could not be prosecuted due to a lack of evidence to prove treason.

Still, the most likely explanation is simpler: The Cubans had regular access to the American diplomatic mission in Havana. The six-story building on the seafront Malecon Boulevard had stood empty for nearly seventeen years. It had housed the U.S. Embassy until diplomatic relations between Castro's regime and the United States were severed and the building shuttered in January 1961, shortly before John F. Kennedy's inauguration. Thereafter, the Swiss government was responsible for safeguarding the facility, but with a small staff in Havana and limited resources, there was not much it could do.

It is highly unlikely that the Americans had left any sensitive CIA records or equipment for Cuban intelligence to pick over when the facility closed. The official CIA history previously mentioned, reported:

> When the break came, the Embassy had three days' notice that it would close on
> January 4. The CIA station had just installed a new incinerator and managed to
> burn what files could not be shipped to Key West. . . . When they were not burn-
> ing papers or smashing technical equipment, case officers were caching radios or
> making advance payments to agents left behind. . . . Station files not absolutely
> essential were crated and shipped back to headquarters. Case officers were work-
> ing fifteen-hour days, seven days a week.[19]

A few colorful footnotes to the hasty American exodus across the Florida Straits are also worth mentioning. The deputy station chief, who anticipated the break in diplomatic relations, was able to make a "special trip on the Havana–Key West ferry to take out his personal car, silverware, and a valuable violin."

Other CIA personnel were not so lucky. They "had maintained houses until the end and lost everything in them." And then the last act was performed ritualistically, the exhausted CIA officers in Havana banding together in solidarity one last time: "On January 4 station personnel met at the embassy, rode in a convoy to the ferry, and sailed to the States."[20]

Years went by, and the beautiful white embassy building stood vacant, regularly doused by Caribbean sea spray. There were no official Americans there during the Bay of Pigs fiasco in 1961, the terrifying missile crisis a year later, and the numerous other confrontations with Castro during the Kennedy, Johnson, Nixon, and Ford administrations.

Finally, limited diplomatic relations were reestablished on September 1, 1977. Jimmy Carter's new administration and Cuba agreed to open "interest sections" in their respective embassy buildings in Havana and Washington. The American legation—known by the acronym USINT, for U.S. Interest Section, Havana—was technically a section of the Swiss embassy. It eventually grew nonetheless, into the largest diplomatic mission in Havana, even though it does not have the status of an embassy and is headed not by an ambassador but by a lower-ranking principal officer. The contrivance is necessary because the United States does not fully recognize the legitimacy of the Castro brothers' government and has not established normal diplomatic relations.

Alan Flanigan, a career diplomat, served as USINT principal officer from 1990 to 1993. In an oral history interview a few years later, he was candid about the vulnerability of the facility even during the years when he served there.

> We were never sure how secure the protection of the embassy building had been. Our assumption was that it wasn't very secure at all, that Cubans had access to it rather freely over those many years, so when we moved back in we had to operate on the assumption that the Cuban intelligence service had the capacity to listen to everything we did there.[21]

Flanigan also recalled that "we had about 120 Cuban employees at USINT." He did not need to add that virtually all of them worked in one way or another for Fidel's intelligence services. Under the circumstances, a revealing Cuban government boast must be taken seriously. According to *Granma*, the television exposés during the summer of 1987 demonstrated how "the activity of the CIA station . . . has been under the surveillance of Cuban security forces at all times."

The phrase "at all times" suggests not only that American personnel were constantly surveilled as they traveled around the island but that a CIA facility had been penetrated and that nearly everything that took place there was being observed or heard, and possibly both. The logical but repellent conclusion is that, when it opened, USINT was peppered with the most sophisticated and miniaturized audio and visual surveillance devices available at the time, honeycombed with tunnels and underground entrances connected to Cuban government buildings nearby, and stripped bare to the DGI's prying eyes and ears. After all, Fidel's men had more than a decade and a half to make the old embassy structure virtually their own.

It is easy to imagine that Castro ventured into the building himself, perhaps late at night, with intelligence officers guiding him and briefing on their handiwork. He has always relished this kind of vicarious pleasure in dealings with the United States. But regardless of whether he actually prowled the premises, it is very likely that DGI filmmakers prepared comprehensive documentaries for him showing the innards of the building. Surely, too, detailed architectural drawings and measurements were compiled. All of that would be of continuing use for future penetration operations.

TWO

ON FIDEL'S ORDERS

WHEN I BEGAN MEETING WITH FLORENTINO ASPILLAGA TWENTY years after his defection, he was sixty, a lean and taut long-distance runner and swimmer. Like so many Cubans, he is animated and broadly expressive, quick to laugh and volunteer deeply felt emotions. When pressed for details about his twenty-five-year career in Cuban intelligence, his description of meeting the CIA officer he had admired from a distance in Havana stoked strong emotions. Even deeper feelings flared as he told me about his flight to freedom with his young lover, Marta.

"Tiny," as he was known to family and a few friends, conducted meetings all day on June 6, 1987, at Cuba Tecnica, the cover company he ran in Bratislava. His principal intelligence agents and informers, and the counterintelligence commissars who monitored the Cuban workers in local factories, gathered to report to him. He had summoned Marta from Ružomberok, the provincial industrial town in eastern Slovakia where she toiled in a textile plant. She had no idea what he was planning and brought nothing with her.

No one in Cuban intelligence had any idea either what Aspillaga intended to do that evening, though the more astute and suspicious might have wondered. Occasionally he had joked with colleagues about someday hurling himself into the clutches of the enemy: "I am going to go over the wall one of these days." They were always amused, confident he was joking, just letting off steam. He was known for his brooding sense of the absurd. And in any event, he was Fidel's most highly decorated counterintelligence officer. It was his responsibility to make sure *they* never contemplated defection.

Soon after his arrival in the Slovak capital the previous November, he had begun to plan his hegira to the CIA. His only previous postings outside of Cuba had been in Angola for about a year in the mid-1970s and briefly in Moscow, but Aspillaga had no chance to make a run to a place where he might find a CIA representative. Bratislava, which is on the Austrian border and only about fifty miles from Vienna and a large American embassy, would be easy to flee.

It had long been part of his plan that when he finally made his move, it would be on June 6, the anniversary of the founding of the Ministry of Interior. He had celebrated on that date in Havana many times with colleagues in the past, at least once or twice as part of a captive audience listening to cheerleading speeches by Fidel or the minister. Now, just as General del Pino's defection had motivated Aspillaga, he wanted to inspire others who might follow. He wanted to goad and enrage Fidel.

"I was inspired to come on June 6. I wanted to get at Castro, to hurt morale."[1]

Tiny—the nickname is probably a variation on Tino, short for Florentino—rendezvoused with Marta in a downtown Bratislava park late in the afternoon. It was a few hours before dark, a warm Saturday evening. Happy strollers and families crowded the grounds, picnicking under shade trees and listening to the tinny music broadcast by state radio. Many Czechs and Slovaks were buoyed that spring with hopes for liberalizing political change. The first whiffs of the reforms that would soon buffet the Soviet Union and communist eastern Europe were stirring.

Fidel, worried about what those changes would mean for Cuba, was pressing ahead with what he euphemistically called the "Rectification" campaign. It might better have been labeled the "Never Here" crackdown. Castro's responses to the liberalizing policies of glasnost and perestroika emanating from Moscow that were beginning to splinter Marxist societies were ideological rigidity and social conformity. The Soviet reforms were lunacy; they would lead to ruin. In self-defense, he adopted the intimidating new slogan: *"Socialismo o Muerte,"* Socialism or Death, shouting it with raised fist at the end of all his speeches. Billboards went up across the island proclaiming it.

Fidel was digging in, closing down micro-entrepreneurs he savagely condemned as "neo-capitalist exploiters." By any measure, their crimes were paltry.

One offender he publicly denounced for selling chocolates in Havana's Lenin Park; another, an itinerant artist, was guilty of sketching caricatures of people for a few pesos; another collected odds and ends at the city dump and made costume jewelry to sell. They were criminal outsiders in Fidel's view, exploiters and violators of the centrally planned economy. Aspillaga never told me that the Soviet and European communist reform movement influenced his decision to defect, but certainly it helped sharpen his hatred of the intransigent Castro.

As a guest worker, Marta's Cuban passport had been confiscated and was kept in a safe at the DGI Center in Prague. This was a standard precaution to discourage defections. Aspillaga would have to smuggle her across the border into Austria, but he knew it would not be difficult. Madly in love with him, she was prepared to do whatever it was he had in mind.

Ignoring the Czechs and Slovaks enjoying the park, he removed the spare tire from the trunk of his official Cuban government car, a little green Mazda 202, and pierced a small breathing hole in the floor. Then he persuaded Marta to fold herself into the cramped space there and quickly closed her in. No one seemed to notice, or care.

The border is only a mile or so from where they started, and he knew the guards on both sides because he often traveled that way showing his diplomatic passport, one of three in different names and cover stories he carried that day. Smiling and joking with the Austrian guards, he was, as usual, waved through. Soon he stopped along the road to let Marta out. She assumed they were embarking on a secret intelligence mission. It was only then, with her seated at his side, that he explained his plan. He broke down and sobbed, begging her to marry him in America, where they would begin a new life together.

"We are going to the United States. You will go many years without seeing your family . . . and they will try to kill us."

He choked up recounting the scene for me two decades later. He was correct that he would soon be targeted for assassination. She was not targeted.

Vienna was less than an hour from the border checkpoint, an easy drive on good roads. Once there, he parked the car, hailed a taxi, and handed the driver a sheet of paper on which he had earlier written the words "American Embassy." But the embassy was dark on a Saturday evening, locked and unwelcoming behind a heavy, ornate iron gate. Aspillaga was not concerned. He knew that Marine guards would be on duty no matter when he arrived, just as he knew they patrolled at all hours at the American legation in Havana. Loitering with Marta near the main entrance, they were soon approached by a well-trained young Marine guard. Marta spoke some English. Aspillaga offered his passports, flashed a thick Cuban intelligence document he had stolen, and, with Marta's help, did his best to hurriedly explain.

"I am a case officer from Cuban intelligence. I am an intelligence *comandante*."

He had crossed his Rubicon. In those moments spent with the Marine he became what is known in American intelligence as a walk-in, in Cuba a *voluntario* (volunteer). Some bring secret intelligence documents with them to quickly establish their bona fides—literally, that they are acting in good faith, are who they claim to be, and have valuable information to share. Aspillaga arrived in Vienna with a sensitive numbered copy of the Ministry of Interior's "Guidelines and Procedures of the General Directorate of Counterintelligence," stamped "State Secret." The duplicate he shared with me is not deeply revealing of Cuban tradecraft or intelligence priorities, but it served to establish his credentials. The stunning secrets he would soon share were all stored in his head.

Some walk-ins are turned away at the doors of foreign embassies when they arrive cold, without warning or sensitive documents. They might be provocateurs, charlatans, or impersonators. The fact that most are understandably nervous and agitated when they arrive does not help to allay those concerns. During the Cold War, the CIA and KGB were wary of such volunteers. In fact, occasionally both spurned genuine, high-level defectors who, later, after making second approaches and being accepted, provided critically valuable information. Vasily Mitrohkin and Oleg Penkovsky are the best-known examples from the Soviet side. Both volunteered to Americans but were not taken seriously at first.

The Cubans, in contrast, usually are less cautious when approached by strangers offering to help. Aspillaga told me that "Cuba is freer"; the philosophy generally is "You take what comes." Exaggerating to make the point, he added, "If a million people come, we would handle the million people." In countries all over the world, true believers in Fidel and his revolution have volunteered their services this way, literally knocking on the doors of Cuban embassies. John F. Kennedy's assassin, Lee Harvey Oswald, was one of them.

With Castro's encouragement, his intelligence officers have tended—to use a popular term of their own—to be *electrico*, or highly charged, on edge, assertive, daring. These are traits Fidel values. He expects the men and women who serve him in clandestine capacities to act audaciously, seizing the initiative, taking risks, pushing against the odds. Ironically, too, these characteristics help explain why there have been so many defectors from the senior ranks of Cuban intelligence.

Aspillaga was confident that what he said next to the Marine guard would hasten his acceptance. It could easily be checked out and confirmed. His bona fides would be verified. He told the young American that he wanted to meet with the CIA officer he had admired from a distance in Havana. He provided the man's name and the European capital where he was then posted.

"Call this guy. He is in the CIA. Tell him I want to talk to him."

Aspillaga had never met the officer, although each had handled the same double agent, known to the Cubans as "Francisco." The American was Francisco's CIA case officer; Aspillaga was his Cuban handler at the opposite end of the double cross. The two agents had peered at each other through the prism of the double they shared. Each learned personal and behavioral things about the other through Francisco. Aspillaga heard the American's voice, surreptitiously recorded during clandestine meetings with Francisco. He had observed him many times in surveillance film and video. And they also worked two other doubles of lesser importance for opposing purposes.[2]

The American spoke Spanish fluently and with a Cuban accent. He easily melded with Latino and Cuban culture and, for Aspillaga, he was a role model more honorable and professional than any of his own colleagues. By observing him so closely, Tiny had grown oddly close to his opposite number.

He respected the CIA man's skills, his integrity, and his family-oriented values. The man's wife had impressed him too. She was like a stock car driver at the wheel of their car, jockeying and accelerating to evade Cuban surveillance. "Whooooosh," is how Aspillaga described her driving skills to me, sweeping his right arm in a wide arc. The CIA officer was *simpatico*. The word means agreeable and pleasant, and when spoken by Cubans it often also symbolizes a verbal *abrazo*, or embrace, that expresses warm admiration. To call someone simpatico is one of the highest compliments gregarious Cubans can pay.

Aspillaga told me with awe that the American's clandestine tradecraft skills were "possibly the best . . . in the entire world. . . . The Russians also said he was the best. I would read it in reports from the KGB." In his memoir, Tiny wrote that his Agency counterpart "was the most dangerous official in terms of his clandestine capabilities and high intelligence that we would confront from any intelligence service."

"Alpinista" was the secret code name Cuban intelligence assigned to the American. It means "mountaineer" or "Alpine mountain climber." Clearly a measure of their respect for him, it also acknowledged his adventurous qualities. He was a master of disguise and evasion and therefore was especially difficult to track. It was known that he handled Francisco and the two other doubles with warmth, charm, and vitality. He behaved like a Cuban.

They also knew he was not skimming from the CIA salaries paid to the double agents he ran. Aspillaga was impressed with his honesty, knowing how lax his peers' ethical standards were. The Cuban doubles were required to turn over all the money they received from the Agency to their government. They were told it would be spent on building new schools, that they would be benefactors of a better educational system. In reality, senior intelligence and Communist Party officials squandered most of these substantial sums on luxury purchases. Double agents who traveled abroad on missions were typically given shopping lists by their superiors for goods not available in Cuba.

The CIA officer was incorruptible. Soviet intelligence had once tried to recruit him. Aspillaga knew from reading KGB reports shared with the DGI that it had once enticed the officer into a tense showdown in a European country where a Soviet agent placed bags of money in front of him and made a crude recruitment pitch. Tiny recalled, "I don't know how many millions of dollars it was."

But the CIA officer remained calm and defiant. He told the KGB, "No. I don't need your money. The only thing I want if I were to work for you is to be the prime minister of Russia."

They were stunned. "What? Why would you, an American, want that? It's crazy. What are you talking about?" He smiled sardonically and leaned forward toward the Soviet agents, his elbows on the table that separated them. "Well, that way I could change Russia and defeat the communist dictatorship."

Both the Soviets and the Cubans declared him an impossible target for recruitment. Actually, by then the DGI had already concluded from what their double agents were reporting, and from their eavesdropping and surveillance, that he was not a good turncoat prospect. They were sure he had no exploitable vulnerabilities. The Cubans and Soviets admired his tenacity and dedication. In Cuban terms, he was too "ideological"—too opposed to communist dictatorships—to be of any use to them.

As Aspillaga recounted these memories to me during our third meeting, he became emotional. It was then that I began to appreciate how his main motive for choosing to join forces with the enemy CIA must have been his admiration for this exemplary American patriot. Switching sides had not been a strictly ideological decision after all for Aspillaga. And it had not been just to hurt Fidel. Tiny wanted to work not only with the Agency but specifically with the agent he so profoundly respected. His competitive mirror-image relationship with the CIA officer had been "very beautiful," he confided. I thought that was a strange, heartfelt admission, especially coming from a hardened Cuban intelligence operative often honored by Fidel as one of his best. And then for emphasis, Aspillaga repeated the thought.

When the CIA man arrived at an American debriefing center in western Europe where the old nemesis he had never met was taken from Vienna, he was so perfectly disguised that Tiny did not recognize him.

"They hadn't told me he was coming . . . he came transformed."

After fifteen or twenty minutes of conversation, the American finally revealed himself. Aspillaga was astounded and delighted.

"And then we began to laugh. He was toying with me to see if I would recognize him."

The rivals were suddenly now professional colleagues, playing on the same team. Aspillaga told me his respect for the CIA officer soared. They hugged in a tight Cuban-style *abrazo*.

There are stranger stories in the shrouded history of intelligence intrigue, but few, I imagine, with the poignancy of this one. Other important defectors during the Cold War, including other Cubans, also admired from a distance the opposing intelligence service they eventually joined. There are comparable stories in literature and military history. I am not aware, however, of any other case of a defection from any country that hinged on the professionalism and appeal of a single personality on the opposing side. The most important *voluntario* ever to abandon Cuban intelligence came to the CIA because of his boundless admiration for an adversary he had never met.

At the American debriefing center, officials could hardly believe the shocking secrets that immediately began to gush from their unexpected Cuban prize.

They listened with stomach-wrenching astonishment as he reported how thoroughly Cuban intelligence had manipulated and deceived the CIA on an unimaginably grand scale and for so many years. Beginning with those first American debriefers, and twenty years later with me, Aspillaga unveiled some of Fidel Castro's most sensitive and incriminating secrets, always with a curious mixture of remorse and pride.

HE IS AN AMERICAN CITIZEN NOW, living quietly and obscurely with a new identity. Providing him that measure of protection after his debriefings by the CIA and FBI was the prudent thing to do. To this day, so long after his arrival in the United States, he still avoids publicity and the torrid polemics and posturing of Cuban exile politics. But even so, and exactly as he had feared from the start, he was targeted for assassination.

The first attempt—in London, on September 12, 1988—was the one that came closest to succeeding. Indeed, Aspillaga's survival was nothing short of miraculous. He still has the tweed jacket he wore that day. He brought it to one of our meetings to show me the holes in its flanks from the bullets fired at him from close range by a former DGI colleague. He is certain that the order for his execution came directly from Fidel. Two other high-level Cuban defectors I interviewed have confirmed that to be true beyond any conceivable doubt.[3]

Juan Sanchez Crespo defected in 2008. He was a trusted member of Castro's security detail from 1977 until 1994 and for a period functioned as chief of his advance team that completed risk assessments before Fidel's international travels. Sanchez told me that "the man who shot at Aspillaga did so on Fidel's orders."

Another highly placed DGI defector shared details of the assassination attempt with me. He and Aspillaga had known each other and collaborated on sensitive operations. This erudite man also lives now as an American citizen with an assumed identity. But even that name will not be revealed here. He has asked for anonymity for his own protection and that of family members, so I will call him José Maragon.

"Fidel was personally involved in that assassination operation, managing and directing most details," Maragon told me. "Fidel ordered the DGI leadership to contact the KGB in Havana and request a special assassination pistol. The Soviets had one at the embassy and gave it to us." It was a Groza, or Thunderstorm, but incongruously named, because it was silent when fired.

A vertically aligned double-barreled derringer, small and snub-nosed, it fired high-speed 7.62 mm ammunition, the same as used in the powerful Kalashnikov rifle. The Groza was designed by the KGB for one purpose: to kill reliably and silently at close range, to carry out what were known as wet operations, or assassinations. The only sound the little pistol makes when fired is a soft *click* of the firing pin.

Describing the weapon to me, Maragon picked up a common fluted glass salt shaker from the restaurant table where we were meeting, enveloping it in his right hand. "The pistol is very small," he said, "about like this."

It was intended to be used by Miguel Medina Perez, a DGI officer assigned to the London embassy as third secretary. Aspillaga told me they had studied together in the DGI intelligence school and had remained friends. Aspillaga considered the baby-faced Medina a candidate ripe for a defection pitch, saying that his loyalty to Castro and the revolution was in doubt. When Aspillaga learned that his old friend was severely depressed that week in London—his stepson had just died in a drowning accident in Cuba—he thought it was even more likely he could persuade him to commit treason.

The two old colleagues met and drank together for four or five hours in a pub. They talked in rapid-fire Cuban Spanish until after midnight, joking and reminiscing. Medina gave Aspillaga every reason to believe he would also defect and finally agreed to do so a few days later at an arranged time and place. But he failed to show up.

In the meantime, he had confessed all to his DGI overseers. "I saw Aspillaga yesterday," he told them. It had actually been a few days earlier, but Medina was desperately trying to protect himself for having met with such a notorious traitor. As penance, a revolutionary auto-da-fé, he was ordered to kill his old friend.

There had not been enough time, however, for the Groza Fidel had requested to reach London in the foreign ministry's diplomatic pouch. So Medina was armed instead with a Makarov. For forty years this much larger and heavier weapon had been the standard-issue Soviet sidearm, which many Cuban military and intelligence officers also carried.

According to contemporary British and American press reports, CIA and Scotland Yard officers were posted in the streets the following Monday afternoon when Aspillaga approached Medina at his home in the fashionable Bayswater district. He would try again to persuade him to defect. Medina opened the door of his apartment and Tiny reached out toward him, to shake his hand.[4]

"Hey, Medina, *como estas,* how are you?" They were no more than five or six feet apart when Medina pulled the Makarov from a hidden holster and began firing, with no words or warning. Unlike the silent Groza, each discharge boomed like a clap of thunder.

But Medina was not a trained assassin. Sanchez Crespo told me that "the man who shot at Aspillaga on Fidel's orders did not know how to use a gun. He was an intelligence bureaucrat, not trained in the use of firearms."

Medina was in fact the indulged and neurotic nephew of one of the early heroes of Castro's revolution; his post in London was a slacker's sinecure. He had no experience with semiautomatic Makarovs or any handguns. Agitated and frightened, under duress to carry out his commander in chief's orders, he fired erratically with one hand, the large pistol wavering and recoiling sharply with each shot.

Fidel, the harshest judge, gave every appearance of believing that it was an authentic murder attempt. He personally received Medina as a hero when he returned to Havana, awarding him a distinguished service medal and a car, an extravagant gift at a time when the Cuban economy was suffering from particularly severe shortages of nearly everything. Castro wanted it understood throughout the intelligence services that, successful or not, Medina had acted heroically, on orders from the top.[5]

Maragon doubts, however, that Fidel was truly convinced Medina had done his best to kill his friend. Always suspecting betrayal and conspiracy, Castro must have wondered if Medina had come close to defecting too. But as it happened so often in the revolution's convoluted history, he needed to make the best of the situation, and thus the weakling he probably despised was briefly elevated to heroic status. Not surprisingly, Medina was never heard from again.

During our second meeting, the lithe and compact Tiny demonstrated for me how he had evaded five or six gunshots that day in London. He darted and jumped and danced in smooth, quick balletic leaps in the room where we were talking. Throughout that spontaneous performance he grinned triumphantly, reenacting his lucky escape fifteen months after Fidel had imposed a death sentence on him. One shot in fact had grazed his right side; he remembers the searing heat.

The leather belt he wore showed signs of having slightly deflected or absorbed that round.

There was another close call, in 1997, ten years after he defected. Fidel was still insisting that the death sentence be carried out. This attempt occurred late at night where Aspillaga was living with Marta, by then his wife, and their two children. Despite all the precautions, the DGI had managed to track him down. Its agents had been diligent and determined, taking advantage of a clerical error made in an American government agency outside of the intelligence community that eventually led them to Aspillaga's hiding place.

He became suspicious after noticing strange men, who looked like young and fit Cubans, loitering near his home. One night soon after, long past midnight, he listened and watched for the intruders he sensed were coming as he sat on guard at his kitchen counter in total darkness. Marta and the children were asleep, barricaded in a bedroom. He heard a slight rustling outside.

Suddenly someone fired at him. He thought the sharp *clap* sounded like an AK-47 round. The shot was wild, striking an aluminum support pole of an awning near the window he was facing.

His luck had held again. The assassins, he believes, were trained DGI illegals, deep-cover agents living in the United States as American citizens with stolen or forged identities. He does not doubt that they were members of an underground network of Cuban agents, the Red Avispa, a sprawling Miami-based "Wasp" espionage complex that was shut down by the FBI one year later, in September 1998. Tiny had no choice but to relocate again with his family.

The second attempt and a third event, according to Aspillaga, were probably orchestrated in Havana by one of his most trusted old friends. They had worked together in intelligence and counterintelligence for twenty-four years. Known to colleagues by the pseudonym "Ricardo," he was recalled as chief of the DGI Center in an African country as soon as his old colleague's defection was confirmed.

"Ricardo" was selected to inflict Fidel's revenge because he knew Aspillaga well and might be able to predict what his friend would do and how he might be found. He would have a good sense of Aspillaga's vulnerabilities and peculiarities. He might even be able to ingratiate himself with Tiny's first wife and daughter, left behind in Cuba, to elicit information that could lead to him. Aspillaga wrote about "Ricardo" in his unpublished memoir: "He was ordered to return to Cuba with the objective that he direct the group in charge of seeking me out, determining my location for the purpose of sending an assassin to kill me."[6]

Tiny's betrayal was also used for motivational leverage in the military's training of commandos and snipers. Lazaro Betancourt, a muscular young member of Fidel's personal security detail, defected through the American embassy in the Dominican Republic in 1999. He told me that he flew out of Santo Domingo on a commercial flight convincingly dressed as a decorated American Marine. Betancourt remembers his elite class of student sharpshooters being berated on the firing range by their military instructors: "Learn this well," they were told, "so *your* shot won't miss when you are assigned to kill Aspillaga."[7]

Aspillaga was still being tracked by DGI bloodhounds and hunters. As long as Fidel was in power, he was determined to exact revenge. That may have changed when he was forced, following debilitating surgeries, to provisionally yield the presidency to his brother Raúl in July 2006, and to definitively step down in February 2008. Under Raúl Castro's less vindictive leadership, the death sentence may have been annulled or simply forgotten. Aspillaga assumes, nevertheless, as he must, that he remains a marked man and will be in the Cuban government's crosshairs until sometime after the Castro brothers and the communist regime have disappeared.

THROUGHOUT THE CIA AND FBI HIERARCHIES, there was never any doubt about Tiny's reliability or the veracity of his revelations. One retired senior officer told me that Aspillaga's "value as a defector was as good or better than any the CIA ever had anywhere. If he had been a Soviet, it would have been the best by far we had in our entire history."

Aspillaga told me he was never polygraphed. "No. They trusted me. The value of what I provided was so extraordinary."

Ironically, however, had he been connected to a lie detector machine and wanted to deceive his CIA handlers, he probably could have succeeded. The manuscript he shared with me devotes an entire chapter to the counterpolygraph training the DGI conducted in a safe house—a *casa operativa*—established exclusively for that purpose in a western Havana suburb. Aspillaga wrote that he had volunteered for the training because the double agents he handled were all routinely enrolled there so they could lie persuasively to CIA polygraphers.

"I wanted to feel for myself the sensations that the agents experience."

With or without an American polygraph exam, defectors often are vetted and verified within hours of their first meetings with knowledgeable intelligence professionals. The fact that he was not a double agent or provocateur would have been established before Aspillaga was spirited out of Vienna.

Later, as he was slowly debriefed, any doubts counterintelligence worriers may have clung to were definitively dispelled. That was because when the CIA was running the agents it believed to be bona fide, some defensive plays had been made, ingenious double checks put in place that later confirmed without a shred of doubt that Aspillaga was a genuine, truthful defector. Those measures are still too sensitive to describe here.

Compounding the shock for the Cuban leadership, Aspillaga was not the only high-level traitor in 1987. Five other ranking military and intelligence officers also fled over several months. Juan Antonio Rodríguez Menier, an honored veteran of intelligence and counterintelligence since the first year of Castro's regime, defected in February from his post as DGI Center chief in Budapest. Later in the year another DGI officer fled from his assignment in a South American capital. Aspillaga told me that two other DGI officers, a married couple, also exited that year, but they have remained silent in exile obscurity. And, as previously noted, Rafael del Pino flew to Florida shortly before Aspillaga departed. All were probably motivated at least in part by the reform movements blossoming in communist bloc nations and Castro's unbending opposition to them.

Every one of the defections was a bitter personal blow to Fidel. As he saw it, they had all betrayed him, mocked and repudiated him by switching sides. At first his intention was to keep their treason secret so that only a few in Cuban intelligence and the military would be aware of them. Del Pino's flight attracted heavy international media attention, however, so there was no keeping it under wraps. Before long both del Pino and Aspillaga were interviewed on radio broadcasts that could be heard on the island. Aspillaga appeared on the American government Radio Martí—a Voice of America news and entertainment outlet—and other Miami commercial stations. In their interviews, both men condemned and ridiculed the regime they had left behind.

The damage done collectively by the six defectors was so great, and the danger of recurrence so ominous, that Fidel could not remain silent. In a rambling four-hour speech on June 24, 1987, only a few weeks after Aspillaga reached the

CIA, he fulminated about betrayal and treason, sounding like a cancer surgeon in the operating room identifying malignant tumors to remove.[8]

"There have been big and small traitors," Fidel said. "I remember three big ones." What distinguished those three from the "small traitors" was that they had all been close to him. They betrayed his trust, not simply communism or the revolution or the regime, but him personally. From his perspective, defections were not just damaging breaches of national security but vile personal affronts.

The first "big" traitor was a peasant named Eutimio Guerra, who had joined Fidel's guerrilla movement in 1957 and turned into an informant for the old dictatorship of Fulgencio Batista. The hapless Eutimio was found out and summarily executed by Raúl Castro on Fidel's orders. It was the second execution of a traitor, or suspected one, that Raúl carried out without question or remorse. In the Castros' Cuba, summary execution on Fidel's orders is all there is of due process for real and imagined offenders.[9]

In a strange believe-it-or-not twist, the other two "big" traitors Fidel railed against shared the exact same name: Rafael del Pino. It is not, incidentally, a commonplace Cuban name, like John Smith in the United States, and one wonders how any others remaining on the island with that name might have fared in the aftermath of Castro's speech. The first del Pino, according to Fidel, betrayed him soon after the triumph of the revolution. He was imprisoned and died in his cell in Havana, supposedly a suicide. More likely he was poisoned or shot.

And there was the air force hero who Fidel berated in the "traitors" speech; he said the general had come from a bourgeois family and, despite valiant contributions, should never have been trusted as a true and reliable revolutionary. The general also now lives obscurely in the United States with a new identity, careful to avoid publicity that might leave him vulnerable to Cuban assassins. He has been targeted at least once on Fidel's orders. During my meetings with him, he has never shown any fear and on a few occasions he has ventured out of his assumed identity to make appearances as himself. But he knows he is the only survivor of Fidel's demonology of "big" traitors and exercises extreme caution.

It was clear to Fidel's listeners in Cuban intelligence that he was also referring in his tirade to the spate of defections from its ranks. He has never mentioned Aspillaga's name in public or referred to his defection, though Tiny was arguably the single most damaging defector from civilian, military, and intelligence careers in the more than half-century history of the Castro brothers' regime. Above all, during his speech Fidel was intent on warning others in the clandestine services contemplating treason that the penalties would be severe. He said: "There will never be an excuse for a revolutionary to cross over to the side of the enemy. We can accept many other things, but not this one. . . . We cannot accept defection . . . the act of defecting while possessing secrets is very grave."[10]

The warning was cautiously parsed. Fidel wanted it to be unmistakably threatening for domestic audiences but did not want to sound like a Stalinist to foreign listeners. Tiny told me that after his departure, he learned—presumably in phone conversations with former colleagues—that Fidel started requiring intelligence officers to sign a blood oath acknowledging they would automatically be sentenced to death—*ajusticiado*—if they were to defect. The speech was Fidel's way of throwing down the gauntlet. The traitor Aspillaga's execution was mandated; he would be made an example to any others who might be tempted to follow him.

Cumulatively, the damage done during Cuba's "year of defectors" was so great that Fidel ordered a sweeping reorganization of the DGI, which was renamed the Directorate of Intelligence. Doubts about the loyalty of many officers intensified, and restructuring continued. It all led in the summer of 1989 to an even more devastating, top-to-bottom purging of the Ministry of Interior. The Castro brothers feared more high-level defections and possibly serious unrest within this bulwark of their regime, second in importance only to the military.

The Stalinist-style crackdown was preemptive, meant to snuff out every trace of support within the secret services for the liberalizing reforms that led in 1989 to the toppling of the Berlin Wall and the disintegration of the communist bloc. Arnaldo Ochoa, Cuba's most decorated and beloved general, was executed on trumped-up charges of drug trafficking. Antonio de la Guardia, a swashbuckling intelligence colonel and a favorite role model for a younger generation of operatives, also faced a firing squad. Why? They had contemplated and perhaps had begun to plot defecting.

The men and women of Fidel's secret vanguard always walked a dangerously fine line as they endeavored to please him. No matter how diligently they carried out his orders—even by achieving remarkable feats in his name—they could never know when they might suddenly fall from grace. José Abrahantes, the faithful minister of the interior when Aspillaga defected and at the time of the 1989 purges, was imprisoned that year and died soon after, ostensibly of a heart attack.

His deputy, Pascual Martínez Gil, a decorated and courageous DGI general, also learned how expendable he was despite his heroism in one of Fidel's greatest victories. Ten years earlier, "Pascualito," as Castro liked to refer to him when he was in favor, was the first man at the head of a commando unit that stormed the heavily fortified bunker of Nicaraguan dictator Somoza, who had fled shortly before. The purged Pascualito is said to be driving a taxi in Havana today.[11]

The DGI went into convulsions and was put under the control of three-star general Abelardo Colomé Ibarra, Raúl Castro's favorite crony. As was usually the case when the Castro brothers unleashed a purge, they had multiple motives. Many DGI officers earned the wrath of government counterparts because of their arrogance and ostentatiously high living standards. They were especially despised by military officers who lived more austerely, earning considerably less. The many easy intelligence successes before Aspillaga's defection had bred institutional hubris. Like all Cuban government entities, the DGI was riddled with corruption. When the worst of the terror had passed, Fidel penned a long editorial in which he complained that the interior ministry had lacked an internal counterintelligence system and that the DGI had become too independent and powerful.[12]

There were many casualties of the purges, including by execution, demotion, banishment, suicide, and inexplicable sudden death. According to the defector Rodríguez Menier, nearly two hundred intelligence professionals were imprisoned. "Everyone I knew in the [ministry], without exception, has been executed, locked up, or retired from power." Another defector, José Ramon Ponce, a psychologist with eighteen years' experience in counterintelligence, says that "thousands" of officers were purged.[13]

Rodríguez Menier also observed that all of the imprisoned officers "were opposed to Castro and were almost to the point of conspiring to overthrow him." They were the "most receptive to change," the most intelligent and best-informed Cubans. He wrote that a coup against the Castro brothers may have been brewing in the intelligence community. Aspillaga also tells of pervading unrest that started within the DGI in 1983 and reached regime-threatening intensity six years later. Others wrote that many of those purged or executed, including General Ochoa, had been attracted to the reform movement then flowering in the Soviet bloc. It was not a coincidence that the Cuban purges began within days of the Tiananmen Square massacre of pro-democracy demonstrators in Beijing.[14]

Another transformational blow that followed Aspillaga's rallying to the CIA was that the nearly free ride the Cubans had so long enjoyed in foreign intelligence operations abruptly ended. Never again would Americans underestimate their capabilities; instead, virtually overnight they became a prime counterintelligence target, respected world-class foes. Aspillaga's defection enabled Americans to better understand—and more easily counter—aggressive Cuban tradecraft. Cuban covert operations abroad were temporarily hobbled, nowhere more calamitously than in Latin America. According to DGI defector Roberto Hernández del Llano, more than 150 Cuban operatives there were compromised and taken out of service.[15]

A few officers who had been especially good friends of Aspillaga's were withdrawn from their overseas posts as soon as it was known he was in American hands. He told me that in addition to Medina Perez in London, a close colleague in Paris was promptly recalled to Havana. Still another, the chief of counterintelligence operations against the CIA in Havana, came under merciless scrutiny, either for misappropriating funds or grave errors of tradecraft somehow related to Aspillaga's defection. With disgrace imminent, that officer put a pistol in his mouth and pulled the trigger.

Almost immediately after Aspillaga's defection, all of the doubles operations went to ground. Cuban moles and agents who feared they had been exposed surely became inactive, some perhaps permanently. The American professor who recruited students for the DGI was probably among them. Ana Montes was an unfortunate key exception. Already a Cuban spy, she had started work at the Pentagon in September 1985, nearly two years before Aspillaga defected, but did not come to his attention. It may have been because she remained in relatively low-level positions at first or because her case was strictly compartmented from the start, possibly even handled personally by Fidel.

Aspillaga did considerable additional damage by identifying a multitude of former associates. He shared with me a by-then somewhat stale directory of more than a thousand Cuban intelligence personnel who were active either on the island or overseas at the time of his defection. Inevitably, a new consensus formed in the American intelligence community. There was no avoiding the ugly truth: Fidel Castro was running exceptionally brilliant covert operations against American interests. In terms of almost every specialty and subdiscipline of human intelligence tradecraft, the Cubans have remained without peer, even after the losses and temporary degradation suffered in the late 1980s.

The nontechnical disciplines have always been their forte: espionage and counterespionage, double-agent and false flag operations, the running of illegals and agents of influence, the insertion of moles, covert action (what the Cubans call *medidas activas*, active measures), deception operations, surreptitious entry, and covert acquisition of technology—along with all of the subsidiary spycraft including, for example, document forgery, photography, disguise, surveillance, and countersurveillance that facilitate such work. Their expertise at double agent tradecraft and counterintelligence is without peer anywhere in the world.

Aspillaga believes that the Cubans are better at surveillance than any other intelligence service, even those of much larger and wealthier countries. "I had some friends who were brilliant," he told me. "No one was better than them, not even the Russians or the CIA, nobody."

In part, he said, it is because Cuba uses cunning psychological and behavioral analysis to anticipate what their quarries are likely to do. "When they are following you, they are examining your attitude. They would know way ahead of time before you would do something."

Some of the espionage footage that was shown on Cuban television after Aspillaga defected was possible because of the use of such advanced tradecraft. Targets were studied and filmed so that staff psychologists could establish a baseline of their normal mannerisms, gait, affect, and other distinguishing characteristics. Any significant changes in their bearing or physical presentation could signal that they were planning to go covert. But to be fair, anyone trying to evade Cuban government surveillance on its home turf—where spies and agents and informers and snitches are everywhere, and where intelligence resources are virtually unlimited—is inevitably at a crippling disadvantage.

Aspillaga wrote about other remarkable elements of Cuban spycraft. Often entire brigades of surveillance specialists are deployed in Cuba to follow important targets, especially Americans known or suspected of being intelligence officers. During one of my visits to Havana, when I was a senior intelligence community official well known to the Cubans, I was followed by a large squad of surveillants all equipped with sophisticated miniature communications equipment. There are virtually no limits on the numbers of street agents who can be deployed. According to Aspillaga, "In many instances a large bus is utilized as it also serves to conceal personnel from view."

The Cubans have elevated the craft of surreptitious entry to a level perhaps unmatched elsewhere. Since a government agency closely tied to intelligence manages all property rentals by foreigners on the island, agents can easily arrange illicit access to private properties. According to Aspillaga, foreign embassies and residences of western ambassadors and other diplomats were routinely penetrated.

Sometimes agents pump supposedly harmless gas under doors or through keyholes or other small openings to anesthetize sleeping residents. Agents can then easily enter and steal or copy documents or install listening devices and the miniature cameras Cuban intelligence calls *visiles*. Fidel himself originally authorized the use of sleeping gas against certain foreign diplomatic representatives in the mid-1960s, and the practice has continued.[16]

Castro's role as Cuba's supreme spymaster extends to all areas of exotic tradecraft. Even foreign heads of state or government are not immune. Aspillaga remembers an especially urgent operation run on Fidel's orders against Yugoslav president Josef Broz Tito, who arrived in Havana on August 29, 1979, to participate in the summit meeting of the nonaligned nations.

Tito, one of the founders of that movement and an independent Marxist never closely tied to Castro's more radical regime, was a vital intelligence target. During a meeting with other nonaligned leaders the previous July, he had sharply criticized Cuban military interventions in Africa. Fidel was worried the old and infirm Yugoslav partisan might openly repeat such criticisms in Havana, possibly even denounce Cuba as an ersatz nonaligned nation because of its close alliance with the Kremlin. Castro demanded that the DGI determine exactly what Tito planned to say in his address to the conference. The resulting covert operation was a stunning success. Aspillaga wrote about it, saying, "Fidel ordered that all of Tito's personal documents be photocopied. A huge operation was prepared which concluded in the penetration of the embassy of Yugoslavia as well as the residence used by Tito."

On August 31, Fidel hosted the Yugoslav leader during a private luncheon. By then he was satisfied that he would not be embarrassed on his home turf as he assumed the chairmanship of the nonaligned movement. The DGI had provided him documentary proof.

Aspillaga wrote that during such searches, residents' personal items carrying their unique scents are routinely stolen and immediately sealed in vacuum containers. They are stored away in DGI facilities and brought out when they might aid in canine surveillance operations. Aspillaga told me, "It would surprise you to know the number of such personal items belonging to North American diplomats and other nationalities that are in storage." I imagine they have my scent on file, some souvenir from my official visits to the island in the early 1990s.

Such shoe-leather skills constitute just one of several main intelligence disciplines, however. As good as the Cubans are at those, they certainly cannot compete with the enormous American intelligence community in scientific and technical collection, operational gadgetry, or airborne systems. Outside of Cuba—with the important exception of Miami—they do not rely extensively on bugs, taps, other sophisticated listening gear, or surreptitious entry.

Advanced code breaking is beyond Cuban capabilities, although in recent years agents have become proficient in secure, high-tech forms of agent communications. Havana does not loft reconnaissance and eavesdropping satellites into space. The Cuban intelligence community is too small to maintain a massive, worldwide communications intercept capability. Nor does it operate in dozens of countries around the world where it has few interests or little chance of penetrating CIA operations.

Rather, like Israeli intelligence, revolutionary Cuba has focused nearly all of its attention on perceived enemies. For the Castro brothers, there are fewer such enemies than the many Arab and Muslim countries the Mossad must contend with. For Cuban intelligence, the perception is that there are just two main adversaries: the American government—especially the CIA—and most Cuban exile organizations and leaders.

That focus permits a concentration of resources, efficiencies of scale, and the development over time of a depth of expertise. American targets are "the reason for being of the Cuban intelligence service," ex-DGI officer Gerardo Peraza has said. All the other defectors I have consulted and interviewed agree. Hernández del Llano, who came to the United States after sixteen years of intelligence service, expressed it to me well: "Cuban intelligence has been targeting Americans— the great enemy—for fifty years. So it is not surprising they have had so many successes."[17]

THREE

ROOFTOP STORIES

ASPILLAGA WAS A RED-DIAPER BABY, STEEPED IN MARXIST IDEOL-
ogy and admiration for the Soviet Union. His father, also named Florentino,
made sure of that. A loyal veteran of the pre-Castro Communist Party, he was a
dedicated activist in its underground campaigns against the Batista dictatorship.

The father inducted his son as a boy of ten or eleven into acts of petty intrigue and street agitation. Together they distributed subversive propaganda, the
boy scampering over fences at the homes of Batista henchmen to slip brochures
under their doors. He got his first taste of the intelligence work he would later
master by one day climbing high into an avocado tree to attach a crude antenna
the communists would use for clandestine communications. When illegal conclaves were held in the family home, the boy played lookout. Intelligence work
would be his natural—and inherited—calling.

Tiny believed his father had long been an informant for Soviet intelligence.
Florentino senior also quickly ingratiated himself with the Castro brothers. Just
three months into their new regime, he was entrusted with sequestering a ranking KGB officer in his home. The Soviet, the first Kremlin representative to arrive
in revolutionary Havana, soon began meeting secretly with Raúl Castro to lay
the groundwork for the alliance that would soon flourish. The father was duly
rewarded with a position in Fidel's inner sanctum, as political chief of his large

security detail. He served the brothers loyally, though with increasing resentment, for many more years.

In November 1986, the night before Tiny departed for Bratislava, father and son had a soul-searching conversation alone on the roof of the son's apartment building in Havana. They knew no listening devices were installed there; no witnesses could eavesdrop. Even the most trusted revolutionaries were never completely immune from suspicion. Tiny told me about some of Fidel's closest advisors and most senior officials whose homes and offices were secretly bugged by counterintelligence on his orders.

Sensing that they would never see each other again, the elder Aspillaga wanted to share with his son defamatory information about Fidel he had never told anyone before. Someone he trusted should also bear the secrets he had preserved for decades. He suspected his son was planning to defect and might even have hoped that details of the incidents he witnessed would eventually reach American ears.

Florentino senior's two remarkable rooftop stories are chilling, incriminating commentaries on the moral void that explains so much of Fidel Castro's behavior since he was in his early twenties. They were among his best-kept secrets.

Fidel was a University of Havana student when the first incident occurred in February 1948. A feared gunslinger, notable in Cuba's noir underworld where student assassins and criminal gang lords mingled, he was usually armed and cocked for action. The elder Aspillaga saw Fidel fatally shoot another youth, also named Castro—Manolo Castro—who was no relation. Manolo was a notorious youth leader, a politically well-connected gangster engaged in graft and believed to be involved in mafia-style mayhem.

He was gunned down outside a Havana movie theater. The two Castros had been violent adversaries, members of opposing criminal gangs that preyed on each other. Perhaps more than anything else in their violent relationship, it must have galled Fidel that his powerful nemesis, so like him in character and ambition, bore the same last name.

Manolo Castro died in the street where he was struck. Aspillaga senior told his son he was there. He had followed Fidel, hidden behind a tree, and, without anyone noticing, watched him pull the trigger. Fearing that he would be killed if he told anyone what he had seen, he kept the secret for thirty-eight years.

Fidel was immediately a prime suspect in the murder. He was known as a sworn enemy of his rival. Acts of extreme violence, carried out with no qualms or regrets, were second nature to him by then. And he had motive to retaliate after narrowly escaping assassination attempts by associates of Manolo Castro. DGI defector José Maragon has no doubt who the killer was. He told me that "everyone I ever talked to about it believed it was Fidel."[1]

Accused by a cousin of the dead man, Castro was detained by the police but released for a lack of evidence. It helped that he had a credible alibi. Yet at least two of his biographers placed him at or near the scene of the crime. One said he was seen leaving the area at the time of the assassination. Another cited witnesses who noticed that "he was hanging around the street that day." Other bystanders "saw him and found him unusually nervous and high strung" near the movie theater. On balance nonetheless, these authors, and several others who have written about the murder, exonerate him.[2]

A more recent biographer, who enjoyed the support of the Cuban government and the Castro family, came to a more ambiguous conclusion, however. He wrote that while Fidel "probably did not directly participate," he "may well have been involved in discussions and planning of the attack." Culpable or not, triggerman or not, he sufficiently feared for his life that he immediately went into hiding, moving from one address to another for the next four or five weeks.[3]

The murder served his purposes and became indelibly part of his legend. His reputation for decisive and menacing action was enhanced. The killing eliminated a despised gangster, and many Cubans were relieved he was gone. Fidel's standing as a courageous if trigger-happy political activist grew. He was able to have it both ways: He could not be charged, but his enemies now took him even more seriously. That pleased him at a time when he was vigorously flexing his political wings and coming to the attention of Cubans as an aspiring national leader.

His rival's elimination also provided a satisfying finality for Fidel. Never again would he have to joust with another man named Castro, not a Cuban or an adversary of any nationality. He would be the only one under the lights on the world stage. But Manolo Castro's name lives on—and on Fidel's orders. Following the triumph of the revolution, a science building at the University of Havana was named after him. Maragon told me he considered that "a sign of Fidel's perverse sense of humor."

Today, after so many years, it is impossible to corroborate or verify Florentino senior's murder story. Unlike virtually everything else I heard from the younger Aspillaga, the account is secondhand from a now-deceased source. (The father died in Cuba in 1994 at the age of seventy-five.) His account is therefore easy to dismiss as just another example of extreme, anti-Castro ranting.

Most sympathizers of the revolution treat allegations of Fidel's involvement in Manolo Castro's death in that way.

Yet the incident is so similar to a confirmed assassination attempt of another student leader Fidel carried out fourteen months earlier in Havana that it rings true. In December 1946, Fidel is known—from undisputed testimonies of contemporaries—to have attempted the cold-blooded, unprovoked murder of Leonel Gomez, a promising younger student who also loomed as a political rival.

Fidel took cover behind a stone wall near the university sports stadium and fired at the youth's back without warning. Shot through a lung, Gomez staggered, seriously wounded, but survived. Max Lesnick, a contemporary close to Fidel in that era—and still, in exile and in his eighties, an enthusiastic supporter—remembered the incident vividly. He told an interviewer in Miami that Castro did it to call attention to himself and to curry favor with rival gang leaders. The attack on Gomez—in fact, everything Fidel did—had a rational explanation, according to Lesnick. His "mind is a logical mind."[4]

Fidel was thinking strategically. His objective was precisely the same in the Gomez and Manolo Castro assaults. He was determined to clear Cuba's political main stage of charismatic young competitors and to acquire powerful allies who could provide protection in Havana's raging gang wars. As would be the case so frequently in later years, his plan succeeded. After Gomez was wounded, Fidel was brought under the wing of one of the country's most notorious gangsters who became his criminal "godfather." According to Lesnick, this new patron gave Castro a pistol and a car and protection from his numerous enemies.

Five months after the Manolo Castro murder, Fidel was identified by a witness in still another killing in which a University of Havana police sergeant was gunned down. The testimony was later retracted, however, and, again, no charges could be filed. It was the last murder allegation Fidel would have to evade or defend against. Never again was he physically close enough to such a crime to be implicated. His hands would always remain clean of the blood spilled on his behalf and on his orders.

He would be responsible, however, for many more killings and attempted ones. He ordered assassinations by a succession of trusted hit men, spectacular commando operations against prominent foreign targets, gangland street murders, and innumerable executions of Cubans by firing squads and in apparent accidents. He deployed Cuban and foreign hit men, including elite members of foreign terrorist and guerrilla groups dependent on Cuba. On his orders, men were marked for elimination (from all the evidence I have been able to gather, there was never a female victim) for the same reasons that motivated him during his university years. In almost all cases he sought to exact revenge or to eliminate powerful rivals and enemies, including serving and former heads of state.

An especially sensitive and reliable covert CIA source reported in November 1962 that Castro was "dominated by vanity, had megalomaniacal tendencies, and possessed a compulsion for revenge that was notorious." The agent added that on occasion, it caused Castro "to reach back as far as twenty years to avenge actions taken against him at that time."[5]

Like Tiny Aspillaga, some of Fidel's targets eluded their assigned assassins. Many others, however, died under mysterious circumstances in countries around the world. They were Cubans, Cuban exiles and defectors, other Latin Americans, and probably some of other nationalities. As in the Manolo Castro case, the evidence trail fades off into confusion and plausible denial in virtually all of these other instances. But these pages will exhume several of the cold cases, based on new evidence provided by Aspillaga and other defectors from Cuban intelligence.

When he was interviewed by one of Castro's biographers in 1984, Max Lesnick had no reservations about describing his friend Fidel's imperative to violence. It was as defining and intrinsic as his smoldering sense of destiny. According to Lesnick, Castro "had precise plans for creating his own place in history. He was always imbued with the conviction that he had to fulfill some transcendental mission, and he was violent but also always calculating."

Lesnick relished telling another revealing story. When he was in hiding after the Manolo Castro murder, Fidel relied on friends to provide safe havens from his enemies. He stayed for a while with Lesnick, in a small room in his grandmother's apartment in Old Havana. It faced the north balcony of the presidential palace, only about a hundred yards away. President Carlos Prío sometimes used the balcony to address crowds below.

One morning as he was reading, Fidel idly glanced out the window of his room. Lesnick was not at home, but his grandmother witnessed what happened next. Castro stood, picked up a broomstick, and pointed it out the window toward the presidential balcony. Holding it up to shoulder height like a sharpshooter, he aimed it as if it were a rifle with a telescopic sight, musing aloud about how easy it would be to assassinate Prío from right there. Lesnick's grandmother was startled but engaged him.

"Well, okay, my boy, and after you do that, what's going to happen to you . . . and to me?" His response was characteristically calculating, and cold-blooded. "*Bueno, vieja . . .*" he began. "Well, my dear old lady. I'll go down these stairs, take the elevator, and leave right onto Prado Street. Nothing at all will happen to me."[6]

He "was obsessed with conquering power, by whatever means," his lifelong friend Lesnick concluded.

It was not the first time Fidel had fantasized about killing a Cuban president on that balcony. Prío's predecessor, Ramón Grau San Martín, once invited Castro and a few other student leaders to confer with him at the palace. He asked them to wait for him on the balcony as he did some other business. Fidel whispered to the others as they stood there alone, "I have the formula to take power once and for all to get rid of this old crook. When the old man comes back, let's the four of us pick him up and throw him off the balcony. Once he's dead we'll proclaim the triumph of the student revolution."

The others were horrified, and refused, but not until Fidel exclaimed, "It's a great opportunity for us to seize power."[7]

The Aspillagas' story about the Manolo Castro murder fits neatly into this peculiar pathology. I cannot vouch for the senior Florentino's reliability as a source, but I have no reason to doubt all of what his son shared with me, including the rooftop stories. There was no reason for the father to exaggerate or fabricate.

I am sure Aspillaga remembered the conversation accurately; it had occurred only seven months before his defection. The father's experiences with Fidel were so startling and vivid, moreover—and, in the retelling, so easily summarized in simple, declarative statements—that it seems unlikely they have been garbled by the son.

The second rooftop story is even more revealing of Fidel at his diabolical worst. It reflects on his willingness to bring down the fury of the gods—to destroy their temple, and himself, like a vengeful, blinded Samson—should his quest for a historic destiny be denied.

Lesnick believed that is essential to understanding Fidel. "I always saw Castro as a man with a destiny; he would either achieve it or die trying." That morbid tension was never more evident than in late October 1962.

THE CUBAN MISSILE CRISIS was entering its final and most dangerous twenty-four hours on the hot and humid night of October 26 and 27 that year.

Fidel was agitated and exhausted. Up before dawn, all that day he had rushed from one military installation to another, issuing orders, hectoring and encouraging Cuban defenders, coordinating island-wide defenses with Soviet commanders. A few hours before midnight he rushed to the Soviet embassy in Havana, his driver and backup vehicles speeding through the dim and eerily deserted streets of the city. Four days earlier he had put Cuba on maximum military alert.

Aspillaga senior was with him, monitoring Castro's personal security detail. They were joined at the embassy by Aleksandr Alekseyev, the veteran KGB troubleshooter and confidant of the Castro brothers, who was also the Soviet ambassador. Alekseyev's aide, another Kremlin Cuba specialist, was with him.

The superpowers were staring each other down across a nuclear abyss. More than forty Soviet medium and intermediate-range rockets, with nuclear warheads, capable of striking Washington, New York, and most major American cities, were on or near launch pads on the island. They had been secretly delivered with Castro's blessing. Discovered when a high-altitude U-2 reconnaissance plane flew over one of the bases, the crisis started in Washington on the morning of October 16 as President John F. Kennedy began meeting secretly with advisors. Six days later he addressed the American public and threw down the gauntlet. He imposed a naval quarantine of Cuba to block any further weapons deliveries and gave the Kremlin an ultimatum: all of its offensive weapons would have to be removed.

Fidel recognized that the crisis was coming to a head, that Cuba was in acute peril. Thirty years later at an international conference in Havana that discussed the events, he recalled his thinking on that last night of the nuclear showdown: "On that night . . . we saw no possible solution. We couldn't see a way out."[8]

He went to the embassy determined to communicate securely with the Soviet premier, Nikita Khrushchev. Angry and bellicose, Castro behaved as he always did when under pressure: He seized the initiative. Until then he had been on the sidelines of the crisis; now he thrust himself into its combustible center. Kennedy and Khrushchev were struggling to reach a peaceful solution, but Fidel remained intransigent, fearing his interests were being ignored. He was not being consulted, and, worse yet, he suspected the Soviet leader was losing his nerve, that he might cave in to the Americans. Fidel recalled:

"I aimed at encouraging him . . . I was afraid that there'd be mistakes, hesitations."

For Castro, hesitation was the precursor of cowardice. "Throughout our revolutionary history," he boasted at the Havana conference, "any time that we have smelled danger, we've taken the necessary steps. And we would rather make the mistake of taking excessive precautions than be taken by surprise because of carelessness." Khrushchev, he was convinced, was not measuring up to those standards.[9]

So Fidel presumed to provide the Soviet leader strategic advice. Still relatively inexperienced on the world stage, the thirty-six-year-old Castro took it upon himself to counsel Khrushchev, the wizened veteran of World War II and survivor of Stalin's purges, who was thirty-two years his senior. The tough old Bolshevik was in charge when the Kremlin lofted Sputnik, the first satellite, and later Yuri Gagarin, the first man into space; he had built the Soviet Union into a nuclear-armed superpower; and he was boldly challenging Kennedy in America's Caribbean backyard. Khrushchev was not expecting carping, unsolicited advice from the upstart Castro.

Alekseyev and his aide, both fluent in Spanish, translated as Fidel scribbled and then dictated what he had written. It was a letter that would be cabled to Moscow, tagged with codes indicating the most urgent priority. The drafting took several hours as Fidel, writing in Spanish with a pencil, corrected and redrafted his message and the Soviets fine-tuned the translation. Near dawn the next morning, October 27, the last full day of the missile crisis, the cable was finally dispatched to the Kremlin. The senior Aspillaga had witnessed the entire process.

Tiny remembered the letter's apocalyptic essence when he recounted his father's rooftop story to me, using the Cuban term for the missile crisis. "Fidel Castro . . . asked Khrushchev to launch the missiles against the United States during the October Crisis."

The father did not provide any elaboration to his son. But the memory, summed up in those few words, was burned into their consciousness. When Aspillaga shared the story with his American government debriefers during the summer of 1987, Castro's letter had not even been whispered about outside of small, elite circles in Moscow. In Cuba, quite possibly only Fidel and Florentino senior knew of it. In the United States, no one had any idea it existed until a few years later. It must have been one of the few things Aspillaga revealed to the CIA that seemed barely believable. The story was seemingly so absurd that it might even have caused the debriefers to doubt his reliability. The opposite, of course, turned out to be true: Aspillaga was the first to tell anyone in the United States about Fidel's letter. His report turned out to be ironclad truth.

The language Castro used in the letter was somewhat more nuanced than what either of the Aspillagas remembered, but it was macabre just the same. The thrust of the message is revealed in just a few sentences in the copy that the Cuban government eventually released.

"Dear Comrade Khrushchev," Fidel began. "From an analysis of the situation and the reports in our possession, I consider that the aggression is almost imminent within the next 24 or 72 hours."

Fidel believed that Kennedy was considering two kinds of aggression:

> The first and most likely is an air attack against certain targets with the limited objective of destroying them; the second, less probable although possible, is invasion. . . . If the second variant is implemented and the imperialists invade Cuba with the goal of occupying it, the danger that that aggressive policy poses for humanity is so great that following that event, the Soviet Union must never allow the circumstances in which the imperialists could launch the first nuclear strike against it.[10]

These are the operative words of what has become known as Fidel's Armageddon letter. Incredibly, he advocated a massive preemptive nuclear attack on the United States, a nuclear holocaust, if Cuba were invaded. Some have argued that he meant Khrushchev should attack in order to save Cuba, to destroy American military capabilities *before* invading troops could occupy the island. Castro and his sympathizers insist, however, that he meant Khrushchev should order an attack *after* an invasion to prevent a surprise American assault on Soviet targets.

Journalist and Castro biographer Tad Szulc, who spent many hours in meetings with Fidel, believed the ambiguous language of the letter could be read either way. On balance, however, he concluded that Castro had advocated a preemptive attack to stave off an American invasion and military occupation of Cuba.[11]

It was not just the missiles on the island that Fidel thought should be launched but also the strategic arsenal based on Soviet soil. Surely he knew that millions of civilians on both sides of the Iron Curtain would die after such a nuclear onslaught. Major American cities would be leveled. Much of the Soviet Union would be reduced to rubble in retaliatory responses from American Minutemen missiles in hardened silos, submarine-launched nuclear warheads, and strategic bombers that survived the initial attack. Clouds of radiation would soak continents. The physical and environmental damage would be incalculable.

There is nothing like the Armageddon letter in the entire history of the nuclear age since Hiroshima and Nagasaki. No other world leader is known to have recommended the use of even a single nuclear warhead since President Harry Truman approved those American attacks on Japan at the end of World War II. Fidel's recommendation to Khrushchev was orders of magnitude greater. He urged a massive, surprise attack in which there could have been hundreds of nuclear explosions, all vastly more powerful than the two bombs dropped on Japan. Even in film and fiction such grotesque thoughts are relegated only to insane Dr. Strangelove–type characters.

Yet, as reprehensible as it was, nothing came of it. Castro was baying into the wind that night at the Soviet embassy. Khrushchev was horrified when he received the letter. He had been traumatized by his wartime experiences and was loath to endure anything like them again. In one of his letters to Kennedy during the crisis, he mused, "I have been in two wars and know that war ends only when it has rolled through the cities and villages, sowing in its wake death and destruction."[12]

Khrushchev's most respected biographer noted that during World War II, "thousands died before his eyes, from simple soldiers mowed down in ill-advised battles to generals who committed suicide in his presence." A year into the carnage in which 27 million Soviets perished, Khrushchev himself was almost killed when German planes bombed his command post. Fidel should have known there was no chance that the Soviet leader would preemptively fire his strategic arsenal at American targets and by doing so provoke a pulverizing nuclear counterattack.[13]

It may be argued, therefore, that the Armageddon letter was not Fidel's greatest crime because nothing came of it. Other more consequential decisions he made were anything but hypothetical. The actions he took early in his revolution to uproot Cuba's entire moneyed class took a horrendous toll. The revolution seized virtually all private property; nearly all of the former owners were propelled into exile with nothing but the clothes on their backs. They were not compensated and have been ridiculed by Fidel and his propagandists ever since as monstrous social deviates. Hundreds of thousands—ultimately more than a million—people were forced from their homeland this way. Even today, twenty thousand Cubans legally emigrate to the United States every year in search of better lives. They are the disposable detritus of Fidel's failed revolution.

Another truly contemptible decision he made, in 1980, was comparable but on a smaller scale. During the mass exodus of Cubans from the port of Mariel, he emptied psychiatric hospital wards and maximum security prisons, then expelled those Cubans by forcing them onto boats going to Miami and Key West. Slightly more than 127,000 people fled the island in that chaotic sealift he ordered. Among them were about 17,000 criminals—including murderers, rapists, and drug traffickers—and people with severe mental illnesses who were abruptly torn from their families and treatments. Only a handful of those so-called excludables was ever accepted back. The rest remain in their adopted country, many incarcerated for committing heinous capital crimes, including mass murders. Only Fidel could have made the decision to force them onto the boats to Florida. He has rarely been challenged to explain it, and he has never apologized or expressed regret.

Those and other egregious violations of human rights committed by Castro are well known. In contrast, for twenty-eight years the Armageddon letter was one of his best-kept secrets. He never expected it to be exposed. It was, after all, a private and secret communication between allied heads of state. He never suspected the Soviet Union would eventually self-destruct and that many sensitive documents would spill forth.

Khrushchev's son Sergei was the first to mention the letter on the public record. It happened during another international conference about the missile crisis, in Moscow, in January 1989. Sergei let it slip that his father had mentioned that Fidel wrote a letter recommending a nuclear attack on the United States.

The reaction to the revelation was fierce. Cuban and Soviet denials were so strident that Sergei felt compelled to retract his words. Alekseyev, the KGB ambassador and translator, told an American reporter, "That's stupid. I wrote the telexes and there was nothing of that kind." The Cuban government joined the chorus with a rebuttal published in *Granma:* "It's ridiculous." Under the weight of the denials, the media furor soon subsided; the allegation seemed just too preposterous to be credible.

Nothing more was heard until September 1990. Glasnost, the policy of greater openness in the moribund Soviet Union, encouraged candor that had not previously been permissible. It was in that spirit that the third volume of Khrushchev's posthumously published memoirs, known by its subtitle, *The Glasnost Tapes,* appeared and finally burst the bubble Fidel had tried so hard to protect.

After his ouster from power in 1964, Khrushchev secretly dictated his life story into a tape recorder hidden at the *dacha,* the secluded country house where he was exiled. The subject he chose to treat first was the one of greatest emotional importance to him: Fidel and the missile crisis. Khrushchev's published words provided an authoritative description of the letter. They seem to support Szulc's interpretation that Fidel hoped for a nuclear attack to prevent an American invasion and occupation of the island. The fallen Soviet leader wrote: "We received a telegram from our ambassador in Cuba. . . . Castro suggested that in order to prevent our nuclear missiles from being destroyed, we should launch a preemptive strike against the United States. . . . We needed to immediately deliver a nuclear missile strike."[14]

Reluctantly at first, Fidel responded, ridiculing the story in a speech in Havana's Karl Marx Theater on September 28. He tried to blame the United States—specifically, he meant the CIA. "They have always used or found ways to create animosity and hatred against Cuba within American public opinion." As usual he worried more about how he would be perceived by important shapers of opinion in the United States than by the Cuban people.

He continued: Alekseyev was not really proficient in Spanish; he had translated the message poorly, distorting his meaning. Fidel revealed, nonetheless, that a copy of the letter had been found and would be released. He no doubt was aware that another copy, in the original Russian, was scheduled to be pulled from Soviet archives.[15]

Khrushchev provided additional incriminating details in his memoirs. He explained that he and Fidel had an opportunity in May 1963 to review the controversy during an extended visit Castro paid to the Soviet Union. Still unable to comprehend how Fidel could have advocated nuclear holocaust, Khrushchev did not mince words with the leader he described as "young and hotheaded."

> I told Castro . . . You wanted to start a war with the United States. If the war had begun we would somehow have survived, but Cuba no doubt would have ceased to exist. It would have been crushed into powder. Yet you suggested a nuclear strike![16]

Oleg Troyanovsky, a senior ambassador and Khrushchev foreign policy aide, received Fidel's cabled letter when it arrived in Moscow. He also wrote about it:

Khrushchev received a telegram from Fidel Castro. The message, written with the typical emotionality of Fidel, was filled with anxiety. I remember calling up Khrushchev who was at home and reading him the telegram . . . I have no doubt that it added fuel to the anxious thoughts preying on his mind.[17]

What Troyanovsky meant, and what other evidence supports, is that the Soviet leader was so disturbed by Fidel's words that he realized he could delay no longer in reaching a settlement with Kennedy. The Soviet leadership knew by late in the day on October 27 that, as Troyanovsky put it, "one spark could trigger an explosion." They had no idea what Castro—acting like a rancorous child playing with fire—might do next.

There had been other alarming developments that day, roughly coinciding with the receipt of Fidel's letter in Moscow. The first shots fired in anger during the crisis were heard in the morning. On Fidel's orders, at first light, hundreds of Cuban antiaircraft batteries started shooting at low-altitude American reconnaissance aircraft. The Cuban media were filled with reports of rallies and a nation preparing for house-to-house combat. Discussing the crisis at the 1992 Havana conference, Fidel remembered how close he had brought the superpowers to actual hostilities.

"War started in Cuba on October 27 in the morning." He preferred violent confrontation even as Kennedy and Khrushchev were desperately trying to avoid it.[18]

That afternoon, an American U-2 spy plane was shot down over eastern Cuba by a Soviet surface-to-air missile. Major Rudolf Anderson, the air force pilot, was killed. Fidel has admitted that he had provoked the incident by stoking a mood of red hot militancy that inflamed both Cuban and Soviet commanders. He later admitted: "We cannot say they were totally responsible . . . the firing started, and in a basic spirit of solidarity, the Soviets decided to fire as well." Without authorization from Moscow, the Soviet missile base commander ordered the plane shot down. In another interview, Fidel stated simply that the plane was destroyed "undoubtedly as a result of a situation created by our decision."[19]

Still, Khrushchev remembered the incident differently. He wrote: "Castro ordered our antiaircraft officers to shoot down a U-2 reconnaissance plane."[20]

In March 1963, a sensitive and highly valued CIA spy who was never doubled and enjoyed access to Cuban leaders was the first to report on the incident.

His account was similar to Khrushchev's. Fidel had seized the initiative; the responsibility for the U-2 shoot-down was his. The source reported that "Castro harangued a Soviet commander" who gave in to the pressure and "to Castro's persuasiveness," and then ordered the plane shot down. The source said "the Soviet command was furious," and the officer was sent home under arrest.[21]

Command and control were breaking down within the Soviet expeditionary forces in Cuba; Khrushchev's commanders were taking orders from Fidel. The combination of that concern, the Armageddon letter, the destruction of the U-2, and the Cuban antiaircraft barrages against American aircraft were too much for the Soviet leader. He knew the crisis he started had to be brought to a peaceful end. Without seeking additional concessions that Kennedy was prepared to make or consulting with Castro, he capitulated. He announced his decision to withdraw the missiles.

FIDEL HAS REMAINED UNREPENTANT. In the September 1990 speech in Havana he blustered: "I do not regret in the least what I did nor what I said." Expressions of shame or sincere regret have always been as alien to him as the possibility of shaving off his signature beard.

During the 1992 Havana conference, he spoke briefly and elliptically about the letter and again was unapologetic. He was asked about it six years later, during an extended interview with CNN News. By then, better rehearsed and with a fistful of relevant documents, he offered the most detailed defense of his actions. He still refused to admit he had been grotesquely wrong.

With a grand flourish, he told the interviewer: "It is the most tremendous letter in history." He was trying to create a new narrative about the incident. He wanted somehow to spin the experience 180 degrees, into something noble. Castro proclaimed: "I think one needed to be very strong, and I would say that one needed great moral courage to say that, because that was the way I perceived things, my perception of what was about to happen."

In these and on a few other occasions when the subject of the letter was raised, Fidel has been adroit in controlling the discussions. He did so by flooding his interlocutors with flows of verbiage, always articulate and precise, and often flattering, while rarely revealing more than what he planned to at the start. Smoothly changing the subject midstream, he tacked in new directions and did not stop talking until the purpose of the original question was forgotten. The result is that during the years that elapsed after he wrote the letter, and before he went into retirement and seclusion, he was never pressed to explain the mystery of what he was thinking when he advocated nuclear war.

Some have argued he must have been irrational that night at the Soviet embassy, an idea easy enough to surmise. One respected American scholar wrote, "A leader who convinces himself that only collective suicide is possible is not acting rationally."[22]

But the senior Aspillaga reported no such emotional or psychotic lapses. He said nothing to his son about Fidel seeming unstable or erratic that night at the Soviet embassy. The truth is he was not out of control. He did not dictate the Armageddon letter in a moment of madness or a burst of magical realism. His assessment of the situation in those final, bleak hours of the missile crisis was coldly, cruelly rational. His friend Max Lesnick had it right: His "mind is a logical mind."

Although Fidel has always calculated his moves carefully, misunderstandings about his most extreme behavior have been common. That is because observers have consistently underestimated his capacity to do the unthinkable, to act aggressively in ways that would be unlikely for any other world leader. All through his career he was masterful at hurling bolts from the blue, astonishing adversaries with his audacity and perfect timing.

When he secretly sent thousands of Cuban troops to fight in Angola in 1975 alongside the Marxist guerrillas he had sponsored, for example, American intelligence was completely surprised. We were not the only ones. Secretary of State Henry Kissinger later wrote in his memoirs that it had been unimaginable Fidel "would act so provocatively so far from home."[23]

That intervention and a similar one in Ethiopia a few years later were just two of dozens of examples of sudden discontinuities, bold strokes in Cuban policy conceived by Fidel. Preempting and eliminating enemies, seizing initiatives, taking calculated risks, going on the offensive, conspiring and manipulating for personal advantage have been hallmarks of his leadership style since his university days. In his prime, Fidel's behavior could rarely be predicted reliably. He was *sui generis,* perhaps the modern world's most idiosyncratic major leader. He was unique because of the limitless grandiosity of his ambitions.

Lesnick recognized that Fidel's quest for a historic destiny would likely only produce two outcomes: either greatness or martyrdom. They are the poles that explain why Castro has eschewed the middle latitudes that are, from his adven-turer's perspective, for ordinary men, those seeking safety and comfort.

Starting on July 26, 1953, when he led a suicidal attack against the Moncada military garrison in eastern Cuba to jump-start his revolutionary odyssey, Fidel veered between these extremes. By his own—exaggerated—count, eighty of the men he threw into that battle were killed. Again, in early December 1956, only a few survived the landing of his expeditionary force on Cuba's southeastern coast that launched his insurgency. In a fundraising speech in New York the previous November, he had promised that "in 1956 we will be free or we will be martyrs." He needed dead heroes and revolutionary pyrotechnics to legitimize his cause. Once in power two years later, it would always be the same.[24]

He expected his followers—whether a few dozen or an entire nation—to join him in triumph or heroic death. Many times he resembled a disturbed fire-and-brimstone evangelist leading his flock to mass martyrdom, all for the sake of his distorted visions and conceits.

In a speech in April 1963 marking the second anniversary of the CIA's Bay of Pigs invasion, Castro recalled the tense end game of the missile crisis, no doubt with the scene at the Soviet embassy in mind. "We are reminded of those days in which all the people, with impressive serenity, prepared to resist the enemy at-tack . . . prepared to fight, and prepared to die."[25]

It is an observation he has repeated many times over the years, actually be-lieving that masses of Cubans would have given their lives for him. In September 1981, for example, he told a Mexican journalist: "The calmness with which the people were ready to die proved touching, and almost incredible to me."[26]

The beauty of mass martyrdom preoccupied him on other occasions too. During the first year of the Reagan presidency he greatly feared, Fidel was again openly seized by forebodings of death and destruction. I wrote an intelligence assessment about his dark moods in November 1981, when I was the principal analyst in the National Intelligence Council. The study was based entirely on unclassified information, mainly his speeches and public performances. I wrote about "his persistent emphasis on themes related to holocaust and apocalypse."

There was abundant evidence in his oratory that he feared the new American administration and its threatening stances toward Cuba. The Soviet leadership, remembering his belligerent behavior during the missile crisis, had notified him that there would be no security guarantee if the United States initiated hostilities. He felt alone, close to a precipice, even as he confronted dire social and economic problems on the island in the aftermath of the Mariel exodus. I knew nothing about the Armageddon letter when I wrote in a now declassified assessment about his black broodings at that critical juncture:

> An apparently despairing Castro has frequently masked his rising fears of con-
> flict with the United States with bravado about how true Cuban revolutionaries
> must fight to the last man. His apocalyptic mood is often quite explicit. He has
> repeatedly used the word "holocaust," has mused about Cuba and the world after
> nuclear warfare between the superpowers and has admonished his audiences
> to increase their vigilance and revolutionary worth in the face of impending
> disaster.[27]

In mid-September 1981 he had said that President Reagan's defense buildup will "lead to nothing but a final holocaust." On October 24 he concluded: "to die honorably is a good way to behave and act." Another time he said, "[I]f they dare to invade, more Yankees will die here than in World War II," and again, that "millions of Yankees will die. . . . We are not like the Christians of ancient Rome who meekly surrendered."

Just as he did twenty-one years earlier when he drafted the Armageddon letter, he was feeling an extreme sense of isolation and abandonment. I noted in the intelligence assessment how on two other occasions he reiterated the same gruesome vision of his and the revolution's denouement. "As long as there is a single armed man," he said, "we will fight to the last."[28]

Castro often fantasized that he would be the last warrior holding out against encircling forces of evil. For decades that was a standard element of his apocalyptic musings. Partly it is attributable to his bravura, to his belief in his personal exceptionalism. But it is also a reflection of the precautions he always takes when in dangerous situations. He shot Leonel Gomez in the back from a distance. His first known kill in the Sierra Maestra during his guerrilla campaign was also from a considerable distance, when he fired a powerful rifle equipped with a telescopic sight. Others who were with him during the attack on the Moncada garrison remember him hanging back, avoiding the worst of the battle, screaming incoherent orders.[29]

And in October 1962 when he drafted the Armageddon letter, he reportedly also played it safe. Anatoly Dobrynin, the well-connected Soviet ambassador in Washington for many years, wrote in his memoirs that Fidel "even suggested that our ambassador withdraw with him to the bunker built at the command post in a cave near Havana." Fidel might well have survived an American invasion there, possibly even a nuclear war.[30]

Another example of his apocalypse complex, also thoroughly publicized in the official Cuban media, occurred in October 1983. About eight hundred Cubans were caught on the small Caribbean nation of Grenada when American military forces invaded, ostensibly to rescue American medical students. Fidel radioed his personnel—military and civilian construction workers—ordering them to fight to the death. Later, when he thought they were complying, he again reached their commanding officer: "We congratulate you on your heroic resistance. Cuban people are proud of you. Do not surrender under any circumstances."[31]

He expected mass suicide for the glory of the revolution, *his* revolution. The top Cuban officer and all but a small number of the others ignored their commander in chief's bizarre orders, however, and surrendered to the Americans. Aspillaga was familiar with the aftermath. He wrote in the manuscript he shared with me that when the survivors returned to Cuba, they were harshly interrogated over extended periods of time.

Some, he knew from a friend who was one of the interrogators, had cooperated with their captors even though they were only held for a brief period in Grenada before being repatriated to Cuba. "At least four," Aspillaga wrote, "confessed to accepting offers to work for the enemy upon their return to Cuba." Some were then turned by Cuban counterintelligence into double agents. At least one officer suspected of having been recruited by American intelligence refused to confess and was reduced in rank and assigned to meaningless work. Aspillaga's interrogator friend told him that the Cubans in Grenada were justified in disregarding Fidel's orders.

Tiny wrote that the investigation in Havana revealed that they "chose not to confront the Americans not only because of the lack of efficient command, but because they did not understand why they had to die if they were not defending their own country."

He added that "all were sentenced to hard labor in constructing roads and other public works in the province of Matanzas. Officers of high rank were sent to highest-risk war zones in Angola."

Fidel expected all Cubans, even the civilians in Grenada, to mimic the ideal Spartan warrior. He required them to be indifferent to hardship and pain, to blindly follow his orders, to die blithely in defense of the fatherland. Loyal Cuban revolutionaries were not to reason why or to second guess him. It was a bitter blow when so few lived up to those expectations.

Yet another period of apocalyptic thinking occurred in 2010, more than two years after Fidel officially surrendered the presidency. In his retirement, he took to penning ruminations about assorted subjects from his Havana convalescent quarters, editorials that then were issued by the Cuban media. They are called "Fidel's Reflections." Nearly all concerned international issues, and some were clearly intended to repair or embellish his image. Between June and November, a dozen of these articles were devoted to his renewed preoccupation with nuclear holocaust. One was titled "The Dangers of Nuclear War," another "On the Brink of Tragedy." On June 16 he wrote that "the sky is growing increasingly cloudy," and on July 11 he brooded that "today everything hangs by a thread."

Then, on August 23, he appeared to return to the knotty matter of the Armageddon letter. He made no explicit reference to it, but his intent seemed clear enough. The article was titled "Nuclear Winter." It was still bothering him so many years later that he had come across as a Cuban Dr. Strangelove when the message to Khrushchev was released. In his dotage he sought another way to be exonerated, to explain it away.

Nearly coinciding with his eighty-fourth birthday, he wrote that he had only recently come to understand some of the most fundamental and commonly known realities of textbook strategic warfare. He said he had consulted earlier in the day with four Cuban experts, including his eldest son—who was once in charge of the Cuban nuclear agency—along with the head of the military's science and technology department. They helped him, he claimed, finally to appreciate what he said that had previously eluded him.

"I should have understood much earlier that the risks of a nuclear war were much more serious than I imagined . . . I had not taken into account one quite simple reality: it is not the same to explode 500 nuclear bombs in 1,000 days as it is to have them explode in one single day."[32]

There is no reason to believe Castro was senile when he wrote or, more likely, dictated those words. It strains credulity, though, that he did not know this simple truth that was for decades clear to schoolboys and girls across the globe. Over the years, he had studied the missile crisis in depth with some of its most prominent American and Soviet decision makers of that time. He participated in the 1992

Havana conference. He presided over one of the best intelligence services in the world and led the most accomplished military from any third-world nation. Fidel prides himself on his photographic memory. And he is a voracious reader. Yet he pretended not ever to have discussed the simple mechanics of nuclear conflict with anyone before or to have read any of the thousands of articles and treatises that have explained it.

With that preposterous, self-exculpating explanation, he apparently hoped to put the Armageddon letter behind him once and for all. He was worried about his legacy, how he would be viewed by historians. No other decision he had made nagged at him as much. He could not bring himself to admit that he had been mistaken in October 1962. He wanted it known that he considered nuclear war abhorrent and despicable.

He had already done his best to seize the moral high ground on that issue. On March 2, 2003, during his only visit to Japan, he went to Hiroshima, where he laid a wreath in memory of the dead at the Peace Memorial Museum. Back home a few days later, during a ceremony in which he was inaugurated for a new term as Cuba's president, he railed against the world's first nuclear power.

"The attack was absolutely unnecessary and can never be morally justified. . . . There was no excuse whatsoever for that terrible slaughter of children, women, old persons and innocent people of any age. . . . Millions of people should visit this site so that the world will know what really happened."[33]

Righteous he was. But there is no denying that he had been willing in October 1962 for millions to perish in a cataclysmic global requiem for the Cuban revolution. By any reading, his letter to Khrushchev demonstrated a cosmic disregard for humanity.

FOUR

COME TO CUBA

IN NOVEMBER 1962, A FEW WEEKS AFTER THE RESOLUTION OF the missile crisis, Florentino senior enrolled his son in the DGI's intelligence school. Tiny was several months shy of his sixteenth birthday. "It was my destiny," he told me, "to work in intelligence." He never doubted his father's wisdom in facilitating it.

All of his fifty classmates were precocious too, most also teenagers, sixteen to nineteen years old. The eldest was twenty-three, and there was another boy who was even younger than Tiny. They were malleable and learned quickly, enthusiastic acolytes in a fledgling intelligence service led by revolutionary stalwarts, most of whom were only a few years older.

Ramiro Valdés, the interior minister at the top of their chain of command, was thirty that year. Manuel Piñeiro—Barbaroja, the American-educated "Redbeard"—who led the DGI from its inception, was twenty-eight. Fidel was thirty-six; Raúl, thirty-one; Che Guevara, thirty-four. Most of the other top-tier figures were also still in their twenties or early thirties, as were the most important DGI operatives abroad. Armando López Orta—the suave "Arquimides"—was typical. A friend of Piñeiro, he was thirty when assigned to run the DGI's large Center in Paris. All were in the vanguard of a generational upheaval that was convulsing Cuban society.[1]

Most older men associated with the prerevolutionary order were expendable. They were viewed as corrupt, supercilious, and beholden to the United States. Impressionable, nationalistic youths—the raw material for Fidel's idealized "new revolutionary man"—would supplant them. The reordering purge was carried out first in the elite intelligence and security agencies and at the top of Raúl's revolutionary armed forces.

Nearly all of the young bloods were peasant and working-class revolutionaries who had rallied to the Castros' insurgency or, like Aspillaga, scions of Communist Party ideologues. Only their uncontaminated, rising generation could be trusted to do Fidel's work with energy and devotion, without looking back longingly to Cuba's bourgeois past.

Most of Tiny's classmates were schooled in intelligence collection tradecraft, propaganda, and active measures. Nearly all were then assigned under diplomatic covers to DGI Centers abroad where they soon came to the attention of CIA officers. Young and awkward, some just beginning to shave, the Cuban boys were lacking in the social graces their diplomatic cover stories ordinarily required.

David Atlee Phillips, a World War II bombardier, flamboyant amateur actor, and playwright before joining the CIA, was sure he would not be fooled by them, as initially he had been fooled by Fidel. In January 1959 when serving under deep cover for the Agency, he stood on a street corner in Havana and, with an exultant crowd of Cubans, cheered Castro's arrival there fresh from his guerrilla victory. That was the contagious attitude in the Agency in those early days of the revolution. A case officer who also served undercover in Cuba at that time confessed to me that "the whole Agency then was pro-Castro. I can't remember anyone who was not pro-Fidel."[2]

A few years later Phillips was assigned to the large Mexico City station, where he began encountering some of Piñeiro's boys. After retiring, Phillips penned an article and a book chapter about them, arguing how dramatically Cuban intelligence had improved since its formative years. Both were titled: "Castro's Spies Are No Longer Teenagers." The callow Cuban agents were easy to spot, he wrote, "with their long hair, unkempt beards, ill-fitting black suits, and invariably, hip bulges which scarcely concealed a Colt .45-caliber automatic pistol."[3]

He may have had one hotheaded nineteen-year-old especially in mind as he penned these words. Rogelio Rodríguez was a DGI officer who served two tours in the Mexico City Center in the early 1960s. In December 1961, according to a CIA biographic file, Rodríguez was involved in a "melee" at the international airport when he rushed to defend a departing courier, no doubt a DGI colleague carrying sensitive materials. Both men packed poorly concealed pistols that were confiscated by Mexican police. Undeterred, Rodríguez threatened to return armed again, shouting "We'll see if you take my pistol then."[4]

Not surprisingly, Piñeiro's tough young charges attracted considerable attention. Former Mexican foreign minister and author Jorge Castañeda, who knew Redbeard well, wrote about them much as Phillips had. The DGI chief's "*muchachos* were generally young, lower middle class, or quite poor, uncouth but bright." Castañeda also quoted a Colombian who knew some of them: "Piñeiro taught these boys how to dress and use knives and forks at the table."[5]

There were no manicured playing fields in their backgrounds, no tennis whites or prom night formals. Most, including Aspillaga, had scarcely any schooling at all. But Phillips, like so many others in the CIA in those days, was deceived again. Too easily dismissed, those Cuban teenagers were rugged true believers in Fidel and his revolution. Thoroughly trained and ready for almost anything, they should not have been underestimated.

Canny and street smart, they had been toughened during the years spent as guerrilla fighters and conspirators in the revolution's urban underground. Some had survived the brutalizing ordeals of Batista's political prisons. Quite a few were adoring acolytes of Fidel or Raúl or of Piñeiro or another top lieutenant who treated them like adopted sons. Castañeda wrote that Piñeiro's boys were "adoring and totally devoted to him."

A CIA officer in Santiago, Cuba's second city at the eastern end of the island, also admired Redbeard when they met on several occasions in 1958. He told me he had a high opinion of Piñeiro. "I thought he was a real nice guy. He was not a communist when I knew him."

This experienced Agency officer had also been deceived. Piñeiro had studied at Columbia University in New York earlier in the 1950s, where he courted and married a Tennessee-born ballerina. He spoke colloquial English and was adept at charming Americans. But later, when he threw in his lot with the Castro brothers, he was a hardcore revolutionary. He shared their antipathy toward the United States and their desire to sow revolution throughout Latin America. Fidel and Raúl had no doubt that he was the perfect choice to get their nascent intelligence service up and running.

Under Redbeard's tough leadership, it did not take the DGI long to achieve something close to world-class excellence. Five KGB instructors played a crucial role in that. Future CIA director Richard Helms recalled that they did "a rather astonishing job."[6]

The Soviets taught the full range of illicit tradecraft. The chief tutor, a short, gray-haired Russian nicknamed "the Frenchman" by the Cubans, spoke good Spanish. With his Soviet bodyguard or aide, he was often seen at Piñeiro's side. Cuban instructors in the intelligence school learned quickly from these KGB veterans, and Redbeard innovated and improvised. The best students completing a course in some operational specialty often jumped to the front of the classroom, where they then taught novices what they had just mastered. The pattern followed class after class.[7]

Soon the eager young Cuban spies were as skilled in intelligence tradecraft as their more seasoned CIA adversaries. Implacably loyal to their commander in chief, their duty was to emulate and please him. And like Fidel, who relished the challenge of taking on the Americans, they were buoyantly confident, convinced they were better, tougher, and operationally more ingenious than the more conventional spies from Langley. Such hubris has been a defining characteristic of Cuban intelligence ever since Fidel's David-and-Goliath triumph over the CIA at the Bay of Pigs.

In the fall of 1963 when Tiny completed his training, double-agent tradecraft was already the Cubans' preferred first line of defense. Originally with KGB guidance and very quickly by dint of Cuban ingenuity and guile alone, the Cubans were turning CIA collaborators in many countries. Others already under Cuban sway were dangled before the CIA as tempting recruitment prospects; if the CIA took the bait, they joined the expanding ranks of Cuban doubles.

Roberto Hernández del Llano, the defector who worked in counterintelligence with Aspillaga, told me how the DGI often managed to stay a few steps ahead of the Agency, laying invisible traps.

"When we learned that a CIA officer was developing an interest in a certain Latin American in a third country, we would beat them to the punch. We'd recruit that person ourselves and then let the CIA believe they were recruiting a good source, who, in reality, we controlled and then used against the Agency."

Enlisting collaborators, especially youthful ones, was relatively easy for Cuba's young spies. The revolution attracted multitudes of acolytes, especially in

Latin America. For them, Fidel's heated denunciations of American "imperialism" needed no elaboration. Cuba was under siege, and no one in Washington was bothering to deny it. The revolution needed the help of progressive men and women wherever they might be. Such pleas were the essence of the pitch Cuban handlers usually made when recruiting new agents.

Enduring operational standards were set in those early days of Cuban espionage. Few spies were paid, for example. One of the major defectors told the CIA that fully 95 percent were not. Then, and ever since, nearly all who have worked undercover for Cuba have believed blindly in Fidel's causes, delighted to work for him pro bono. The most they have generally expected to receive are reimbursements for out-of-pocket expenses. Many Americans have been brought into the clandestine Cuban fold as true believers. Hernández del Llano says, "Americans have always been relatively easy to recruit. So many are naive about Cuba, and predisposed to its myths and propaganda."[8]

The public record of Cuban clandestine inroads bears this out. As many as half of the Americans who flocked illegally to the island in the 1960s and 1970s as volunteers to cut sugarcane or work in construction brigades "were eventually recruited by Cuban intelligence," according to Hernández del Llano. Some of those political pilgrims were converted into reliable, long-term undercover assets. Others became witting or unwitting agents of influence, energetic and convincing apologists for the revolution. Many settled into academia. By the mid- and late 1960s, communist Cuba was embraced on campuses across the United States, viewed as an innocent, beleaguered victim of American imperialism. The professor who handed one of her students over to the DGI for recruitment was, therefore, hardly an unusual case, except that her treachery was exposed after Aspillaga defected.

By 1963, active measures, covert actions to bolster Cuban causes, were lavishly funded by the Castros. Copies of Fidel's speeches and glossy literature extolling the revolution and its leaders were pumped out of Havana in many languages for local distribution.

But the CIA was watching closely. In February 1963, its tough anti-Castro director, Republican John McCone, told the House of Representatives Foreign Affairs Committee that every month twelve tons of such propaganda was being intercepted and destroyed in Panama alone. Another ten tons were being sent to Costa Rica. Presumably, most of this propaganda was to be distributed to other countries in the region. Radio Havana and Prensa Latina, the DGI-dominated Cuban news service, were also engaged in "a massive propaganda effort," McCone testified.[9]

Cuban agents put into play clever disinformation campaigns to indict the CIA in foreign capitals. They enlisted sympathetic journalists and broadcasters to push Cuban lines. Prominent intellectuals and pundits enamored of Fidel and the revolution, and hostile to the United States, volunteered their services to Piñeiro's boys or were easily enticed to help. In Paris, the Cuban embassy operated its own lively cabaret on the Left Bank showcasing Cuban food, music, cigars, and tropical island bonhomie. Not incidentally, it also provided cover for espionage and influence operations.[10]

The DGI's overseas presence expanded quickly. By 1963, it was present in dozens of countries, wherever Cuba had official representation. Center chiefs operated independently of ambassadors, taking orders only from headquarters, the Principal Center in Havana.

The Paris embassy was typical. Because he was a boyhood friend of Fidel's, the ambassador there in the mid-1960s was more freewheeling than a typical Cuban envoy. Yet López Orta, the DGI chief, was more powerful still. Whenever there was a dispute over priorities in the embassy, the rule, according to DGI defector Orlando Castro Hidalgo, who served under López, was that "the illegal has precedence over the legal."[11]

In countries where Cuba did not have embassies, the DGI recruited foreign agents, referring to them as "illegals" and running them through its Illegals Department. Most of them—university students, labor leaders, and intellectuals, bureaucrats, politicians, and military officers too—were infected by the myths of the Castros' revolution and the day-to-day drama of its struggles with Yankee "imperialism." With DGI help, these deep-cover operatives traveled clandestinely, usually by way of Prague, to Havana, where they learned basic intelligence tradecraft while being steeped in revolutionary ideology.

Home again, their missions were to penetrate governments and important political groups and to target the CIA. Most also provided support for Cuban-sponsored insurgent groups operating in their own countries or neighboring ones. The scope of this early Cuban effort was enormous even by the standards of much larger intelligence services. During just five years in the early 1960s, at least 650 foreign illegals traveled, most by way of communist Czechoslovakia, to

Cuba for training. Vasily Mitrokhin had the hard documentary evidence to prove it. A KGB archivist, he stole a trove of secret Soviet records and shared them with British intelligence when he defected in 1992.[12]

After the missile crisis, the DGI began dispatching another kind of illegal: Cubans posing with false identities as foreign nationals. This is the way the term "illegals tradecraft" is normally understood. William August Fisher, the deep-cover spy for the Kremlin, best known as Rudolf Abel, is one of the most familiar exemplars. He was arrested and convicted in New York in 1957 for running a large and productive spy ring. A few years later he was exchanged for Francis Gary Powers, the American pilot of a CIA U-2 spy plane shot down over the Soviet Union in 1960.

The work of such classic illegals is expensive, tedious, and dangerous. As a result, major intelligence services generally use them sparingly. KGB defector Oleg Kalugin has said that "even in the worst years of the Cold War, I think there were no more than ten Soviet illegals in the United States, probably fewer." No doubt he was correct, yet, in June 2010, exactly that many Russian illegals—a new generation—were apprehended by the FBI in several American cities. Like the Cubans, who run a surprisingly large number of classic illegals, Vladimir Putin's Russia today also seems willing to play for higher stakes.[13]

The DGI learned the intricacies of classic illegals tradecraft from the KGB. One of the Soviet advisors working with "the Frenchman" at DGI headquarters used the name Vladimir Grinchenko. He taught in Havana after having lived for ten years as an illegal in Argentina. Some DGI officers, like the defector Gerardo Peraza, were enrolled in specialized espionage schools in the Soviet Union. Peraza told a Senate investigating committee that one of his KGB instructors was an expert in illegals tradecraft. That Russian had spent twenty years living under an assumed identity in the United States.[14]

In those early days, Cuban illegals prepared for overseas assignments far more rapidly than their KGB counterparts. Mitrokhin, the KGB archivist, told British intelligence the reason was partly because the DGI paid less attention to devising defensible "legends"—the characteristics and paperwork supporting an invented identity. Even so, Aspillaga's young classmates would not have qualified for such advanced duties. The DGI has always selected older, worldlier intelligence officers for illegal assignments. In recent years, the methods used to choose, train, and back them up have become much more sophisticated.

Legends have been validated with exquisitely forged documentation. Posing as, say, Dominicans, Venezuelans, Argentines, or Puerto Ricans, Cuban citizen illegals easily transform themselves. Acquiring the inflections and slang and learning customs unique to their adopted nationalities are the highest hurdles they have to surmount. They blend in quickly, naturalizing into their adopted countries, some gaining significant influence in political and media circles. For obvious reasons, it has been easier still for Cuban illegals to meld into the Miami exile community.

Piñeiro did not initiate such penetration operations until early 1964. When the CIA welcomed Vladimir Rodríguez Lahera, the first knowledgeable defector from the DGI that April, he revealed that there were three Cuban citizen illegals finishing training programs and preparing to begin living their new identities. He said one was slated to settle in Mexico; the others elsewhere—he did not know exactly where—in Latin America. The three were the vanguard of a covert operational specialty Cuban intelligence has mastered to a degree seemingly unrivaled by almost any other foreign intelligence service.[15]

When he defected, Aspillaga knew of two "really good" Cuban illegals living with false identities and operating beyond suspicion in California, presumably in Silicon Valley. He was not sure if they were posing as American citizens or possibly as Latin American legal residents. Although the FBI must have made determined efforts to track them, I am not aware that they have ever been uncovered.

The DGI constructed the Wasp network, centered in Miami and the Florida Keys, around a devoted team of illegals. The largest Cuban spy ring yet to be dismantled by the FBI, it targeted exile groups and Defense Department installations while its members also allegedly carried out special assignments, including the assassination attempt against Aspillaga at his home. Gerardo Hernández, a ranking intelligence officer, performed ably as the Wasp leader. He used two aliases, backed up with false passports and meticulously rehearsed legends, both identifying him as a Puerto Rican and therefore an American citizen. Just in case, he also carried a forged Texas birth certificate.

Hernández is serving two life sentences in a federal penitentiary for espionage. Two of his top associates, also Cuban illegals posing as American citizens, were sentenced with him, along with two Cuban Americans. An additional five members of the net cooperated with the prosecution and received lighter sentences. Twenty more—some of them also documented DGI illegals—were able to escape to Cuba before they could be arrested or went underground in the United States. Flight was easy; typically the DGI equips its citizen illegals with at least one backup set of false documentation to be used if the primary alias is compromised.

Since those prosecutions, the five imprisoned ringleaders have been heralded incessantly in the Cuban media as *"Los Cinco Heroes,"* the Five Heroes. The regime insists they were doing nothing more sinister than trying to prevent acts of terrorism on the island by militant Miami exiles. By keeping the bright propaganda spotlight on them, Cuban leaders seek to reassure all their undercover operatives that, if apprehended, they too would never be forsaken.

DGI defector José Maragon recently told me about a third category of DGI illegals tradecraft; "true identity" illegals. Starting in the mid-1980s, Cubans with dual nationalities—most of them also American citizens—were identified and recruited on the island where they had lived since childhood. They were trained intensively for a number of years, their loyalty to the revolution tested and re-tested to eliminate any doubts. They probably also were polygraphed to be further probed and vetted. Maragon said that his former service wanted "to reduce the costs and serious difficulties of creating true, believable illegal officers from scratch" as they did with Wasp leader Hernández. With this new approach, professional Cuban intelligence agents could legally travel to the United States with American passports and begin their espionage duties.

The best-known case of a "true identity" illegal is René González, one of the five principal spies in the Wasp net. He was born in the United States and moved with his family to Cuba as a child, and thus claimed dual nationality. A skilled pilot, he successfully infiltrated two prominent exile organizations. Convicted of conspiracy, he served thirteen years of a fifteen-year sentence in a federal penitentiary.

THROUGH MOST OF THE 1960S, Fidel had another clandestine priority just as important as planting penetration agents in Miami and Washington. His passion for promoting Latin American guerrilla movements had been evident since his first few months in power. Small bands of Cuban-supported insurgents sallied from the island, landing on the coasts of four Caribbean countries during the first six months of 1959. The plan was to spark new *fidelista*-style rural insurgencies.

They were all quickly extinguished, but Fidel's interest in such violent interventions only grew and became better organized. CIA director McCone emphasized in his congressional testimony in February 1963 that "today the Cuban effort is far more sophisticated, more covert, and more deadly."[16]

A DGI department, appropriately named Liberacíon Nacional, or National Liberation, was established solely for that purpose. It quickly became the largest entity in Cuba's spy services. There was no chief in 1963 because Piñeiro and his deputy presided over it personally, managing the numerous subversive programs in the region in close collaboration with the Castro brothers and Che Guevara.

Raúl often visited Piñeiro, his close friend and former guerrilla comrade, at National Liberation headquarters in Havana's Miramar district. There was much to coordinate; the armed forces ministry operated guerrilla training schools in a joint venture with Redbeard. (His beard and hair were not merely red, I've been told by a Cuban who knew him; they were "almost orange.") Raúl also made sure the young Latin American volunteers got real-world combat experience. During the early and mid-1960s, many were sent for tours of counterinsurgency duty in the Escambray Mountains of central Cuba.

Soon after defecting, Rodríguez Lahera told the CIA: "They're taken there [into the mountains] and incorporated into regular Cuban army units, so they can adapt to the life of the countryside and take part in operations against anti-Castro guerrillas in that area." These young Latin Americans provided useful, nontraceable support for Raúl's armed forces as they went about exterminating organized opposition on the island. Rodríguez Lahera knew of Salvadorans and Guatemalans who had fought for the Castros this way. When foreign trainees were killed in action, their families—who rarely had any idea they had gone to Cuba in the first place—never knew what had become of them.[17]

Aspillaga wrote in his memoir about two young Latin Americans who went to Cuba to train and never returned home. They were from the same country, but he was not sure of their nationality. After coming under suspicion in Cuba, they were sent to a DGI safe house to be polygraphed. They had been noticed "acting very strange." Under the stress of confinement and aggressive examinations, each one confessed that he was actually an undercover agent working for the armed forces of his country. They were shuttled off to Villa Marista, a pre-Castro Catholic boys school, later a prison and counterintelligence headquarters in downtown Havana. Interrogated again, the men were soon made to disappear, executed by a military firing squad.

Fidel was even more involved than his brother in the National Liberation department's violent activities. Piñeiro had to report to him regularly and coordinate anything involving expenditures for arms or other costly initiatives. The commander in chief was deeply interested in the minutiae of these operations. He intervened to be sure that a group of Guatemalans he met during his visit to the Soviet Union in May 1963 would receive guerrilla training. And, bypassing the DGI bureaucracy, he and Piñeiro arranged that year for militants from the East African island of Zanzibar—later incorporated into Tanzania—to also receive guerrilla training.[18]

The CIA collected solid information about the Cuban schools for subversion. McCone testified that "at least 1,000 to 1,500" young Latin Americans from every country "with the possible exception of Uruguay" went to Cuba for training and indoctrination in 1962. Speaking in February 1963, he said that an even larger number had already arrived thus far that year. The largest contingent—as many as two hundred—were from Venezuela, then Fidel's principal target. Some of the training courses, McCone said, "are as short as four weeks . . . others last as long as a year."[19]

He described Cuban methodologies:

Castro tells revolutionaries from other Latin American countries: "Come to Cuba; we will pay your way; we will train you in underground organization techniques, in guerrilla warfare, in sabotage and in terrorism. We will see to it that you get back to your homeland. Once you are there, we will keep in touch with you, give you propaganda support, send you propaganda materials for your movement, training aids to expand your guerrilla forces, secret communications methods, and perhaps funds and specialized demolition equipment."

The CIA had evidence that recruits returned home clandestinely with forged passports and documents. The DGI taught them how to acquire weapons and ammunition illicitly from the uniformed services of their countries and to rob banks for funds. They learned the basics of upholding cover stories, *trabajo de manta* (literally blanket or undercover work).

Nearly all were instructed in how to concoct and use invisible ink in secret writing and how to use accommodation addresses and *agentes de buzon,* mail box agents, to communicate covertly with their handlers in Havana. In those early days, few Cuban assets were given radio communications equipment or the kind of sophisticated computer programs Ana Montes, the Cuban spy in the Pentagon, would later use.

McCone was also persuasive when briefing President Kennedy and his national security team on Cuba, as he did often in 1963. The message was always succinct and hard-hitting, based on reliable evidence from intelligence sources. Fidel was pursuing boldly interventionist policies. He was expending enormous energies and resources to subvert his neighbors. The CIA chief and his entire analytic team were convinced that if Fidel was not stopped, he would succeed in overturning one or more Latin American governments and replacing them with revolutionary Marxist regimes beholden to Cuba. The targets were not just the military dictators Castro routinely condemned—they were "gorillas" or "apes," he liked to say—but also civilian, democratically elected leaders.

The Venezuelan president Rómulo Betancourt was Fidel's most despised target. A progressive social democrat and former communist, he was a deserter from the Marxist causes of his youth. Worse yet, in Caracas in early 1959, Betancourt recalled that Fidel "visited me at my home" and pleaded with him to join in an anti-Yankee crusade, what Castro characterized as "the master plan against the gringos." Instead, Betancourt allied enthusiastically with the Americans. He was President Kennedy's favorite Latin American leader, a scrupulous and popular reformer, and thus the most credible sort of adversary a revolutionary Marxist could face.[20]

Fidel's memory for such enemies is long, and he never forgives. Forty-six years after Betancourt survived everything the National Liberation department hurled against him—saboteurs, terrorists, assassins, pirates, and rural guerrillas—he was still on Castro's mind. In February 2010, exactly two years after Fidel had definitively surrendered Cuba's presidency to his brother, he wanted posterity to remember just how much he still loathed Betancourt. In a published commentary, he wrote about the long-deceased Venezuelan: He was "the most abject and vile people's enemy," a "fake and a pretender."[21]

The CIA scored some stunning successes against Piñeiro's subversive operations. But there was one glaring gap in what was known. A large number of ranking military officers, all veterans of the Castros' own insurgency against Batista, were secretly fighting side by side with Latin American guerrillas. A reading of McCone's many briefings, along with what is available in the thousands of pages of once highly sensitive and now declassified CIA records on these subjects, allows no other conclusion. Until 1967 the Agency knew almost nothing about the exceptional Cuban warriors who infiltrated other countries as guerrilla advisors, exemplars, and combatants.

The CIA director did tell Congress about three Cubans who were involved in a violent labor strike in Peru that caused "some four million dollars worth of damage" to an American-owned smelter. Clearly they were Piñeiro's boys. One was "directing armed invasions of big ranches in the Andean highlands by land-hungry Indians." That was all McCone was able to say about Cuban volunteers stirring up revolutionary violence. If he had had information, even tentative or qualified reports, about the presence of Cuban military officers serving incognito with regional guerrillas, he surely would have revealed it.[22]

Unknown to the CIA, in the 1960s there were as many as three dozen such officers. All were proven warriors, some were close associates of top Cuban leaders. They were expected to demonstrate their mettle, their loyalty to the revolution, by volunteering for foreign adventures—"internationalist" duty, as it came to be known. They constituted a fourth category of illegals: "elite illegals." Unlike other illegals, they were not tasked with conducting espionage operations, but with overthrowing Latin American governments.

Many were delivered by ship, generally Cuban fishing vessels, to their target countries, landing in small craft on remote beaches and then trekking through wildernesses to jungles and mountain ranges. Others used elaborate covers and legends to travel on commercial flights and then go underground to join with guerrilla forces in the hinterlands of several Latin American countries.

One of those Cuban elite illegals, Raúl Menéndez Tomassevich, later revealed: "Fidel ordered us not to carry more than thirty-five pounds of gear, including our rifles that weighed ten pounds, and ammunition." As usual, Castro was certain he knew best, intervening at the most rudimentary operational level, imposing his indomitable will.[23]

However lightly equipped, it was not always easy for the Cubans to rendezvous with the guerrillas they went to help. Menéndez, who had served prison time in the early 1950s for embezzlement and bank fraud and later became one of Raúl Castro's favorites, was interviewed years later about his experiences as a mercenary in three countries. He was most intent about recalling a large DGI infiltration mission in May 1967 at an isolated beach called Machurucuto, on the Caribbean coast of Venezuela.

Menéndez survived the landing, but others perished, and two Cuban military officers were captured after a fierce firefight with Venezuelan security forces. The principal casualty was Antonio Briones Montoto, the leader of the expedition and founder—on Fidel's birthday in August 1963—of the Ministry of Interior's Special

Troops. The regime's elite first-strike commando assault force, they were incorporated into the defense ministry during the 1989 purges. The Cuban counterintelligence school was later named after Briones.

I have learned from three knowledgeable defectors—my only sources of information about this—that the Machurucuto calamity was the result of a CIA
penetration in the Cuban military. Francisco Carballo Pacheco was an army captain, a cartographer, who was recruited in Mexico during the first year or two of
the revolution. He was ideally placed, working at the military mapmaking agency
created with American assistance during the Batista era and later converted into a
military institute. For years the mapmaker was a legendary villain—known as "El
Espia Pacheco," Pacheco the Spy—his name often invoked during special forces
training courses as an abject lesson in treachery. According to Fidel's former commando bodyguard Lazaro Betancourt, Pacheco was considered the most damaging spy ever to have penetrated the armed forces.[24]

He provided the DGI—and apparently the CIA—with geographic coordi-
nates for Machurucuto, where the ambush force, rather than Venezuelan guerrillas, would be at the ready. Pacheco, eventually apprehended after he tried to flee
Cuba on a raft, confessed under torture. Betancourt told me he viewed a training
video about the case in 1978 when he was enrolled in a Cuban artillery school.
Every student, he said, was required to watch it, and later all military officers were
as well. Raúl Castro is featured in the video, stripping Pacheco's rank insignia off
his shoulders. Then Pacheco is shown kneeling on the ground as he is shot in the
back of the head with one of the first AK-47s in the Cuban arsenal.

Pacheco is also depicted in the Special Troops museum in Siboney, outside
of Havana. It is in a former barracks building, turned over to the Ministry of
Interior. Betancourt had been there and told me: "There were many displays that
will never be known publicly." He remembered in particular a world map on the
wall with colored pins representing every successful Special Troops mission completed. He said: "There were pins everywhere, all over the world."

Raúl Menéndez and the other survivors of the Machurucuto landing—four
Cubans and four Venezuelans—wandered for three and a half months in the Venezuelan wild before finally reaching the Marxist guerrillas they were sent to help.
Conditions got no better once they joined forces. The pudgy Menéndez wasted
away to just a hundred pounds, barely surviving by eating worms, snakes, and
monkeys. That hardship was partly the commander in chief's doing. Fidel had

insisted that his expeditionaries limit the amount of the food they carried in their packs to just two and a half pounds.[25]

Menéndez was so emaciated when he finally returned to Cuba that Raúl Castro plotted a macabre joke. He would announce his friend's death, lay him out in a coffin for his colleagues to view, and then, with dramatic fanfare, they would witness his miraculous "rising from the dead." Known for his bizarre sense of humor, Raúl wisely thought better of the idea. Menéndez recovered and eventually was rewarded with promotion to two-star (division) general rank in the army.[26]

He and the other military volunteers were the best the revolution could muster, all fiercely loyal to the regime and its inflammatory doctrine of exporting revolution. Havana believed they were so good that they would tip the balance of power to the insurgents wherever they went. They would be inspirational, like Greek gods, arriving deus ex machina to vault an insurgency into power.

In 1975 a wiser David Phillips told a special Senate committee chaired by Democratic Senator Frank Church of Idaho that fourteen Cuban guerrilla volunteers served in Venezuela in the 1960s.[27]

As a young man, Arnaldo Ochoa, a dashing officer with an infectious sense of humor—and a military record unrivaled by anyone in Raúl's armed forces—had been one of them. That was revealed for the first time in 1989 during the disgraced general's trial for treason. In the end, his faithful internationalist services in Venezuela and several other third-world conflicts did not save him from Fidel's wrath.

Two of the other Cubans who infiltrated Venezuela were also eventually promoted to general officer rank. A fourth would later wear the insignia of an army colonel. Today, the most prestigious of them—Ulises Rosales del Toro—is a three-star (corps) general, vice president, and super minister in Raúl Castro's government. For fifteen years he was Raúl's right-hand man as armed forces chief of staff. He may not have achieved any of those distinctions had he not volunteered as a young man to fight with the Venezuelan guerrillas. To get ahead in the Castros' Cuba, that was obligatory service.

Rosales was one of forty-one flag-rank military officers who sat in judgment on their colleague Ochoa in a so-called honors tribunal. They concurred unanimously in the death sentence Fidel had demanded. Rosales, Lazaro Betancourt told me, sat directly opposite the defendant in the hearing room; it was "another of Fidel's Machiavellian acts of vengeance." Those must have been difficult moments for General Rosales. During their guerrilla service in Venezuela, Ochoa had saved his life, carrying him on his back to safety when he was too weak and emaciated to walk. Twenty-two years later, Rosales could do nothing to save his friend.

Other surviving veterans of National Liberation department interventions also now occupy influential posts. Communist Party politburo member Abelardo Colomé Ibarra, Cuba's minister of interior since 1989 and the country's second or third most powerful figure, volunteered in 1963 as a guerrilla organizer and advisor to an incipient Argentine insurgency. With false Algerian and Bolivian documentation and legends, he traveled to a remote region of Bolivia, close to the Argentine border, and set up an operational base.[28]

Yet like all the other insurgencies Cuba supported in those days, it was annihilated and many of its leaders and foot soldiers were killed in action or captured and executed. Colomé Ibarra—known to most Cubans by his childhood nickname, "Furry"—has never explained publicly how he managed to escape. When he set out on the mission, he was just twenty-two and a favorite of both Raúl Castro and Che Guevara.

Despite the adventures of these elite illegals, it was not until Guevara, the most gloried of them all, was tracked down and executed in Bolivia in October 1967 that the CIA came to appreciate just how audacious the Cuban interventions had been. Che was the ultimate illegal expeditionary, leading a force of about twenty Cubans, including five members of the Communist Party's central committee and two deputy government ministers. They ventured into uncharted Bolivian backlands with the intention of forging an insurgency that would take hold in that Andean nation and then metastasize across the South American continent.[29]

It is not known how many Cubans were killed by American-assisted government counterinsurgency forces in Venezuela, Bolivia, Colombia, and Guatemala, and possibly other countries where they fought or how many others succumbed to the rigors of life on the run. To this day the Castro brothers' government has failed to acknowledge the sacrifices of all but a few of them. Despite efforts that continued until Guevara's failure in Bolivia, there was not a single guerrilla victory and there were few tactical battlefield successes anywhere the Cuban-sponsored insurgents operated.

Many hard lessons were learned. When Raúl Menéndez stopped over in Paris on his circuitous way back to Havana from Venezuela, he met with DGI Center officers to review what had happened. He told them of all the ways in which the Venezuelan guerrillas had been inadequate brethren. Marxists, *fidelistas* all, trained in Cuban guerrilla warfare schools, infused with the mythology of the Cuban revolution, supported with arms and ammunition from Raúl's stocks— they turned against their Cuban advisors who had sacrificed so much to help. The DGI defector Orlando Castro Hidalgo remembered what Menéndez shared in Paris about the Venezuelan guerrillas: "They would not believe that we Cubans had come only to fight as soldiers. Always there were the misgivings, the fears that the Cubans were going to take over."[30]

Guevara's experience in Bolivia was similar, a hopeless, virtually suicidal calamity. Like Menéndez and Rosales, he was emaciated and ill, barely able to walk at the end. He had been unable to recruit a single Bolivian peasant to his guerrilla cause. There were no military victories to brag about, only bloody skirmishes that steadily picked away at his little band. The field diary he kept was a saga of unrelieved hardships and failures.

Guevara wandered for months, leading Cuban and Bolivian stragglers of the pretentiously named National Liberation Army as they fled from the slowly encircling forces of American-trained Bolivian rangers. Two Cuban exile veterans of the Bay of Pigs, working again for the CIA, advised the Bolivians in the field. Félix Rodríguez was one of them. He tried to save Che from execution and was the last person to speak to him. These were exotic cold war footnotes: Cubans pitted against Cubans in the remote hinterlands of eastern Bolivia.

Although not a DGI officer, Che was a master of covert tradecraft and had been enmeshed in clandestine operations since the first weeks of the revolutionary regime. He traveled clandestinely to Bolivia using two forged Uruguayan passports, each in a different name and the same legend of a middle-aged, slightly paunchy businessman. Once in Bolivia, he used the nom de guerre Ramón. An Argentine until granted Cuban citizenship in 1959, for him, posing as a native of neighboring Uruguay was no challenge at all.[31]

The DGI did an artful job of confecting his new identity. Jon Lee Anderson, one of Che's biographers, wrote that a prosthesis was put in Che's mouth to change the shape of his face. His hairline was painfully made to recede as hairs were plucked one by one with tweezers. His signature beard was shaved. Unchar-acteristically, he wore a suit when in the role of the Uruguayan.

With his disguise complete, a few days before he was to leave Cuba on the Bolivian crusade, he met with a group of government officials in Havana, all of whom knew him well. Anderson wrote that Fidel introduced the disguised Gue-vara to the group as a foreign "friend." No one recognized him. Later, still in dis-guise, he shared a lingering farewell lunch with his children. The DGI's work was so good that even they did not know him.[32]

When he was captured, wounded and lame, his appearance and false iden-tity as the urbane Uruguayan businessman had shredded. His hair was matted and rangy. He was filthy, his sagging flesh mottled. He was miserable, depressed, hungry.

"I am Che Guevara," he growled, head down, to the Bolivian peasant soldiers who had cornered him. They knew he was their quarry but almost nothing about him. In contrast, in the cities of Europe and the Americas, he was a legend. The romantic imagery of "el Che" sprang from photos and posters of him brooding in a dark beret, from his sweet-and-sour poetry and memorable prose, and from the curiously monosyllabic name the Cubans had invented for him. He was one of a kind. There was no other Che. But the aura that surrounded him elsewhere never glowed much in Bolivia.[33]

Piñeiro's Liberation Department—later renamed the Americas Department to seem less confrontational—had little to do with the adventure. Redbeard never thought much of it. Markus Wolf, the East German communist spymaster who rivaled Fidel as perhaps the best to have served anywhere during the twentieth century, worked on joint operations with Piñeiro.

Wolf quoted Redbeard in a memoir he wrote after the two Germanys were united and he had retired. He was familiar with the Cubans' theory of revolu-tion; Che's Bolivian escapade was supposed to have unfolded the way Cuba's own insurgency did in the late 1950s. It would spring up in the countryside, at-tract peasant and other support, wage guerrilla warfare, and finally seize power in the capital city.

But about Che Piñeiro admitted to the German, "Cuba was unique; I think we all knew that even before he went."[34]

So, according to this reliable account, even Fidel realized that Che had scant chance of succeeding in Bolivia. The countries were about as different as any two in Latin America. In any event, Castro's preferred target was Betancourt; he and Piñeiro focused on Venezuela, which was so much like Cuba but, with its oil and mineral wealth, the biggest possible prize in the hemisphere. Fidel always thought strategically, many moves ahead, like a grand master moving pieces on a giant chess board. Venezuela was an opponent's queen; Bolivia, a pawn.

Che could steal off to that impoverished, landlocked Indian country and try his hand. Fidel was comfortable with that. He would be well served no matter how it turned out. If by some fluke Guevara were to win, he, Fidel, could take credit for sponsoring and masterminding the victory. And if the roving Argentine incendiary were die in the quest, that would reverberate even more enduringly. Cuba would have a martyred patron saint.

Che and all of the illegals sent out from Havana in the 1960s were the precursors of the tens of thousands of "internationalists" who followed in later years. Cuban military interventions in Angola and Ethiopia with large ground and air forces that fought pitched battles, and smaller military missions in Nicaragua and a few other countries, succeeded in their immediate goals of establishing Marxist revolutionary regimes. In all of those conflicts, the Special Troops of the Ministry of Interior led the way.

Cuban doctors, medical personnel, technicians of all sorts, and intelligence advisors fanned out to a score of countries beginning in the 1970s. Typically too, the Ministry of Interior provided expert presidential and leadership protection in nations that came under Cuban influence. All of this is still true today. Hugo Chávez's Venezuela hosts many thousands of Cubans, mostly medical, intelligence, and security specialists who play a crucial role in upholding the socialist regime. In return, Chávez provides Havana with oil and investments valued at an average of between $3 and $5 billion annually. That support is comparable to the subsidies the Soviet Union provided Cuba for three decades.

The unusual alliance with Chávez stands out as the single most stunning foreign policy success in Fidel's long reign. Without the Venezuelan lifeline, Cuba's economy would crumble, and Raúl Castro's regime might collapse. The support of Chávez, who was recently under treatment for malignant cancer, is vital. Without the support he has provided, Cuba would be thrust into the economic and geopolitical void that it faced after the Soviet Union dissolved.

Little is known publicly about how Chávez, a career Venezuelan military officer, became Fidel Castro's adoring disciple. There is a good chance, however, that either he or his older brother, Adán, was spotted and recruited as a sleeper agent by the DGI years before he won power. As a recruited Cuban illegal either man might have received clandestine training in Cuba.

Hugo Chávez is known to have traveled frequently to Cuba, lodging in a luxury guest house, in the years after he was released from prison following an unsuccessful military coup in 1992. He had tried to overthrow Carlos Andrés Pérez, Rómulo Betancourt's internal security minister, a leader of his Democratic Action political party, and a successor in the presidency. I do not have any hard evidence that there was a Cuban hand in that coup attempt, yet it is difficult to imagine that Chávez mounted it without outside help and inspiration.

The Cuban military today is island bound, smaller by orders of magnitude and bereft of the massive quantities of Soviet equipment that was provided gratis for about three decades. However, today senior officers and retirees can form for-profit enterprises—many in the tourism sector—which result in higher levels of corruption and malaise in the ranks than ever before. Commanders are elderly, with most of the top generals in their late sixties and seventies and a few, including Raúl himself—Cuba's only four-star general—eighty or more. This gerontocracy remains the controlling political class.

They have served the revolution since their youth, dedicated fighters on the front lines of what Fidel always portrayed as a life-and-death struggle with Yankee imperialism. But no Cuban warriors made as much difference, beginning in the early 1960s, as Piñeiro's teenage intelligence recruits and all of the DGI secret operatives. A number of Aspillaga's original classmates were among them.

FIVE

AT DAGGERS DRAWN

ASPILLAGA'S ADVANCED TRAINING PROPELLED HIM IN VARIOUS directions. He studied counterintelligence tradecraft for nearly a year, becoming expert in the arcane and technically challenging work of communications intercept and direction finding, known as *radio localizador*. Under the tutelage of KGB instructors and using World War II–era Soviet equipment, he learned Morse code and wireless telegraphy, burst communications, the workings of shortwave radio, and the fundamentals of counterespionage.

Graduating in October 1963, he immediately began work in two primitive little commo huts. The secret installation was adjacent to what was later known as Punto Cero, Fidel's isolated family compound at the beachside hamlet of Jaimanitas, near Siboney, on Havana's western fringe. The area is more developed today; the fashionable Hemingway Marina is just a little farther to the west.

Tiny was sixteen, several months shy of his seventeenth birthday. Like so many of Piñeiro's boys, he was trusted with significant responsibility from the start; at first his main duty was to pinpoint the source on the island of covert CIA communications. About a dozen agents were in radio contact with the Agency, using miniaturized modules, each about the size of a carton of cigarettes. Applying direction-finding skills, Tiny became proficient at locating the agents' positions while they broadcasted, which sometimes resulted in their apprehension by security forces.[1]

That year the CIA introduced two faster and more secure wireless telegraphy systems for their agents to send and receive ciphered messages. The first, a one-way voice link known as OWVL, is used over standard shortwave frequencies. It relies on the transmission of a series of seemingly random numbers. The numerical "soup" could be deciphered only if the agent on the receiving end had a one-time pad corresponding to one used by the CIA sender. Somewhat later, burst transmissions added another layer of protection by mechanically accelerating the speed of messaging. In burst transmissions, an encoded tape is fed through a small transmitter at a speed so fast that direction finders less adept than Aspillaga were generally stymied. The principle is simple: the more rapid the transmission, the smaller the chance that it will be detected and the sender put in jeopardy.[2]

Tiny told me that the popping electronic bursts he was taught to track rarely lasted more than eight seconds. He claimed exceptional skills at locating the senders within that brief window of opportunity. Proud of his work at Jaimanitas, in time he eventually became the Cubans' foremost expert at tracking CIA communications, including those with the double agents he went on to expose.[3]

He told me: "I was the only one who knew all about the CIA, all about CIA communications."

Seining the airwaves, he was quick at tweaking the dials and sliding the needles of his equipment until he got a "lock." He was like the young chess masters and math and musical geniuses—and today, computer programmers—who astound their elders by performing breakthrough feats at tender ages. Chopin, Mozart, and Mendelssohn all reached heights of extraordinary musical creativity in their mid- and late-teenage years. Tiny was an equivalent, a radio counterintelligence prodigy.

He was assigned to track maritime targets too. Exile infiltrators launching from CIA ships off Cuba's coast radioed onshore collaborators to arrange rendezvous and deliveries. These were regular occurrences in the fall of 1963. Ted Shackley, chief of JMWAVE, the giant CIA station in Miami, revealed in his memoirs that "our paramilitary teams and boat operators were in and out of Cuban waters all the time."[4]

Tiny labored alone. Other than Castro's large security detail, he was the only person allowed on the dusty lane that some years later led to the commander in chief's secluded residence. There was a second building nearby, used by Fidel's security, and beyond, nothing but vacant fields clogged with marabu, a thick and spiny tropical bush. Earlier, the undeveloped land had been the location of a capitalist-era golf course. Tiny traveled to Jaimanitas daily by bus along Quinta Avenida, Fifth Avenue, a major artery roughly paralleling the north coast, then walked the short distance from the bus stop to his listening post.

He rarely saw Fidel during the many years he worked there and then only from a distance as Castro raced by, slouched in an armored vehicle or in a convoy at the wheel of a jeep. The two had no contact. I heard much more from Aspillaga about Castro's paramour, the young and strikingly beautiful Dalia Soto del Valle.

Mother of five of Fidel's sons, all now in their thirties and forties, she has been described in recent years as his wife. Tiny admired her, and he was smitten during the years he worked nearby. He described Dalia warmly, as an exceptional beauty, a "good and noble person." She lived modestly and inconspicuously, never seen in public with Fidel, and she has always remained all but invisible to the Cuban people.

Dalia often walked alone along the same short route Tiny took to the bus stop on Fifth Avenue, sometimes at the same time he did. Fidel would not provide her with a car and driver, so instead she stoically took public transportation into Havana where she worked or studied anonymously at the university.

She and her youthful admirer spoke only to greet each other, always formally. *"Buenos días, cómo está?"* "Good morning, how are you?" Hardly anything more.

"I never tried to talk too much because I knew who she was . . . and you know . . . he can kill you."

Aspillaga smacked the palm of his hand hard on the table where we were meeting, dramatizing how Fidel was to be feared and never crossed. The memory was electrifying. He was reminded of the close call in London with Miguel Perez Medina and the other attempts on his life. Flirting with Fidel's much younger lover could be recklessly dangerous.

Young and unattached, enthusiastic and determined to succeed, Tiny toiled fourteen and fifteen hours most days in a small, windowless space crammed with electronic gear. As a youth, a journeyman at his counterintelligence trade, he believed fanatically in the revolution and the doctrinaire Marxism passed down by his father. José Maragon, who also began in the DGI as a teenager, remembered his colleague unfavorably. Aspillaga, he told me, was "a true believer, harsh, didactic." He castigated other Cuban agents when they secretly kept small amounts of hard currency acquired during overseas missions. He "was a radical communist, given to preaching vows of poverty," a "*tipo duro,*" a hard-liner. Maragon could not explain why Aspillaga later changed so fundamentally.[5]

Tiny was doing everything by the revolutionary book and succeeding. His direction-finding equipment was connected to a thicket of antennas arrayed in a treeless field nearby, close to the sea, and with unobstructed sight lines to the north. The antennas usually were oriented toward Agency facilities outside of Washington and at JMWAVE in Miami. After dark they also monitored a wide arc of the waters in the Florida Straits, off Cuba's northwestern coast. The charge was to catch American spies and infiltrators in the act.

THAT GENERALLY HAPPENED ON MOONLESS NIGHTS when the tides were right. CIA mother ships—most often the *Rex* and the *Leda* out of West Palm Beach—silently approached the island, lurking several miles offshore, in international waters. The *Olga Patricia* and the *LCI*, christened the *Barbara J* during her Bay of Pigs service, sometimes substituted. Between 150 and 200 feet at the waterline, they discharged smaller fast boats that sped close to isolated beaches and mangrove swamps with Cuban exile commandos and saboteurs on board. The final leg to shore was usually on small, black inflatables propelled by nearly silent motors.[6]

Ted Shackley's JMWAVE operated the third largest navy in the Caribbean, including a midget submarine, tenders, patrol boats, and a swarm of high-powered intermediate-size craft. They were crewed exclusively by Cuban exiles, sailing from the Miami River, the Keys, and Florida ports as far north as Tampa and Fort Pierce. All hands were experienced seamen; three of the ship captains were 1960 graduates of the Cuban naval academy who defected and took to sea against their loyalist classmates.

"Five hundred people were involved in maritime operations," Shackley told the Church Committee. The CIA navy was about the same size as Castro's Soviet-supplied fleet, but generally it was faster and more skillfully manned. The cover stories used to camouflage its operations were not compromised until many years later. Shackley's stealth naval force and his sprawling Miami station remained secret to all but a few outside the clandestine fold.[7]

Their "charter was to conduct offensive operations against Cuba," according to a top CIA manager at the time. The battles with Castro's forces were even more aggressive than the ambitious but failed campaigns based in western Europe during the early cold war years, when rolling back communism in Stalin's satellite states was a top Agency priority. Sam Halpern was a ranking CIA officer on the front lines of the Kennedy-era Caribbean conflict, a scrappy, fast-talking New Yorker who was always brutally candid with his bosses. He later described what he experienced without circumspection. "We were fighting a war against Cuba, undeclared or otherwise, but we were fighting a war." Castro and his policies were anathema to the Kennedy administration because of the subversion he sponsored in Latin America and his military alliance with the Soviet Union.[8]

Always reluctantly and elegantly, Richard Helms made clear in numerous sworn testimonies in the 1970s, after he had stepped down as CIA director, that the authority to wage this war came straight from President Kennedy and his brother Robert, the attorney general. "The Kennedy brothers wanted to unseat Castro by whatever means," he told a commission chaired by Vice President Nelson Rockefeller. There was "a flat-out effort ordered by the White House, the President and Bobby Kennedy . . . to unseat the Castro government, to do everything possible to get rid of it by whatever device." Helms went slightly further in testimony before the Church Committee, saying "[N]o limitations were placed on the means."[9]

Under oath he also said, "Let us not for a moment think the Kennedy administration wasn't dead serious about getting rid of Castro's government. Certainly President Kennedy wanted to get rid of him." Helms testified that in 1963, almost "the entire energy" of the clandestine operations directorate he headed from 1962 to 1965 was devoted to ousting Castro. "That was the reason for mounting the large operation in Miami."[10]

The Cuban exile mecca so close to the target was the obvious place to locate the JMWAVE station. But there was no precedent for mounting peacetime paramilitary operations from anywhere on American soil. A much smaller station had operated in Puerto Rico for a while, with a mission that is still shrouded in secrecy, but it closed in 1958. Larry Houston, the CIA's general counsel, was consulted; would a booming covert installation in Miami violate the laws that established the Agency and assigned it to operate exclusively abroad?[11]

Houston was a refined old hand, admired in Washington social circles and close to the seventh-floor leadership at headquarters in Langley. He was regularly in touch with Bobby Kennedy and therefore knew how important overturning Castro was to the White House. He never said so, but it may have been the attorney general who gave him the go-ahead to establish the station. "You guys are responsible and reporting to the President," Houston told the Cuba team, "so set it up any way you want to." With that blank check, JMWAVE quietly opened in September 1961, structured and treated just like the Agency's overseas stations, although soon it was vastly larger than all of them.[12]

Shackley in Miami reported to Desmond FitzGerald, chief of the cryptically named Special Affairs Staff at headquarters at Langley. SAS had no responsibilities other than to run espionage, paramilitary, and other intelligence operations against Castro from Washington, Florida, and a number of CIA stations around the world. Jim Angleton, the venerable counterintelligence czar, told the Church Committee that SAS handled its own affairs and was a power unto itself. He surely resented that it had its own large counterintelligence staff and maintained independent liaison with the FBI.[13]

Angleton managed to keep a hand in Cuban operations nonetheless. He arranged for Israeli intelligence to install one of its own experienced agents in Havana, a young man "born in Bulgaria . . . a source totally unknown to everybody," Angleton recalled. Only Helms and one other CIA officer knew of "his existence or identity." The Israeli spoke Russian and other languages and later rose to a senior position in Mossad. Whatever intelligence he collected was communicated securely to Tel Aviv and then immediately passed on to Angleton.[14]

FitzGerald's SAS quickly grew into the CIA's largest geographic entity with more than 150 headquarters staffers, bigger than regional divisions responsible for a dozen or more countries, bigger even than the Soviet division. Cuba was that important to the Kennedys.[15]

The budget was enormous, four times the total spent in all twenty of the other Latin American and Caribbean countries combined. According to an Agency assessment from that era, Cuba would continue to be "the highest priority for all components of the clandestine services." That meant other divisions and staffs were also expected to seize every opportunity to recruit agents and run operations that could hurt Fidel. There were many and far-flung successes. But as late as July 1962, CIA director McCone told the attorney general and others in a White House meeting that "no high level penetrations of the Cuban government have yet been attained."[16]

A declassified covert planning document dating to late 1963 or early 1964 revealed, however, that many Cuban diplomatic and commercial missions abroad had been compromised. The report cited fifteen recruited agents, eleven audio operations, and fourteen telephone taps in Cuban legations. Mexico City and Paris were the most thoroughly penetrated, but Cuban diplomats and intelligence officers in a total of seventeen other world capitals were also being heard or monitored clandestinely. The hope in Langley was that "some of those now recruited will be returned to Havana to a high level foreign office or other government post."[17]

SAS teams were posted to several CIA stations where Cuban targets were plentiful. The busiest by far was in Mexico City. Dave Phillips remembered that nearly every Cuban embassy officer there had been targeted for a recruitment pitch. They were mistakenly believed by the CIA to be all but naked to intrusive prying. Agents intercepted their mail, photographed people going in and out of their facilities, and snatched and picked over their trash. Embassy telephones were tapped—"covered completely," according to an Agency history completed under Phillips's auspices when he was Latin America division chief, following his service in Mexico. But the boast turned out to be exaggerated in several historically important respects.[18]

Seven microphones hidden in the Cuban embassy were pumping out sensitive conversations, one of them from the leg of a coffee table in the ambassador's office. Through one or more of these technical operations, the CIA unmasked a spy reporting to the Mexico station—really a double agent working for the DGI. The Agency bombarded Cuban officers in the Mexican capital and three regional consulates with disinformation and propaganda.

FitzGerald managed all this from a maze of cubicles and dark little offices in the basement at headquarters, the "G," or ground-floor, level. A Harvard graduate and transplanted Park Avenue socialite, he was known to all as "Des." Close to President Kennedy and his brother, the men supposedly were distantly related through Rose Fitzgerald Kennedy, the Kennedy family matriarch. Helms recalled that Des and Bobby "got along well; they had no difficulty communicating." In fact, the younger Kennedy stayed at the FitzGerald home in the exclusive Georgetown neighborhood of Washington during his brother's inauguration.[19]

Shortly after taking over SAS early in 1963, Des traveled to the front lines in Miami to get acquainted with the burgeoning station. Shackley commanded six hundred Agency staff employees and as many as a thousand contractors. In an interview after he retired, he said that up to fifteen thousand Cubans "were connected to us in one way or another." They were supported by three or four hundred cover companies, including boat maintenance providers, arms dealers, real estate firms, and travel agents. JMWAVE's own uniformed guard force protected the facilities. More than a hundred cars were leased.[20]

Shackley, who seemed sinister to some of his colleagues, was the perfect field adjutant. Abrasive, cold, and impatient, he demanded more than most of his subordinates could deliver. His Agency alias was appropriately Teutonic: Andrew K. Reuteman. For some obscure reason, the Miami Cubans nicknamed him "Tequila." His biographer David Corn adds that he was also known by a melodramatic moniker that he hated, the "Blond Ghost."[21]

A University of Maryland graduate, fluent in his mother's native Polish, Shackley and the debonair, white-shoe FitzGerald were incompatible opposites. Des surely was pleased therefore that their offices were a thousand miles apart; small talk or cocktails together in Georgetown would have been unimaginable for him. But Shackley did not hesitate to do the dirty work that was demanded. Unabashedly ambitious, he was aware of his place as the saluting subordinate to a much higher-ranking FitzGerald. Their mission was simple, Des told him in Miami: "regime change in Havana."[22]

Nearly everything was permissible toward that end. Shackley was smug when he told the Church Committee, "[I]t would not have been contrary to our policy to supply weapons to someone who might have access to Castro." He admitted too that exile revolutionary groups he supported and militant refugees on the Agency payroll might have independently carried out assassination attempts. He was right about that.[23]

As JMWAVE's maritime operations accelerated in 1963, both sides were taking heavy casualties. The CIA was losing many of its frogmen, saboteurs, and reporting agents behind enemy lines on the island. It was getting progressively harder to protect and exfiltrate them safely. Tiny and other young Cuban intercept operators were getting better at their craft, so the CIA's clandestine communications were no longer as secure as they had been. Frequent firefights lit the Caribbean night as exile intruders were intercepted by Cuban security forces.

Losses in October 1963 appear to have been higher than during any month since the Bay of Pigs debacle two and a half years earlier. Understandably, Aspillaga has not told me whether he had a hand in those or any other fatal successes against the CIA and its Cuban exile operatives. But the chances are that on occasion he had intercepted agent communications and alerted security forces in time for them to take defensive measures. That, after all, was his principal responsibility. And his location at Jaimanitas was ideal for detecting CIA communications in western Cuba and the surrounding waters.[24]

By November 1963 it was known that at least twenty-five JMWAVE contract agents had been captured or killed that year. The actual number, including many others missing in action, was likely much higher. No one in the Agency or the high policy circles where the sabotage and penetration operations were approved in advance could have had illusions about the fates of those captured. Few would have been spared summary execution. To survive meant agreeing to be doubled and turned back against the CIA, all the while not knowing how long the diabolical pardon would be honored.[25]

Many of the men in Miami and Langley who were sending courageous young exiles to their deaths were torn, morally confounded. It was "enormously frustrating. You have no idea how frustrating," Helms told the Church Committee, "trying to find people who could . . . land on the coast and be alive the next day." But the pressure from the Kennedys to get Castro was overwhelming, irresistible. In another testimony, the proud and dignified former director and ambassador was forced to admit: "If the attorney general told me to jump through a hoop, I would have."[26]

No one knew the ugly innards of post-Bay of Pigs covert Cuba policy better than Helms. His preeminent role began when he was surprised by McCone at a morning staff meeting in December 1961 and learned that he would be the Agency's new "man on Cuba." Sam Halpern remembered that his admired boss "looked like a thunderbolt had hit him." It was the last thing he had wanted. Helms was a supple survivor, graduate of a Swiss boarding school and Williams College, a journalist who interviewed Hitler in Nuremberg in 1936, and a veteran of the wartime Office of Strategic Services (OSS). He joined CIA at its inception and began his rise to the top. A tall, thin patrician presence in the CIA rough-and-tumble, his alias, Fletcher M. Knight, suited him well.

Helms's operator's instincts rarely failed him; they had screamed to steer clear of the Bay of Pigs, and he did. Countless CIA careers were ruined in that disaster. He had hoped also to avoid the Kennedy brothers' punitive Operation Mongoose, their successor to the Bay of Pigs, the second chapter in their bloody covert war against Fidel. It was a yearlong campaign of paramilitary and espionage operations that geared up in November 1961 under Bobby Kennedy's command. This new effort was brutally contentious, and Bobby was at Helms's throat.

The attorney general lived a mile or so from headquarters and liked to drop in unexpectedly to confer on Cuban operations. Helms said he "regularly called middle- and lower-level CIA officers" he knew by name to "give instructions." Incredibly, Kennedy's secretary at the Justice Department sometimes called on his behalf to issue orders to case officers. SAS leadership invariably acquiesced in those interventions.[27]

Helms, who dealt with Bobby constantly, described him as the president's always-demanding "right hand man in these matters." He was constantly "putting pressure to get more action, and I'd be the one to try to think up excuses" when we could not meet his expectations for boom and bust in Cuba." They were "adversary proceedings." Though they were friends, Bobby also hectored FitzGerald. Tom Parrott, who worked at the White House and knew them both, recalled that Bobby was "a thorn in FitzGerald's side." Des "would just be seething sometimes." Marshall Carter, the army general who was McCone's deputy at the Agency, recalled that the attorney general was the president's "hatchet man" who "operated as a sort of rat terrier."[28]

In the administration there was a prevailing "hysteria" about Castro after the Bay of Pigs, according to Robert McNamara, the defense secretary. The Kennedys were unaccustomed to losing, he said, and they wanted to avenge their humiliation. Helms remembered it the same way. He testified that the foiled exile invasion had "whetted the appetite of the administration to get rid of Castro by some other device." The author Garry Wills has written that "Castro brought out every combative instinct of the Kennedys." He quotes the president's most trusted advisor and ghostwriter, Ted Sorensen, saying that "Castro made Kennedy lose his normal cool." Helms's new assignment as McCone's chargé d'affaires for ridding Cuba of Fidel meant there would be no shirking the White House's demands.[29]

DURING DOZENS OF HOURS of sworn testimony on fourteen occasions in the 1970s, Helms was the essential witness about his Cuba work for the Kennedys. Testifying was always agony for him. He was accustomed to doing his most sensitive business in private and off the record. So, with members of Congress, he was elegantly evasive when he needed to protect CIA and administration secrets.

Senators and senior staff of the Church Committee were once caught on tape commenting on Helms's forensic skills as they prepared to begin another hearing. The committee staff chief noted dryly that "yesterday, trying to hold him onto a question was difficult." The senior counsel chimed in: "[H]e is a very, very intelligent witness and if you ever want to pin him down on precise facts, he knows very well how to make that difficult." Seeming to enjoy the contest about to be joined, chairman Frank Church fired the starting gun: "Alright, let's have him in."[30]

Helms was the repository of the most intimate knowledge of Cuba. FitzGerald and Shackley worked for him, and his only superiors, McCone and General Carter, were content to have handed off the Cuba hot potato to him. He was always especially uncomfortable, though, when pressed to testify under oath about the Kennedys. By the time of the Senate hearings, it was no secret that the CIA had orchestrated murder plots against Castro in the early 1960s. It also became known that FitzGerald had dreamed up other bizarre killing schemes that never made it beyond back-office brainstorming.

Helms had to volley questions about what the Kennedy brothers knew of the attempts against Castro. Had they mandated them? Did they know the details? No one other than Helms could provide the answers. McCone and Carter had been cut out of the assassination planning, probably on Bobby Kennedy's orders, and Des was dead by the time of the hearings.

Helms, the loyal presidential servant, refused to implicate either Kennedy brother in assassination plots. And in his otherwise thorough posthumously published memoirs, he glides right over the subject. But there was no misunderstanding what he kept saying between the lines when he was pressed and under oath in congressional hearing rooms. "Getting rid" of Fidel was his preferred evasion. It hovered somewhere between a clever euphemism and a flat-out admission that murdering Castro was indeed the administration's goal.

Senator Church summarized what he thought he had learned about that in one session of his hearings:

Our testimony from Mr. Helms shows two things . . . that he believed the policy of the government was to bring down Castro by whatever means, and he himself was satisfied that this included assassination. The testimony also shows that Helms was never . . . instructed to assassinate Castro by Robert Kennedy.[31]

Still, in another of Helms's appearances, Church had asked whether the attorney general "ever [told] you to kill Castro?" "No," Helms responded, "not in those words. I don't want to put those words in a dead man's mouth. It's not fair of me." The inference was clear enough. It was the closest Helms ever came to implicating Bobby.

The Rockefeller and Church investigations, and another investigation a few years later by the House of Representatives Select Committee on Assassinations, never got any closer to the raw truth. By protecting the attorney general, Helms was also immunizing the president. That has always been the "eleventh commandment" in the executive suites on the seventh floor at CIA headquarters. To implicate one Kennedy brother was to involve both.

Everyone who worked with them understood how Bobby mirrored and mimicked the president. There was never any doubt either about who made all of the most important foreign policy decisions. Jack Bell, a journalist friend, once asked the president who in the administration made foreign policy. "It's made right here," Kennedy responded, pointing down at the floor of the Oval Office. That was especially true regarding decisions about Cuba.[32]

Several CIA officials told the Church Committee that they knew or believed from whispered conversations in Langley that the attorney general's demands to get rid of Castro originated with his brother. "We were keeping those things out of the Oval Office," Helms confessed. The committee obliged by doing so as well.[33]

But if he had been asked by a subsequent president where the assassination authority had come from, Helms undoubtedly would have told the truth. The distinguished historian Max Holland suspects that such a conversation did occur between the then CIA director and President Lyndon Johnson during a White House meeting on May 10, 1967. Helms was there to inform the president about the CIA inspector general's ultra-sensitive report cataloging CIA plots and schemes to assassinate Castro. There were eight of them, described in flat bureaucratic prose that hinted at just how mortified the authors had been when reporting on their colleagues' behavior.[34]

Helms's meeting with Johnson lasted nearly an hour, but almost nothing of what was said was recorded. Yet Holland writes that if Johnson had asked under whose authority the CIA acted, Helms would have said Robert Kennedy "personally managed the operation" to assassinate Castro. In 1975, Helms used similar language in a meeting with Secretary of State Henry Kissinger. A document stating that, perhaps the only one surviving anywhere that explicitly ties Bobby to the Castro assassination planning, is stored at the Gerald R. Ford Presidential Library in Michigan.[35]

OPERATION MONGOOSE WAS TERMINATED during the missile crisis when wiser heads feared that some errant JMWAVE sabotage raid might be misunderstood as the opening shots of an American invasion of Cuba. Yet Castro was not off the hook. After a pause of several months, the third stage of the Cuba wars was launched. Helms testified that it began in spring 1963. Tom Parrott had been an Agency man since 1949 and had served in the Kennedy White House as secretary of the secretive committee that approved covert actions. He testified that Mongoose had been designed "to keep the pot simmering" in Cuba. The following spring, the pot would be brought to a boil.[36]

In an internal Agency interview in 1988 that was declassified eleven years later, Sam Halpern, the perennial special assistant to the Agency's top brass, remembered the ratcheting up. "After the missile crisis everything was just dead in the water." But soon the pressures built again. "'Castro is still there. Do something.' So that's when we started all over again."[37]

The Kennedys were outraged that Fidel had given Cuban territory over to Khrushchev to install nuclear missiles. The president had no knowledge of the Armageddon letter, but if it somehow was leaked as he was preparing for reelection in 1964, his Republican opponents would have had a devastating issue to raise against him. It was bad enough that Cuban subversion in Latin America was reaching new intensity and that the Kremlin was refusing to remove the several thousand stay-behind troops it kept on the island. If Kennedy had lived, these would have been white-hot campaign issues.[38]

The president's journalist friend Charles Bartlett, who was often privy to his thinking, remembered in an oral history interview that Kennedy "really did not think it was going to be easy" to be reelected. "It would have been an interesting campaign . . . I think he would have debated Cuba." Some opinion polls were showing distinct vulnerabilities. A Harris survey taken in October showed that only 42 percent of the respondents believed that Kennedy was doing an excellent or fairly good job at "handling Castro." Still in power, still goading, denouncing, and confronting the "imperialist enemy," Fidel would have been a delicious Republican campaign issue, just as he had been for Kennedy in the 1960 campaign against Richard Nixon.[39]

So, the war to rid Cuba of Castro was renewed in March and April 1963. On balance, this third and final thrust to oust Fidel proved to be the most ambitious, and the most sinister.

"There'd have to be something more sophisticated," Helms testified. And, recalling those days, he said again that "no limits were placed on what we were attempting to do. We were never told, don't do this, or that." He understood the enmity that had grown between Castro and Kennedy like an abscess. Their rivalry for influence in Latin America, the many forms of subversion each practiced against the other's interests, and the vivid memories of the missile crisis kept them in a state of virtual war.

Their priorities collided in Latin America. Kennedy devoted more time to that region than to any other part of the world and obsessed about another country falling under Fidel's sway. During his truncated presidency he managed to meet face-to-face with fifteen of the eighteen Latin American chief executives beyond Cuba, travel three times to the region, and consult in the White House with countless Latin ambassadors, politicians, and intellectuals. He met twice with his favorite among them, the endangered Venezuelan president Rómulo Betancourt. Kennedy established the Alliance for Progress, a massive aid program that urged social and economic reforms on regional leaders as a means of shoring them up against Cuban subversion.

Kennedy and Castro vied for influence, especially among the younger generation of Latins. There were few remote corners anywhere that Fidel's name and image were not familiar, even among the poorest and least educated. But Kennedy also fared well. The journalist Laura Bergquist recalled that during her frequent travels, she talked to "barn-burning young revolutionaries who were pro-Castro" but found that, surprisingly, they also empathized with Kennedy. She said it "was amazing how he got across to people, not only in the United States, but all over the world."[40]

Thomas Mann was the U.S. ambassador to Mexico and hosted the president's state visit there in June 1962. He too was impressed with Kennedy's enormous appeal. Mann wrote in unpublished memoirs that Kennedy's visit was an unparalleled success. He had never seen "anybody make such an impression on the people of another country, anytime, anywhere," as Kennedy did with the masses of rapturous Mexicans who greeted him. C. Allan Stewart, the American ambassador to Venezuela, remembered the "electrifying effect" Kennedy's inaugural address had there and more widely throughout Latin America.[41]

Because of the Cuban threat, Kennedy once referred to the region as the "most dangerous area in the world." Egged on by McCone and gloomy CIA assessments, the president did not doubt that one or more Latin American countries were immediately vulnerable to Cuban inroads. A Special National Intelligence Estimate issued in mid-November 1963 warned that "Castro will not reduce to any significant degree his incitement to subversion." In short, Helms believed, as he once testified, that Castro and Kennedy "were at daggers drawn." They were like street brawlers, each prepared to inflict a fatal blow or, if they knew one were coming, to look the other way.[42]

ON NOVEMBER 12, 1963, the president was updated on the progress of the new covert campaign against Cuba. Just ten days before he was assassinated in Dallas, it was the last of the many high-level meetings on Cuba he attended. FitzGerald sat in the briefers' chair at the long, ornate table in the White House Cabinet Room, a civilian general reporting to his commander in chief.

The Kennedy brothers were joined by seven cabinet and ranking sub–cabinet-level officials, including the secretaries of state and defense and the chairman of the Joint Chiefs of Staff. Such a top-heavy turnout was unusual. The Pentagon's McNamara, for example, rarely attended such sessions on Cuba. But this one was billed as of crucial importance. The White House and the CIA believed that D-Day was approaching in the covert war against Castro. A number of operational plans were converging, and there was a palpable sense of urgency.[43]

It was CIA's show, so five top Agency officers were also in the room. McCone and Helms, and Bruce Cheever, FitzGerald's deputy in SAS, were there. Shackley flew up from Miami. It was a full-court press because the stakes were so high.

McCone opened and FitzGerald took over a few minutes later. He stated, "Cuban counterintelligence efforts have intensified during the past months. Our losses have increased. This is particularly true with regard to the 'black' (covert) teams. The Cuban control system and ration system make the teams' continued existence more and more precarious."[44]

Agency spies and intruders faced a survival problem similar to those that felled Cuban volunteers fighting with foreign guerrilla groups: hunger. Finding sufficient food while on the run was nearly impossible without betraying one's subversive purposes. The official White House transcript of the meeting emphasized that. "The reasons for these casualty figures are the increasing effectiveness of Castro's internal security forces and discovery brought about when agents try to obtain food."

Regardless, FitzGerald assured the Cabinet Room gathering, SAS would "press forward with all the other types of intelligence operations." They ran the gamut of everything CIA had learned and practiced all over the globe, as well as tricks and feints that had never been tried before. The plan was described as a "six-point integrated program against Cuba." Meeting participants knew its general parameters and purpose, but most of the details would have been new to most of them.

Cheever was the Agency's note taker; his SECRET memorandum, now fully declassified, is a comprehensive record of what was discussed. No other CIA document reveals so dramatically the magnitude of the undeclared war against Cuba on the eve of John Kennedy's death. It leaves no doubt about the president's complicity in that brutal and violent campaign. Ironically too, his brother, the chief law enforcement officer of the United States, was its most demanding advocate.[45]

Covert collection of intelligence was the first item on FitzGerald's brief. He felt reasonably good about how SAS was performing. Despite the losses to Cuban security, there was still a diverse complement of spies on the island. He mentioned seventy-four singleton agents operating alone and "reporting directly to us." Those communicating by radio were the main targets of Aspillaga's direction-finding efforts. Another seventy-nine subagents residing in Cuba worked in espionage networks. A commando "black" team with fifty-five subagents in its net was operating in the westernmost province of Pinar del Río.[46]

Two other items, propaganda and sabotage programs, were intertwined in FitzGerald's brief. Programming was not crafted around passive, high-minded themes of democratic values and human rights or how Cuba had become a vassal of the Soviet Union. It was calculated instead to incite the populace, "to stimulate low-risk sabotage" and resistance. Radio Swan, broadcasting from a small western Caribbean island later ceded by the United States to Honduras, was on the air thirteen hours daily. Programming was focused on specific groups: students, the Cuban military, workers, and others.

The effort was considered a success. There had been "a slight upturn" in sabotage. The Agency had reports of 109 such acts perpetrated since the previous April, including "derailing locomotives, destroying high tension poles, burning trucks and factories." Des said that some of the recent attacks had been successful against "a power plant, oil storage facilities, and a sawmill. An underwater demolition operation was run against a floating crane" in a Cuban harbor. The propaganda seemed to be working; Cubans on the island were stimulated to mount their own destructive attacks against the Castro regime independently. But there was another reason for the upturn in sabotage that Des did not acknowledge.[47]

In his memoirs, Shackley told of creating from scratch an exile paramilitary group he dubbed the Comandos Mambises, after the late nineteenth-century Cuban guerrillas who fought for independence against Spain. The Miami station designed a shoulder patch for them depicting a stylized Cuban flag and a guerrilla fighter on horseback. Shackley's Comandos specialized in underwater demolition techniques and were run out of JMWAVE. They began attacking Cuban targets in late summer 1963, ferried by the covert navy. In April, Shackley had approved the use of limpets—five-pound explosive devices that exile frogmen attached magnetically to the sides of ships below the water line.[48]

Over the next few months, a number of hits were scored, including on an oil storage depot and pipelines, a sawmill, and coastal patrol boats. Some of the targets were among those FitzGerald had mentioned. But Shackley wrote that it was difficult to distinguish between the sabotage operations run by his new teams and violence carried out independently by disaffected people on the island. He did claim that "spontaneous events tended to occur shortly after a Comando Mambises operation."[49]

Des was particularly pleased with the efforts devised to squeeze life out of the Cuban economy, the fourth item on his list. He told the White House gathering that, on balance, this "government-wide program probably had a greater impact" than anything else being done to topple Castro. Most provisions of the economic embargo—including a travel ban affecting most Americans—are still in effect at this writing, fifty years later, reinforced and extended twice by legislation during the 1990s. No other country has ever been targeted by the United States with such punishing economic sanctions and aggressions as Castro's Cuba was during the Kennedy years.

Covert programs complemented the many declared ones to economically strangle the regime. In polite policy circles it was all referred to as "economic denial." Cruder language was used in SAS's gray-painted corridors. The gruff General Carter used the term "testicular grip" in a congressional hearing. Among friends he and others probably preferred more commonplace, locker-room versions of that phrase.[50]

Almost nothing was off limits. There was high-level talk about using biological agents to eradicate Cuban crops. Carter remembered that McGeorge Bundy, the president's national security advisor, told the Agency there was "no worry" about that. I know of no evidence that any such plans were ever carried out, although to this day Fidel has not ceased insisting that they were implemented on a ravenous scale.

Still, many cruel and petty acts of terrorism were routinely inflicted. It was bandied about in Langley that stray cats were dunked in gasoline and set afire to run crazily torching dry sugarcane fields. Agents in many countries were tasked to foul the engines and gas tanks of vehicles purchased by the Cuban government before they could be loaded on to freighters.[51]

Bill Sturbitts, a World War II veteran and desk analyst in the CIA's analytic directorate, was recruited by FitzGerald to stir this witches' brew. Some of the punishing initiatives the two came up with were conducted within the bounds of American law; others were criminal by any measure.

One effort consisted of selling sabotaged and defective industrial replacement parts to Cuba through third countries. "We had our agents get the Cuban orders all over Europe," Sturbitts later admitted. He also mentioned a "target of opportunity"—a freighter hauling Cuban sugar to the Soviet Union that accidentally took a hole in its hull and had to put in to Puerto Rico for repairs. SAS arranged for a harmless substance to be applied covertly to the sugar, turning it sour and worthless. The Agency was commended for its initiative and daring.[52]

Sturbitts ran what he called a preemptive purchase program. "If there was a single source of supply for a particular good, we would go in and buy it to deny the Cubans that market." One such operation blocked the purchase of a badly needed heavy oil, known as bright stock. Agents approached more than six hundred American companies to persuade them not to sell spare parts to Cuba through their foreign subsidiaries. Sturbitts remembered that not one refused to cooperate. He also told of successful efforts to prevent Cuban government auctions in Europe and Canada of valuable art collections and racehorses that had been confiscated from wealthy families. "We ran legal operations, got the owners and had them hire attorneys and bring them (the Cuban government) to court."[53]

FitzGerald also professed to be pleased with the progress of so-called autonomous anti-Castro groups—another of the euphemisms used by the Agency and in policy councils. Two prominent exile leaders—both favorites of Bobby Kennedy—had been encouraged, with substantial arms and financial support from JMWAVE, to run sabotage attacks and espionage from bases in Central America. Their activities would, therefore, be easily deniable. Des was upbeat. He told the president and the others gathered in the Cabinet Room that "these groups will relieve some of the pressure on our operations which we believe will be most beneficial."

Shackley, however, was a skeptic from the start, in no small measure because the "autonomous groups" operated beyond his control. One of them, he explained in his memoirs, was never able to do much of anything. The other, led by Manuel Artime, a Bay of Pigs survivor, initially seemed more promising, but Shackley sneered that the support he provided Artime "turned out to be a labor of love that produced no tangible results." He told author Don Bohning that it was a Bobby Kennedy operation, "an exercise in futility."[54]

Shackley again was right. Fidel revealed in a speech in March 1966 that the DGI had penetrated the heart of Artime's group at its inception three years earlier. The admission was a rare example of Castro publicly boasting of Cuban intelligence triumphs. He said all of the arms caches covertly delivered to the island by Artime, in seventeen different infiltration operations, were retrieved and later used by Cuban security forces. With a Delphic swipe at CIA and a rhetorical bow, he added, "No one knows how we know, but we know, and *we* know how we know."[55]

The last of FitzGerald's briefing items was intended to be the coup de grace. It was the covert initiative in which he had made the greatest personal investment, putting both himself and the attorney general at considerable risk. SAS and JMWAVE were endeavoring on several fronts to sow discontent and rebellion in Raúl Castro's armed forces. That had been a major policy goal, approved at the highest levels, since earlier in the year. The objective, of course, was a coup.

"Slow but encouraging progress is being made," FitzGerald intoned. His staff, working jointly with the Defense Intelligence Agency, had completed detailed biographic studies of 150 Cuban military officers. Forty-five of them were of "particular interest," and FitzGerald added that "we are currently in direct contact with three 'Heroes of the Revolution.'" That was not a title in use in Cuba at the time, but Des was correct; SAS indeed had contact with a few military leaders, who "need[ed] to be reassured . . . that, 'should they overthrow Castro' they will be viewed favorably in the United States."[56]

The most important of these men was Rolando Cubela, a prominent if eccentric revolutionary hero. A wounded veteran of the anti-Batista insurgency, admired leader of revolutionary students, and a medical doctor, he wore the insignia of a *comandante*—literally a major or commander—which, until the 1970s when general officer ranks were introduced, was the highest in the armed forces.

Cubela had been meeting secretly with CIA case officers in foreign capitals since early 1961 and recruited as a trusted agent in August 1962. As noted, until then the Agency had no high-level sources in the Cuban regime. Shackley admitted in his memoirs that "our assets were NCOs [noncommissioned officers], logisticians, and food handlers, useful in the past but hardly what we would need for a coup." Another Agency document from that period revealed that none of the assets "is high level or privy to the basic political and military decisions." Cubela was thought to be pure gold.[57]

The White House war council lasted little more than a half hour. The president asked if the maritime attacks were worthwhile and were contributing to the objective of routing Castro. Robert Kennedy was supportive of the raids. He believed the Agency's efforts "had produced a worthwhile impact." Defense Secretary McNamara agreed. It was Secretary of State Dean Rusk who expressed the only reservations about what he preferred to call "the hit-and-run raids." In the end, the president authorized additional sabotage attacks. One would target a wharf and another a sawmill. They were scheduled for the next weekend, November 16 and 17.

Thus, the president of the United States, his brother—the attorney general—and the national security cabinet had all calmly listened to and, without objecting, collectively became complicit in acts that constituted a deliberate and massive campaign of international terrorism. Historians have written of the president's silent confidence that he would get Fidel. Garry Wills noted that "the one option the Kennedys never considered . . . was leaving Castro alone."[58]

TINY ASPILLAGA WAS AT WORK alone in his little hut in Jaimanitas ten days later, early Friday morning, November 22, 1963. Around nine or nine-thirty, as he still vividly recalls, he received a coded message by radio from his *jefatura*, or headquarters. There was no phone in the building where he did most of his work. The message instructed him to go over to the second little structure he used, a hundred yards away, and use the secure phone there to call back for instructions.

He was ordered to stop all of his CIA tracking efforts. During the month or so of his work there, and for the next dozen years, his only targets had been the Agency's spies on the island and incursions by sea. Nothing else mattered. That morning in November 1963 would be the only exception he later remembered.

"The leadership wants you to stop all your CIA work, *all* your CIA work." He was told to redirect his antennas away from Miami and Agency headquarters in Virginia. It was broad daylight so he did not need to monitor seaborne incursions by JMWAVE saboteurs that always occurred after dark.

He was ordered instead to listen to communications from Texas.

"I was told to listen to all conversations, and to call the leadership if I heard anything important occur," Aspillaga told me. "I put all of my equipment to listen to any small detail from Texas. They told me Texas."

He said, "It wasn't until two or three hours later that I began hearing broadcasts on amateur radio bands about the shooting of President Kennedy in Dallas."

Kennedy was shot at about 12:30 P.M. Dallas time, or 1:30 P.M. Havana time. Aspillaga told me he had tuned in to Texas frequencies about three hours earlier.

"Castro knew," he said. "They knew Kennedy would be killed."

SIX

TYRANNICIDE

THE TWENTY-SEVEN-YEAR-OLD DGI AGENT PRESENTED A FALSE
Cuban diplomatic passport in the name of Vicente Ramírez López. His true
name, as the CIA would soon discover, was Vladimir Rodríguez Lahera. He was
the first person ever to defect from the heart of Cuban foreign intelligence.[1]

Rodríguez Lahera did not speak a word of English when he stepped off the
Cubana Airline flight in Halifax, Nova Scotia, on April 21, 1964. He nervously
scanned the tarmac for a Canadian government official he could approach to
signal that he desperately sought political asylum. There would be very little time,
and probably just this one chance, to persuade the authorities his life would be in
danger if he were forced back on the plane.

Halifax, about midway on the long North Atlantic haul between Havana and
Prague, was a refueling stop for Cuban government airliners. Transiting passen-
gers from communist nations had sprinted to freedom there before. But escape
would be risky. Rodríguez Lahera knew from his work at DGI headquarters that
several of his countrymen on board, including the stewardesses, were agents or
informants of state security trained to watch for defectors.[2]

His life was on the line. If he were snared by Cuban agents before he could
plead his case, he would be guilty of treason, doubly or triply compounded. He
would be branded a thief as well as a traitor, as he carried a small trove of secret
DGI documents jammed into a briefcase and a two-inch wad of money stolen from

official accounts. Among his meager possessions were 127 American twenty-dollar bills and a smaller amount in *colones,* the currency of El Salvador. Summary execution in a dank island prison would be his fate for this combination of crimes if he were thrust back into Cuban hands.[3]

Once processed in Halifax, he was relocated to Ottawa, where he made clear that he hoped to move as soon as possible to the United States. He had relatives in New York and Miami and wanted to share with American authorities all he knew about Cuban intelligence and subversive operations. Like Aspillaga and most other Cuban defectors who would follow, Rodríguez Lahera had learned to despise Castro and the system he created.

From a poor, rural family in Oriente Province, at the eastern end of the island, Rodríguez Lahera had eleven years of schooling. Letters to his wife Luisa, whom he left behind in Havana, demonstrated that he was smart and creative. Some of that correspondence is included in his once highly sensitive CIA files, which were declassified in the late 1990s. They reveal in remarkably fine-textured detail everything he knew about Cuban intelligence as well the dangerous work he performed for the CIA after he switched sides. There is no other intelligence defector of any nationality whose operational history has been so completely bared.

According to a CIA performance appraisal, he was "personable, intelligent, and foresighted." Lahera had "proven himself self-confident and courageous . . . quick thinking, and had performed excellently in all tasks." A Cuban American friend from that era remembers him as "very sociable, not a bragger." He had been toughened in the Castros' revolutionary movement, which he joined in 1957 as a twenty-year-old. Rising from private to lieutenant, he first engaged in urban sabotage and propaganda operations, served a sentence in a Batista prison, and then went to the sierra to fight against the dictator as a guerrilla. There he joined Huber Matos, one of the revolution's most popular commanders.[4]

But Matos ran afoul of Fidel just nine months after their victory when he criticized the growing influence of communist apparatchiks in the new government. Convicted by a kangaroo court, the ascetic Matos was sentenced to twenty years in prison. Rodríguez Lahera's estrangement had its roots in those events. His hero had fought on Castro's side, but for a free and democratic Cuba. The old dictatorship was gone, but a new one was forming. Matos's only offense had been to speak the truth about Fidel's duplicity.[5]

"Laddie," as Rodríguez Lahera was soon nicknamed by his new American friends, had served as a DGI staff officer for only about nine months when he defected. But he was observant and curious, had a retentive memory, and, not long into his brief intelligence career, was already planning on eventually assisting the Americans. CIA debriefers were amazed at how much detailed knowledge he brought. About 320 finished intelligence reports about the inner workings of Cuban intelligence were issued based on what he told them. Information of operational value was even more bountiful.

Until Aspillaga's defection twenty-three years later, Laddie was the CIA's most valuable Cuban acquisition by far. I never met him, but as a young CIA analyst working Cuba, I was familiar with much of his groundbreaking reporting and relied on it as gospel. Ray Rocca, Jim Angleton's deputy in the Counterintelligence Staff, was right when he exuberantly described Rodríguez Lahera as "an operational gold mine."[6]

The mother lode of Cuban secrets he brought was for CIA eyes only, and once in Ottawa, he did not have to wait long. Harold "Hal" Swenson, a tall and athletic CIA officer with leading-man looks and a loose, confident gait, was on a flight out of Washington almost as soon as word of the defection reached headquarters. Brooklyn-born and street smart, the forty-nine-year-old Swenson was chief of the large SAS counterintelligence unit.

He had tallied almost a quarter century of such work, beginning as an FBI agent before Pearl Harbor. One of his first assignments, according to his daughter Sally, was to search for suspected secret Japanese air bases in Baja California, in northwestern Mexico. Fluent in Spanish, he was later assigned by the Bureau to a remote area of Argentina before he joined the Marine Corps when the United States entered World War II.[7]

His first meeting with the Cuban was on the night of April 23. Swenson's preliminary report, communicated to Langley the next day, was positive but not effusive. A lawyer with a degree from Fordham, he was cautious, a doubter trained to sniff out deception and worry about worst-case possibilities. Loath to elevate expectations too high at Langley, initially he could not be sure he was dealing with a genuine defector rather than a Cuban dangle. Swenson was always more alert to that possibility than Des FitzGerald or anyone in SAS.[8]

In cable language shorthand, he told headquarters the Cuban was "eager go US and cooperate" and that "local authorities willing permit him do so."[9]

On May 1, still in Ottawa awaiting immigration clearances, Swenson securely sent twenty-three reels of tape-recorded interviews to headquarters. Once transcribed, they formed the foundation of the massive Rodríguez Lahera archive. Thousands of pages of administrative, operational, and information reports and cables to and from Agency field stations would bloat the files devoted to this prize defector. From a starting point of profound ignorance of Cuban intelligence personnel, structures, and workings, suddenly CIA was awash in inside information.[10]

Swenson later told the Church Committee that the defection had been a watershed. Until then "[w]e didn't know there was a DGI; our knowledge was quite fragmentary." Even among Cubans on the island, Laddie told Swenson, "very few people know anything about it or are even aware of its existence." He said Cuba's hidden spy service was generally referred to by code, as "M," rather than its true name.[11]

Indeed, it was shrouded so well that the Agency had not previously confirmed its identity. Langley had no doubt that Cuba was running sophisticated intelligence operations of many kinds against American interests. But even after Rodríguez Lahera described the DGI to Swenson, the closest anyone could come to pinpointing its pedigree was that it had been established "sometime in 1961."

Most of its operating methods had also been beyond the Agency's ken. Before leaving Ottawa for a CIA safe house in suburban Virginia, Laddie began explaining the missions, internal structure, leadership, and unique tradecraft of Cuban intelligence. He told how agents communicated and traveled. He identified dozens of his former colleagues—although not always by true name because they all used pseudonyms, even among themselves. (His was Victor.) He knew of the DGI's then-limited capabilities for forging and fabricating passports and other documents and shared a wealth of details about Cuban subversive operations.[12]

Laddie gave the Agency detailed descriptions and floor plans of the previously unknown DGI headquarters that occupied an entire walled city block in Marianao, a close-in Havana suburb. CIA learned for the first time of the innards of the three operational components of its adversary service. The Legal and Illegal Departments were patterned closely on KGB models, but the National Liberation Department was a Cuban innovation.

Swenson—known in the declassified CIA records by his pseudonym, Joseph Langosch, and to Laddie as Mr. Safely—was certain he was dealing with a genuine

and truthful defector. The best ones, no matter their nationality, are able to as-
suage doubts within a few hours. It helped that Rodríguez Lahera had never been
a member of the Cuban Communist Party or engaged in operations that imperiled Americans. And he had brought revealing DGI documents.

All the same, he was polygraphed, some years before the Cubans had developed the skills to defeat the lie detector. Thirty-six questions were put to him,
including one designed to confirm that he was not a double agent: "Do you have
any secret missions unknown to us?" By all measures he answered truthfully.
Swenson wrote the CIA security director "there is no question in my mind" that
he is a "bona fide defector or that he has furnished us with accurate and valuable
information." After that, there would never be questions from any quarter about
his reliability.[13]

Rodríguez Lahera's swift transformation from a Cuban to an American intelligence operative soon became official. An oral contract was concluded, presumably sealed with a handshake. He began earning $300 a week and was provided a
modestly furnished apartment.[14]

Around the same time, his cryptonym—AMMUG—was randomly pulled
out of a database. Occasionally, however, the choice of a crypt carried an obvious,
even mischievous, connotation, perhaps for the amusement of Agency officers
who alone are familiar with them. Fidel, for example, was AMTHUG; Raúl Castro, AMLOUT; and Che Guevara, AMQUACK. The DGI came to be known as
the sonorous AMAPOLA, the Spanish word for "poppy." There were hundreds of
others in the AM series during the early 1960s. That two-letter prefix referred to
something or someone relevant to Cuban operations.[15]

In August 1964, using his true name, the CIA reassigned Rodríguez Lahera
to JMWAVE. He remained on the CIA payroll for a few more years, assisting,
among other duties, in recruitment operations against former colleagues. Even
then, years before Aspillaga's experience in London, it was dangerous work
against armed and edgy DGI operatives. Laddie received an Agency commendation for the "courage" demonstrated in his travels, a well-calculated boost to his
sometimes-sagging morale.[16]

For most operatives, defection opens a lifelong wound. Nearly all, regardless
of nationality or background, present dismaying and continuing problems for
the intelligence services that receive them. Adjustment issues, feelings of guilt and
estrangement, and ultimately a sense of abandonment contribute to emotional

distress. For those who leave family members behind, the anguish can be debili-tating. Rodríguez Lahera was no exception. After nearly three months of debrief-ings, when there was nothing more to be squeezed out of him, he complained of being underutilized and neglected. He had made only a few friends, remaining closest to Hal Swenson, always a calm, reassuring father figure who counseled and encouraged the Cuban during his most painful periods.

He was "amicably terminated" from service on November 30, 1967, and re-ceived generous separation bonuses. The Agency even took a number of com-plicated steps to return to him the $2,540 he had stolen from the DGI. Creative finance officers, surely enjoying the challenge of legitimizing the theft, reim-bursed him for the federal taxes due on that "income" as well as accrued interest. He moved to Miami and found work there as a driver with a trucking firm. An American citizen by then, he seems to have left his two-chapter intelligence career permanently behind, blending inconspicuously into the Cuban American com-munity. According to reports I have not been able to verify, Laddie died sometime later, still a relatively young man.

HIS DEATH MAY HAVE BEEN from natural causes. But the mysterious demise of his friend and Agency comrade Miguel Roche, AMNIP–1, leads directly to the top of the Castro regime. Roche was a teenage veteran of the anti-Batista urban underground, a distant relative of Redbeard Piñeiro who recruited him for po-lice and intelligence work and later protected him when he ran afoul of fanatical revolutionary ideologues.

At the age of twenty-one, Roche was promoted to lieutenant and put in charge of internal security in Camagüey Province. Later he managed a govern-ment-controlled import company used for intelligence purposes and may have had responsibility for local gambling operations. Quick with calculations and financial transactions, he easily played at black-market currency manipulations to the advantage of the new regime. Had he remained in the Cuban service, he probably would have risen to its top ranks, becoming a DGI colonel or general.[17]

Gradually disaffected, however, he took asylum in the Ecuadorian embassy in Havana in December 1961 and later gained safe passage to Brazil. He was contacted there almost immediately by Hal Swenson and brought to the United States. Dangerous overseas assignments for CIA soon became his specialty. In mid-June 1964, Swenson wrote for the record: "I explained to MUG that in the immediate future I would like him to work with Roche in identifying members of Cuban intelligence . . . and I explained it might be necessary . . . to make trips outside the US to contact persons of operational interest who might be recruited or defected."

Laddie and Roche became close friends, both residing in the northern Virginia suburbs of Washington, near CIA headquarters, and often traveling abroad together on joint operations. They were an impressive pair. Miguel, from a well-off commercial family that lost everything to the revolution, was the dominant, buoyantly self-confident senior partner. Five-foot-ten-inches tall and weighing over two hundred pounds, he towered over the diminutive Laddie.

Clever, charming, and gregariously persuasive, Roche was a born street operative and was soon cutting to the DGI's quick. His widow told me that during the next several years he traveled abroad as often as twice a month carrying out Agency missions. She remembers that he went to Europe as well as Canada, Africa, Mexico, and South America. Declassified records confirm that at least one successful recruitment resulted. An agent, known as CAPRICE 1, was pitched by Roche in 1964 and formally enlisted several years later. Judging from how aggressively the Cuban regime responded to Roche's efforts, there were probably other successes too.[18]

In June, Roche traveled to Mexico City and Santiago, Chile, to meet DGI officers considered good recruitment prospects. The hoped-for rendezvous in Mexico never materialized. But soon after Roche huddled in a hotel bar in Santiago with two Cubans, one a known intelligence officer. It was a tense, high-stakes face-off, with recruitment pitches flying in both directions. Interior Minister Ramiro Valdés and other officials in Havana had "a high regard for him," Roche was told, and they "deeply regretted his defection." The Cubans wanted him back in the DGI fold as a double agent . . . or so they claimed. But, in a sign of what was to come half a dozen years later, he was also crudely threatened. The CIA station in Santiago cabled headquarters that Roche was warned: "Cuban intelligence has long arms and could kill him anyplace, anytime if he played false."[19]

The meeting had apparently been authorized and scripted by the senior leadership in Havana. Cuban figurehead president Osvaldo Dorticós told a CIA asset, "Oh yes, we know all about 'El Cojo' Roche's [recruitment] attempt . . . on behalf of the Americans. . . . We know all about his activity." (Cojo means "cripple" or "lame"; Roche walked with a limp after being thrown through the windshield of a car when working for Cuban intelligence in Havana.) The high-level interest meant that his work for the CIA had become so fruitful that he was a marked man.[20]

Undeterred, Roche remained operationally productive and brazen until his death. But with each approach he made to a Cuban, he put himself in greater peril. A thick dossier cataloging his efforts became the source of increasing outrage in Havana. He and Laddie had crossed two Rubicons: They had defected to the "imperialist" enemy with valuable information, and they went on to taunt and subvert their former service. By unforgiving *fidelista* diktat, they were committing capital crimes. Roche's were compounded many times over.

He received threatening letters at his home indicating Cuban authorship. He was warned: "We know what you are doing . . . so one way or another we will take care of you." His widow still has one of the letters. Roche was only thirty-one years old and in robust good health when he collapsed in front of his home in Falls Church, Virginia, in September 1970. He was dead by the time of arrival at a local hospital. Earlier that day, his widow told me, accompanied by an FBI agent, he had had an operational lunch meeting at a Mexican restaurant with one or more mysterious Cubans. It was just hours before he died. His widow was kept in the dark about whom Roche met, and why, but to this day she has no doubt that her husband was poisoned by Cuban intelligence. Autopsy reports she shared with me suggest that she is right.

Roche's blood tested negative for alcohol. His cardiovascular system checked out as normal; he had never been diagnosed with heart or circulatory problems. "He had been perfectly healthy until the day he died," his widow says. The toxicology report stated that 90 percent of the hemoglobin in his body had been contaminated. Cyanide, I am told, can have that effect. Extreme inflammation was found throughout the cells of his respiratory system. The examining pathologist, a medical doctor, told Roche's widow that he believed the damage "was caused by some unknown poison."

There was no police investigation, and CIA was unable to do anything despite powerful suspicions of foul play. Perhaps, however, Roche's untimely death persuaded the Agency that future star Cuban defectors would have to be provided new identities in order to live more safely beyond the reach of Castro's assassins. The dueling work that Rodríguez Lahera and Roche performed when trying to suborn DGI agents was much more dangerous than was thought at the time.

RODRÍGUEZ LAHERA'S GREATEST CONTRIBUTIONS were in exposing Cuban subversive operations. With almost no background or training other than his own guerrilla experience, he had been assigned to run the El Salvador desk at DGI headquarters.

Governed by a tenacious military-plutocratic elite, that little Central American country was a much lower priority for Fidel and Piñeiro than Venezuela or Guatemala, where guerrilla insurrections were taking root. Revolution in El Salvador was not as promising; the Cubans thought, correctly, that an upheaval there was still years in the future. Still, small Marxist cells and knots of Cuban-inspired youths were eager to take up arms.

Before his defection, Laddie kept busy supporting them. He worked with guerrilla combat trainees, illegals, and members of the Communist Party who clandestinely made their way to Havana. Their mentor and principal facilitator, he quickly became the DGI's resident country expert. His knowledge of espionage tradecraft extended to the workings of the Mexico City Center, which served as the conduit and clearinghouse for Central Americans seeking passage to Cuba.

His defection was a boon for the counterinsurgency experts at Langley. He identified about 120 aspiring guerrillas and DGI illegals of a half dozen nationalities, all by name. He knew seven of them well enough to describe quirks and vulnerabilities that made them easier prey for CIA recruitment or, failing that, nullification as viable Cuban assets. In mid-June 1964, it was noted in an "operational target analysis" that "we have already undertaken action." The kind of action was not specified.[21]

Partly on the basis of Rodríguez Lahera's reporting, the United States was able to grind down, all but annihilate nascent insurgencies in a few countries. The most drastically thwarted were Cuban subversive efforts in El Salvador and Nicaragua. Laddie passed on the names and descriptions of about thirty-five Salvadorans working with the DGI, most of them graduates of guerrilla training camps. He also identified twenty-three trainees from Nicaragua. Those exposed constituted nearly the entire trained revolutionary cadre in the two countries; it would be another fifteen years before Cuban-supported insurgents could regroup and fire up viable insurrections.

One of Rodríguez Lahera's most valuable tips concerned a brooding young Salvadoran firebrand. Roque Dalton, author of more than a dozen volumes of prose and poetry, is still recognized as a talented Latin American literary figure and martyr for revolutionary causes. He is the most honored poet ever to emerge from El Salvador.

Dalton was recruited in Cuba as a DGI agent in October 1963 and codenamed "Montenegro." Rodríguez Lahera, his case officer, arranged for training in secret writing, radio transmission and reception, and other clandestine tradecraft. Like so many of his generation of Latin Americans, Dalton also completed courses in guerrilla warfare.[22]

He had studied at universities in Chile, Mexico, and El Salvador. Twenty-eight when Rodríguez Lahera began describing him to the CIA, he was an attractive figure with an authentic legend that even Piñeiro himself could not have invented. According to CIA records, he had "a long thin face, black eyes, two gold teeth, and black hair parted on the left side." Oddly, the description failed to mention his most distinguishing physical characteristic, his long Pinocchio nose.

Dalton must have been one of the most promising of the DGI's Central American recruits: fit, young, charismatic, and admired by Salvadoran youths and intellectuals. When he was singled out, he was surely thought of as just the kind of romantic hero who could lead a Cuban-style guerrilla revolt in the volcanic mountains of his country. He might even prove to be a successful Salvadoran Che Guevara.[23]

But Dalton dismayed the Cubans. It turned out he had been poorly motivated from the start. "He has a weakness for women and the easy life, and a generally weak nature," according to the CIA vulnerability analysis. Dalton "is very intelligent," Rodríguez Lahera told the Agency, "but never showed a real desire to learn during his Cuban training."

He had been given $600 to purchase a sophisticated radio set when he returned covertly to El Salvador and instructed to transmit coded messages on the second Monday of each month. The frequencies he was to use were recorded on seven scraps of microfilm concealed in a hollow in the heel of his shoe. Despite the elaborate training and the DGI's high hopes, the poet never communicated. Swenson reported in his first debriefing dispatch from Ottawa that once back in his country, Dalton "took a little trip for himself, lived high, and spent the money."[24]

Of all the foreign revolutionaries who had come to his attention, Rodríguez Lahera considered Dalton the "leading candidate for recruitment by us," according to a CIA report. It was speculated that "subject would not be a too difficult target to hit," meaning to approach and recruit as a double agent against the Cubans.[25]

But why would Dalton work more diligently for CIA than he had for the Cubans? That obvious concern was noted in the records: "his failure to perform for the DGI . . . might mitigate against our use of him." But on balance, it did not matter. The concern, after all, was motivation. He was like all the other DGI agents and illegals over the years who got paid only for expenses and perhaps an occasional small honorarium. A substantial flow of American dollars might be sufficient inducement for him to play a double game.

Soon the Agency concluded that Dalton's membership on the central com-mittee of El Salvador's Communist Party was reason enough to keep him in its sights; "it makes him an operational target for that reason alone." A headquarters memo in November 1964 expressed the range of what the CIA hoped to achieve: "Our object is to double, defect, or nullify Dalton." Indeed, after he was arrested and imprisoned in San Salvador earlier that year, Rodríguez Lahera and a CIA of-ficer—probably Swenson—interrogated the poet, determined to turn him against the Cubans. He "was much shaken" and "begged" to be released, promising to abandon politics, according to a CIA field report cabled to headquarters. Yet, even in the presence of his former DGI case officer, Dalton was adamant in denying any association with Cuban intelligence. But this is where the declassified record runs dry. If he was eventually recruited, if Dalton was persuaded to cooperate in any way with the Agency, nothing of it has been revealed, and most likely it never will be.[26]

On the surface, he was a model revolutionary. For a number of years after his time in prison he lived in Havana and Prague, and most likely remained on the DGI's rolls despite his failings as an agent. Most of his writings were published in Havana by the Casa de las Americas, the government's publishing and cultural arm that has always been entwined with intelligence.

In late 1974 he returned yet again to El Salvador to take up arms against the government and penned some of his most didactic underground verse. A few lines from his poem "The Violence Here" are typical:

Violence will not only be the midwife
of History in El Salvador.
It will also be the mother of a child-people.[27]

Dalton was often a focus of flattering Cuban propaganda, awarded literary prizes and featured at international symposia. His public posture remained purposefully militant. For all appearances he was a true believer in *fidelista* causes, particularly violent revolutionary warfare in his own country.

Yet, in the hall of mirrors of international espionage, the obvious often is a mirage. He actually may have had reasons to cooperate somehow with CIA. His father was an American who emigrated to El Salvador. Three of his brothers were American citizens, one of whom is said to have fought against Japan in the Pacific during World War II. And the circumstances surrounding Roque's death in May 1975, when he was just days short of his fortieth birthday, have kept speculation alive that he in fact had some kind of CIA connection.

Back in El Salvador, he joined an emerging guerrilla movement. But soon he was in strident conflict with its leaders. They staged a secret revolutionary trial, finding him guilty of insubordination or treason. Dalton was executed the same day in San Salvador, and his body was never found. He had strayed far beyond his literary talents, a victim of the fantasy that his twin muses of poetry and revolutionary warfare could happily cohabit. He was another of the many doomed acolytes of the 1960s revolutionary fevers, a willing victim of Fidel's morbid incantations to revolutionary violence.

Those who imposed the death sentence spread the word that the poet had to be killed because he was a CIA agent. That may have been contrived as a sure way of justifying their actions; or they may have been convinced it was true. I am not aware that the killers ever elaborated on the charge or provided evidence. Certainly nothing ever leaked from CIA vaults about Dalton that would have compromised him. And the archived records where I found descriptions of CIA operational interest in him were not released until 1998.[28]

Ironically, there is a good chance that the killers were victims themselves—of a masterful deception operation. If so, the most likely perpetrator would have been the brutal Salvadoran military dictatorship. The generals and army intelligence had ample motive to plant false evidence linking Dalton to CIA. They would have calculated that it could hobble the insurgency, further dividing the guerrillas and putting one of their most appealing leaders in mortal jeopardy. In 1960s and 1970s Latin America, almost anything was permissible in guerrilla and counterinsurgency warfare.

And yet there is another possibility: The Cubans may have been responsible for Dalton's execution. He was a mercurial dilettante, had abused DGI tutelage, and may have run afoul of Fidel and Piñeiro. If Cuban intelligence concluded Roque had been secretly involved with CIA, nothing would have been more certain to result in a death sentence. As a trained DGI illegal, he would have been marked just as surely as the traitors Aspillaga and Roche were.[29]

The possibility is strengthened by the subsequent execution—on Fidel's orders, it appears—of another prominent Salvadoran revolutionary. Salvador Cayetano Carpio, "Marcial" to his brethren, the "Ho Chi Minh of Central America" as he liked to boast, was the most intransigent hard-liner among the guerrillas. He was blamed in 1984 for the gruesome ice-pick assassination of "Ana Maria," the nom de guerre of his Salvadoran guerrilla deputy and rival. Shortly after attending her funeral in Managua, Carpio was also found dead, of a gunshot wound, in the Nicaraguan capital where the Marxist Sandinista regime was in power. His death was explained away as a suicide.[30]

But Juan Antonio Rodríguez Menier, one of the 1987 DGI defectors, believes differently. He is sure it was Fidel who issued the death warrant. Ana Maria's murder "was investigated by top Cuban officials" in Managua, he says. According to other sources, Piñeiro was among those investigating officials. Rodríguez Menier adds that Fidel "then ordered that the man responsible be executed."[31]

Carpio had been dangerously at odds with the Cubans over political and military strategy. And he objected to their aggressive meddling. Just months before the two murders, he is reliably reported to have repudiated Fidel's bullying, telling him "to go to hell." That is not the kind of rebuke the vain Cuban leader suffers lightly. Jorge Castañeda, the former Mexican foreign minister and an expert on the Latin American radical left, wrote that Carpio "had been fighting the Cubans ... for months."[32]

Fidel was accustomed to exercising patrimonial influence over the guerrillas and to getting his way. Notably, in 1979, he brought leaders of their competing factions to Havana, where, with cajolery and promises of munitions, he forged the insurgent alliance that became known as the Farabundo Martí National Liberation Front, or FMLN.

Joaquín Villalobos, leader of one of the factions, was there. He told me how two representatives of each of the guerrilla groups were met at the Havana airport by Cuban intelligence officers and taken separately in Mercedes limousines to guesthouses. Together, all of them later met with Castro in the presidential palace with Piñeiro attending. "Carpio was the problem; he challenged Fidel; he'd been drinking," Villalobos told me during a meeting in November 2011 in Toronto. Another Salvadoran guerrilla commander later recalled that "had it not been for the Cubans, especially Fidel Castro, it would not have been possible to attain unity."[33]

After building up their capabilities, on January 10, 1981, just ten days before Ronald Reagan's inauguration in Washington, Fidel presumed to act as the guerrillas' commander in chief. From a DGI war room in Havana, he relayed orders to their fighting units as they launched what was optimistically called the "final offensive" to topple the military government. A former American intelligence officer with direct knowledge of the Cuban role told me, "They [the Cubans] were running the whole thing, receiving intercepts on Salvadoran military movements and operations, and communicating with the rebels. They were highly confident the FMLN would be victorious."

Plans had been in the works for over a year with as many as five hundred Salvadorans being trained and readied in Cuba. They received hundreds of tons of arms, channeled through Nicaragua. Seasoned Cuban advisors were on the ground with them. Fidel's audacious plan was to present the new American administration with a revolutionary fait accompli. The fighting over several days was savage, but the government's military forces beat back the onslaught.[34]

Apart from Rodríguez Menier's assertion, I can find no evidence linking Fidel to Carpio's murder. But everything else the defector has revealed appears to be reliable. His story about Carpio's death is consistent with Castro's violent behavior since his university days and with the seigniorial privilege he wielded over the Salvadoran rebels. Assassinations and attempts against enemies, rivals, and traitors were as characteristic of his governing style as speechmaking and grandstanding. During his decades in power, Fidel authorized the executions of a long list of offenders, including two of his intelligence chieftains who died under mysterious circumstances, probably on his orders.

Redbeard Piñeiro allegedly was one of them. A well-connected former Cuban government official who worked with the spymaster for many years claims that Piñeiro was murdered in 1998 on the orders of either Fidel or Raúl Castro.

Like so many others in the brothers' entourages over the decades, Piñeiro had strayed from their rigid orthodoxies and had been shunted aside. But "he was impossible to retire," my source told me. He knew too much; he was writing a book, and he made the mistake of telling others about it. His whole career—more than forty years—had been in intelligence and intrigue. Everything he had done was as Fidel or Raúl's proxy in covert operations in dozens of countries on several continents. What else could he have been writing about?

The day after his death, security personnel searched his home in Havana, "as if he were a dissident" or a conspirator, and "kept all kinds of papers," according to the former Cuban official who now resides in Florida. He also told me that Piñeiro's home "was surely bugged" and that he had been talking too freely.

Redbeard's bodyguard, who doubled as his driver, was also certain his boss had been murdered. Piñeiro was said to have fainted at the wheel of his car, resulting in a single-vehicle accident on the streets of Havana. He survived with minor injuries and was taken to a government executive hospital for observation. A day before the accident, the transportation ministry had instructed his driver to take some time off: Piñeiro would drive himself. My source told me the distraught driver lamented openly: "They knew. They knew." The regime said that Redbeard died of a heart attack in his hospital bed. The story is reminiscent of brutal scenes in the *Godfather* movies that Aspillaga told me were shown in his day for DGI training purposes.

ASSASSINATION OPERATIONS HAD ALWAYS BEEN Fidel's personal bailiwick. None could be conducted that he did not authorize and help plan. The means for carrying out this most sinister of secret Cuban capabilities were always decentralized and rigidly compartmentalized. In the 1950s and early 1960s, the KGB's infamous Department 13 killed traitors in what the Soviets called "wet operations." But when I asked Aspillaga if Cuba had created anything similar, he laughed: "The Russians in that respect are more vulgar." It was not scruples that concerned Fidel but the need for airtight deniability.

The Cubans used DGI-controlled illegals, surrogates of other nationalities, as executioners. They carried out some of the most sensitive missions overseas, especially against high-visibility, well-protected targets. Death squads drawn from Latin American terrorist and revolutionary groups beholden to Cuba could be relied on, deniability compounded by degrees of separation. Carefully screened, the foreign assassins were trained at secret Cuban bases, learning to kill in gangland-style hits, elaborately orchestrated paramilitary operations, commando strikes, and sly poisonings.

In the most sensitive operations, when even greater deniability was desired, Fidel did rely on carefully screened Cubans. In the 1970s and 1980s, according to Aspillaga, a super-secret four-man squad of assassins reported exclusively to Castro. With few exceptions, including Minister of Interior José Abrahantes, who succeeded Valdes in 1985, no one else was aware of these professional hit men, Tiny told me. It was dangerous for any Cuban to share the commander in chief's most incriminating secrets. No wonder perhaps that, like Redbeard, Abrahantes also died under mysterious circumstances. His death received just a few memorial lines in the official media. In our meetings, Aspillaga described two of Fidel's secret assassins. One he knew in the 1980s was nicknamed "El Chiquitico," the Little One. Another was familiar to him only as "El Chamaco," the Kid. In one of our recorded interviews, Aspillaga said of Fidel, "When he chooses someone, he takes his personality and dominates you . . . he controls you mentally. That's what he did to those four assassins." They had been molded and brainwashed, Aspillaga believed, into blindly loyal killing machines.

I asked him for examples of their handiwork.

Fidel, he said, "had generals in Bolivia who were involved in Che's death killed." CIA analysts had come to that conclusion years before Aspillaga defected. Four Bolivians—two generals, an army captain, and a peasant—who had materially contributed to Che's demise were assassinated, for all appearances, by death squads. Another general, René Barrientos, the popular president of Bolivia when Che was hunted down, died himself a year and a half later in an unexplained helicopter crash.

In the late 1960s, we CIA desk analysts knew nothing about Castro's personal team of assassins and, frankly, little about his compulsion for lethal revenge. But the number and pattern of the killings of the Bolivians, Fidel's obvious motive, and the professionalism of the executions all suggested official Cuban involvement. These were not the kinds of mysterious deaths that could have been explained away as heart attacks, suicides, or accidents. We had no doubt that the Bolivians had been murdered by killers intent on avenging Che.

The first to die after Barrientos was Honorato Rojas, a subsistence farmer in the backlands where Che's insurgency had struggled for a toehold. At first Rojas assisted a band of guerrillas commanded by one of Guevara's lieutenants, agreeing to guide them through the tangled terrain. But a Bolivian army officer persuaded him to betray the strange, bedraggled intruders, most of them Cubans. On August 31, 1967, Rojas led the guerrillas straight into a killing ambush at the confluence of two swift rivers. A half dozen of Guevara's dwindling band were killed instantly, and others were captured. Che's lover, a German Argentine woman known by her war name, "Tania," was among them. It was one of the decisive skirmishes in the lopsided Bolivian conflict and was followed five weeks later by Che's capture and execution.[35]

Rojas's betrayal was key to the failure of the entire revolutionary endeavor; the ambush he arranged eliminated a third of Che's force. For Fidel, the Bolivian farmer was appallingly reminiscent of Eutímio Guerra, the Cuban peasant who had betrayed him to Batista's army, one of the "big three" traitors he would publicly condemn in 1987. In July 1969, Rojas paid the ultimate price for his treachery, as Guerra had a dozen years earlier. The luckless peasant was gunned down by unknown assailants claiming to be members of a Bolivian revolutionary front.

The next target was Roberto Quintanilla, a Bolivian army intelligence officer who played a role in Che's failure. He was murdered in Germany in 1971. The best known victim was General Joaquín Zenteno, commander of the army division that pursued Che. Zenteno was shot in Paris in May 1976 while serving as his country's ambassador. The previously unknown Che Guevara Command claimed responsibility; it was never heard from again. Two weeks later another general, Juan José Torres, a top Bolivian staff officer who had ratified the order for Che to be executed, was murdered by an Argentine death squad. All the cases quickly went cold.[36]

General Zenteno was doubly anathema to Fidel. Assisting him in his hunt for Che were two Cuban exile contract CIA operatives, both veterans of the earlier clandestine wars across the Florida Straits. They were well known to Cuban intelligence. In his memoirs, Félix Rodríguez admitted participating in an assassination plot against Fidel in 1961, and he believes he was targeted for death by Castro after Che's execution. Gustavo Villoldo, the second Cuban exile advisor to General Zenteno, also published memoirs, and told me that he was targeted for death on three different occasions by Cuban operatives, most recently in 2003 during a visit to Bolivia."[37]

There is no evidence of Cuban government participation in the murders of the Bolivians. It is possible that all the death squads acted independently of Havana, each incident entirely separate from the other. Latin American and European terrorists were enchanted with the iconic Che, wanted revenge, and could have acted on their own. But, on balance, Cuban responsibility for at least four of the cases seems likely.

Arranging for the executions of defectors, traitors, worthy enemies, and even an occasional foreign general was commonplace in Fidel's nearly fifty-year career in office. Targeting serving and former heads of state was a more daring undertaking.

Since the Middle Ages and early Renaissance period, regicide practiced by a national leader against enemy monarchs and chief executives has been rare. Bill Harvey, one of the CIA's legendary operatives—who twice in the early 1960s plotted Castro's death with Mafia gangsters—told the Church Committee that even Soviet dictator Joseph Stalin must have eschewed such risky behavior: "I cannot personally document or testify to a single Soviet assassination of a leader of a foreign state."[38]

But through most of his years in power, Fidel played by his own vengeful rules. At least four sitting or former presidents of Latin American countries were the targets of meticulously planned Cuban "black" operations. Probably other such operations left no traces.

Knowledgeable exile sources have told me that Fidel for years had his predecessor, Batista, marked for execution. The old dictator, living in exile in Portugal and Spain, was the target in 1973 of an elaborately rehearsed Cuban plot. Fidel had compelling motive. In the mid-1950s he had spent nearly two years in one of Batista's prisons. The dictator had authorized untold numbers of executions of Castro's supporters in the late 1950s. After the triumph of the revolution, hundreds of his henchmen were put up against execution walls in retaliation. Had he not escaped in time, Batista assuredly would have stood before a firing squad himself.[39]

Fidel's plan was not to assassinate him but to snatch, or kidnap, him alive. It would be a Cuban version of the justice meted out to Nazi mass murderer Adolf Eichmann, who was kidnapped by Israeli intelligence in Argentina and convicted in a show trial in Jerusalem in 1961. Cuban commandos and DGI operatives were ready to seize Batista from the walled compound near Lisbon where he lived or when he ventured out. He would be drugged, smuggled to Havana—probably on a Cuban merchant vessel—displayed and humiliated before a revolutionary tribunal, and then executed.

I learned of this previously untold conspiracy from a ranking DGI defector. For his safety and that of his family members, I will call him Francisco Compostela. Now living in the United States under an assumed identity, he learned of the Lisbon plot from another senior DGI officer with knowledge of what was in the works. Compostela told me, "The plan was ready to be implemented. We had a squad of illegals set up in a safe house, ready to seize Batista and take him to Cuba . . . or assassinate him if the plot could not be fulfilled. It was elaborately planned." Ironically, Batista died of natural causes during a vacation at a Spanish resort town in August 1973 shortly before the operation was to take place.

Fidel always denied any intent to seek vengeance against his predecessor. During a fundraising speech in New York in November 1955, a year before he set sail from Mexico to begin his insurgency, he told an audience of Cuban exiles: "We do not practice tyrannicide."[40]

He meant Batista, of course. And then, quoting a hero of Cuba's nineteenth-century independence wars, he elaborated: "The man who exposes himself to death and can kill his opponent on the battlefield does not use the treacherous and disgraceful means of assassination."

The "battlefield" reference is key to Fidel's thinking. That is where he believes he has spent his entire adult life. As he tells it, his personal saga has been a protracted life-and-death conflict with powerful enemies bent on destroying him and his work. His preference was always to seize the initiative against them, to go on the offensive, and to give no quarter. Tyrannicide, therefore, was merely one of the many forms of homicide he believes to be justifiable—in self-defense, in warfare, but more precisely in revolutionary struggle. When an enemy poses a grave threat, assassination is justifiable—not only in what he would characterize as a just war but also against a foreign leader he considered heinous.

The savage Dominican dictator Rafael Trujillo was an early example. He was a genuine tyrant from almost any perspective, including John F. Kennedy's. Trujillo authorized the torture and merciless killing of his opponents. The grudge Fidel held, however, was due to Trujillo's sponsorship of a clumsy coup attempt against him in August 1959. Castro even then—his first summer in power—was running double agents, one of whom kept him informed of Trujillo's conspiracy.[41]

Rumors of Fidel's desire for revenge against his Caribbean nemesis circulated for years. But until recently, I was not aware of persuasive evidence. The new information comes from Dariel Alarcón Ramírez, still known by his nom de guerre, "Benigno." A faithful foot soldier who fought with Che in Bolivia, he was one of a handful who survived the debacle, managing, after tortuous peregrinations, to get safely back to Cuba. Later, though, like so many other experienced DGI officers, he defected. He has firsthand knowledge of an attempt on Trujillo's life.

Benigno recently told me: "I know of direct Cuban participation in an assassination attempt against Trujillo in 1959." A prominent veteran of the Castros' insurgency, a *comandante* named Derminio Escalona, was allegedly the leader of the failed attempt. Benigno also confirmed what Aspillaga told me about Fidel targeting the errant Bolivians.[42]

For Castro, however, there were no more deserving objects of his wrath than two of modern Latin America's most reviled dictators. Also both generals, Anastasio Somoza, the durable Nicaraguan dictator, and Augusto Pinochet, the Chilean president from 1973 until 1989, were for years high on Fidel's most wanted list.

Somoza, commander of Nicaragua's National Guard before inheriting the presidency in 1967, had done much to earn Fidel's wrath. Working with the CIA, he had provided training facilities and an air base for the Bay of Pigs brigade in 1961. Two years later he allowed Manuel Artime's "autonomous" exile group to train and launch sabotage attacks on the island from a base on Nicaragua's Caribbean coast. As noted, Fidel knew all about it from a Cuban double agent. Somoza's was the kind of mercenary belligerence that Castro cannot forgive.

The DGI mounted the first serious attempt against the dictator in 1964. But it was not until sixteen years later that a perfectly executed commando operation succeeded in assassinating the former Nicaraguan leader. The armored car in which he was being chauffeured in the streets of Asunción, Paraguay, was incinerated in a coolly calibrated bazooka attack on September 17, 1980.

Jorge Masetti, one of Piñeiro's boys—his godson, in fact—has written about it. Masetti was the son and namesake of a fallen Argentine guerrilla leader who had been close to Che. Following in his father's footsteps, the younger Masetti was for years a roving DGI warrior and operative. After defecting in 1990, he described Somoza's murder. It was a precision attack, conceived, planned, and practiced to perfection at a secret base in Cuba.[43]

The executioner "knelt in the middle of the street," according to Masetti. "His shot hit the mark dead center, but the projectile was a dud. And then, amid the ensuing crossfire . . . he calmly reloaded and made the second shot that killed Somoza. The guerrillas then hastily withdrew according to plan." Masetti knew them; they were a group of Argentine terrorists, DGI illegals. "They were my *compañeros*," he wrote."[44]

With Somoza gone, Pinochet rose to the top of Fidel's demonology. Leader of the September 1973 coup that overthrew fervid Cuban ally Salvador Allende, the Chilean president would prove less vulnerable than the exiled Somoza. There may have been other failed attempts, but the one that came closest to success occurred in September 1986.

It was a paramilitary operation similar to the one against Somoza, conducted at the curve of a road in the outskirts of the capital of Santiago with an arsenal of heavy weapons. Two Cuban defectors—former top DGI operative José Maragon and Lázaro Betancourt, a commando and sharpshooter—know details of the meticulously planned attack. They told me the guiding Cuban hand was common knowledge in their intelligence circles.

Betancourt was familiar with the failed attempt because it was used as a case study in his commando training. His instructor had prepared the Chilean terrorists who conducted the assault. They were members of the Manuel Rodríguez Patriotic Front, one of the South American terrorist groups the DGI used for special operations that could not easily be traced back to Cuba.

During the explosives phase of his course, Betancourt was posted at Punto Cero, a secret military base in Guanabo, east of Havana. (It has the same name as Fidel's family compound at Jaimanitas but is entirely distinct.) Betancourt told me:

> They explained to us the assassination attempt on Pinochet and why it had failed. It was because the Chilean terrorists changed the attack plan at the last minute. They should have placed the explosives in the path of Pinochet's motorcade and then used firearms to finish him off. But they reversed it, and fired first. My instructor said that if they had done it right it would have been successful.

No Cubans participated. But the planning and training had all been done at the Cuban base. Cuban Special Troops delivered the Vietnam-era American weapons used—aboard a vessel of the Cuban fishing fleet—to an isolated spot on Chile's northern Pacific coast.

The *Guardian* newspaper in London described the assault as "dramatically cinematic in its execution." Pinochet's heavy armored vehicle came under a rain of machine-gun fire and was jolted by at least one grenade explosion. Reportedly bazookas and rocket launchers were also used. The dictator, accompanied by his young grandson, was slightly wounded but went on to serve another three years in office. Five of his bodyguards were killed and eleven others were wounded. According to Maragon, "the escape plan worked very well." All the attackers managed to flee safely back to Cuba.[45]

SEVEN

MOUTH OF THE LION

THE VLADIMIR RODRÍGUEZ LAHERA AND MIGUEL ROCHE STORIES probably would never have been known outside of a small CIA circle—and soon forgotten by nearly all—had Laddie not traveled to Mexico City a month before defecting.

Under diplomatic cover, he went there from Havana to meet clandestinely with a group of Salvadoran Communist Party leaders. Patiently he waited, expecting to hear the password "Mauricio" that would authenticate them as Cuban assets. But they never arrived. The work of field operatives is often like this: planning for meetings that fail to materialize, whiling away days at a time waiting for a phone call in shabby hotel rooms in faraway cities.[1]

He lingered in the Mexican capital from March 14 to 23, 1964. It was his first trip outside of Cuba, and he was delighted to make the best of it at the DGI's expense. Meetings with Nicaraguan revolutionaries were arranged, other operational tasks carried out; otherwise, he mingled with colleagues at the DGI Center. It operated out of the consulate building, adjacent to the embassy, on the same square-block compound in the downtown Condesa neighborhood. Once he was in CIA hands a month later, that experience assumed critical new importance.

Laddie's knowledge of the Center's personnel and procedures made him a figure of enduring interest in investigations into John F. Kennedy's assassination. This is why virtually all of his CIA files were declassified in the 1990s under the

legislated authorities of the Assassination Records Review Board that was established to make publicly available all federal government records considered relevant to the assassination. Rodríguez Lahera was important because he and Lee
Harvey Oswald dealt with some of the same Cuban intelligence officers at the
DGI's Mexico Center.

Kennedy's assassin went to the Cuban consulate on three occasions while in
the Mexican capital between September 27 and October 2, 1963, seeking a visa to
travel to Cuba. Laddie was at the Center six months later, and was already familiar
with its operations because of his work at DGI headquarters. He was a unique
and reliable source of information about one of the most vexing matters still
under scrutiny by the Warren Commission. Could Cuban intelligence have had
a hand in the president's assassination? Chief Justice Earl Warren and six other
American notables were in the late stages of their investigation into Kennedy's
death when Laddie defected, preparing to issue their much-maligned report the
following September. CIA considered Laddie such a sensitive source, however,
that he was shielded from commission staff. He was not interviewed, nor was
Swenson. Worse, the most valuable information he brought that was relevant to
the investigation was not fully aired or analyzed at the time. Notably, Laddie was
convinced that Fidel had lied when he publicly denied any knowledge of Oswald
prior to the assassination on November 22, 1963.[2]

In two speeches over the next few days after Kennedy's death, Castro insisted that he had known nothing about the assassin. By nightfall on the day the
president died and Vice President Johnson had been sworn in to succeed him,
Oswald's Marxist convictions, defection to the Soviet Union, and pro-Cuban pas-
sions and activism were reverberating in the news media. Castro knew he needed
to preempt the inevitable charges that Cuba had somehow been involved in a
conspiracy. So, speaking of Oswald on the evening of November 23 from a Havana television studio, Fidel was unequivocal: "We never in our life heard of him."

Knowing the stakes were dangerously high, Castro had gambled. Few people
could credibly contradict him. Only a handful of Cuban officials had the knowledge to refute their leader, and who would dare? No one, of course, anticipated
that Laddie would defect a few months later. As in similar instances over the years
when the pressure was intense, Fidel calculated that through bluster, bombast,
and well-crafted lies, endlessly retold, he would be believed. The government's
propaganda machine—and DGI active measures campaigns that echoed his

position—were rolled out almost immediately. The lie was perhaps an understandable retreat from the heat of the moment, but it has only compounded the doubts: What else was Fidel hiding?

In early May 1964, Swenson reported up the line what Laddie knew about Fidel's deception, condensing it into just a few words. Hal added no commentary and made no effort to highlight the information. Oddly, he did not consider it important, and there is no evidence in the declassified records that anyone else in CIA did either. No one informed Cuba specialists in the analytic directorate. As a result, my predecessors there did not include any details in the sensitive intelligence publications they drafted for Washington policy audiences. The two subsequent congressional investigations of the Kennedy assassination and independent researchers also overlooked the anomaly. Fidel's deception was buried away in the Rodríguez Lahera archive, where it remained unexamined—until now.

LADDIE KNEW THE WORKINGS of the Mexico Center well. With at least ten case officers, it was the largest Cuban Center in the world. CIA believed that even the gardener worked as an intelligence asset. Laddie revealed that the DGI also staffed busy consulates in the Mexican gulf coast ports of Veracruz and Tampico, and in Mérida, the principal city on the Yucatán peninsula. The Cubans enjoyed "quite a lot of freedom of movement and action in Mexico in those days," Helms's deputy told the Church Committee.[3]

Laddie knew Manuel Vega Peréz, the corpulent Center chief, and his deputy, Rogelio Rodríguez López. They were among Piñeiro's most ruthless and proficient operatives, handpicked by Fidel. Two independent sources told CIA handlers that in February 1964, the two masterminded an assassination attempt against Anastasio Somoza, then commander of his country's National Guard. It was to be carried out by Nicaraguan illegals under Cuban direction. That attempt failed, or never coalesced—the declassified record is incomplete—but the DGI's merciless hunt for the archenemy continued. Vega and Rodríguez López, and their accomplices, could claim no credit for the ex-dictator's fiery annihilation years later, but their efforts were probably as seriously planned.[4]

Laddie identified other Mexico Center intelligence officers. In Havana, he had known Luisa Calderon, a vivacious and attractive young woman, before the DGI transferred her to the Mexico Center. A senior DGI official at headquarters believed "hers was a peculiar case," and Laddie knew enough about her to agree.

She went into seclusion immediately after Kennedy's assassination. When she returned permanently to Cuba a few weeks later, Laddie said that Calderon continued to be paid "a regular salary by the DGI even though she has not performed any services." She was living in an expensive Havana neighborhood. He thought she may have had dealings with Oswald.[5]

Swenson reported that Laddie "had no personal knowledge" of Kennedy's assassin, though he had learned from Vega about Oswald's second and third visits to the Cuban consulate. They would have been memorable to all within earshot.

In 1978, Silvia Duran, the Mexican receptionist there told staff of the House of Representatives Select Committee on Assassinations—investigating the deaths of President Kennedy and Martin Luther King—that Oswald created angry, boisterous scenes when denied a visa. Eight Cubans—including Fidel—were also interviewed by committee representatives.[6]

Two of them remembered Oswald's visit vividly. Vega's replacement, the incoming Center chief, DGI officer Alfredo Mirabel, told the committee that each of Oswald's confrontations lasted from fifteen to twenty minutes. Cuban consular officer Eusebio Azcue said he argued with Oswald, "violently or emotionally." "We never had any individual so persistent." When refused a visa during his last visit, Oswald slammed the door in a rage as he departed.[7]

He was a baffling case for the Cubans. Duran remembered how hard he tried to convince them he "was a friend" of the revolution. Supposedly he carried a book of Lenin's writings under his arm when he appeared. He also carried a packet of letters, documents, press clippings, and membership cards. Oswald had never joined the American Communist Party but brought a forged identification claiming that he had done so. He showed the Cubans that he was a legitimate, card-carrying member of the New York–based Fair Play for Cuba Committee. It was known by the FBI to be funded and manipulated by the DGI, although Cuban officials have denied that.[8]

Oswald tried to create an unauthorized branch of the Fair Play group in New Orleans, but he, his Russian-born wife, Marina, and the fictitious A. J. Hidell were its only members. Hidell—it rhymed with Fidel—was also the alias Oswald used to purchase the rifle used to kill Kennedy. A DGI captain who was among the officials monitoring the House committee during its representatives' visits to Havana volunteered that the "A" in the Hidell name was short for Alejandro, Fidel's nom de guerre during his insurgency. The Cuban commented, "I think it was well chosen." How the captain knew what the initial referred to has never been explained.[9]

Oswald had been enthralled with Fidel since his late 1950s service at the El Toro Marine Corps Air Station in southern California. It was there, just before Christmas 1958, that Nelson Delgado, a Brooklyn-born Puerto Rican, struck up a friendship with him. Delgado was one of the few people who ever thought of the acerbic, unpredictable Oswald as a real buddy. He told the Warren Commission: "We started talking . . . got to know each other quite well." The glue between them was the attraction they felt for Castro and the guerrilla struggle he was then in the final week of waging against Batista. Delgado said they had "many discussions regarding Castro." Oswald "actually started making plans . . . how to get to Cuba. . . . He started studying Spanish . . . and kept asking me how he could go about helping."[10]

"I didn't know what to tell him," Delgado remembered, so "the best thing I know was to get in touch with the Cuban embassy . . . I told him to go see them." Delgado believed Oswald reached Cuban government representatives in Los Angeles. "After a while he told me he was in contact with them. . . . He was telling me there was a Cuban consul . . . and he started receiving these letters." Later Delgado remembered that Oswald had a civilian visitor at the marine base whom he suspected was a Cuban. "They spent about an hour and a half, two hours talking." It appears that reports about these alleged contacts found their way into the DGI's case files on Oswald.

Batista was ousted on January 1, 1959, so it was too late for Oswald to find his way to Cuba to fight as a foot soldier in Fidel's insurgency. An alternate plan materialized. Delgado recalled that they mused about volunteering as guerrilla fighters in other Caribbean countries. They talked about "how we would like to go to Cuba and . . . lead an expedition to some other islands and free them too." For Delgado, their bravado may have been mostly idle, romantic fantasizing; for Oswald, it reflected his authentic militance and desire to abandon the bourgeois America he despised. In October 1959, he defected to the Soviet Union.

His infatuation with Fidel and Cuba endured. Marina first noticed it during their courtship in Minsk, today the capital of independent Belarus. Oswald was incensed when the CIA's brigade of Cuban exiles landed at the Bay of Pigs. He took Marina to see a Soviet film about Cuba, telling her he considered Fidel "a hero." Authors Jean Davison and Gus Russo wrote that he sought out Cuban students in Minsk.[11]

Back in Texas and Louisiana after redefecting in 1962, Oswald's interest in his hero grew. He hung a picture of Fidel on the wall of his apartment in New Orleans. He mused about naming the couple's unborn first child Fidel. Absurdly, he tried to talk Marina into helping him hijack a plane to Cuba so, she recalled, he could fight for "Uncle Fidel." He read copious amounts of print propaganda about his idol and was adept at repeating it. Translated speeches by Castro, photographs of him, booklets, and other published materials extolling the revolution were found among Oswald's possessions after his arrest.[12]

At the consulate in Mexico City, he struggled to persuade the Cubans of these revolutionary bona fides and brandished a photo of himself from a New Orleans news story published a few weeks earlier. He had been arrested after a street altercation with Cuban exiles as was he passing out pro-Castro leaflets. Marina remembered that he was proud of the disturbance he had created and the night spent in jail as a result. She told the Warren Commission that he "was smiling" when he came home the next morning. "It was advertising," she said. "He wanted to be arrested." She believed he had staged the event just so he would have proof of his militance to show the Cubans. When he realized that embassy representatives were not impressed, however, Oswald denounced them. They were just "bureaucrats." He, in contrast, "had been in jail for the Cuban Revolution."

The fixation was especially strong during the summer months the Oswalds spent in New Orleans, just before his Mexico trip. "Fidel Castro was his hero," Marina told the House committee. "[H]e was a great admirer . . . he was in some kind of revolutionary mood . . . he would be happy to work for Fidel Castro's causes." Oswald's "devotion and ardor for Cuba knew no boundaries," according to Kennedy assassination expert Vincent Bugliosi.[13]

In Mexico, Oswald told the Cubans that he had defected and lived in the Soviet Union for two and a half years. He had appeared on New Orleans radio and television programs professing Marxist beliefs and proclaiming that "Cuba is the most revolutionary country in the world today." He had demonstrated in the streets of Dallas when he lived there, wearing a handmade placard that read "Hands Off Cuba! Viva Fidel!" He may have told the Cubans that he had learned about the U-2 spy plane he observed during military duty at an American air base in Japan.

All of that would have made him of interest to the DGI. In the universal language of intelligence, Oswald was, therefore, a classic walk-in, a *voluntario*, a defector when he showed up at the consulate. He wanted to be useful to the bearded man he idolized. He was eager to take up arms for Fidel. Marina was asked if Oswald often spoke about the Cuban revolution. "Yes, when Lee obtained a rifle, I guess that is somehow in my mind associated with some kind of revolution."[14]

Oswald purchased the Mannlicher-Carcano rifle he used to kill Kennedy on March 12, 1963. He first fired it with homicidal intent on April 10, against retired army Major General Edwin Walker, an extreme right-wing, anti-Castro agitator who had demanded just days earlier that Kennedy "liquidate the scourge that had descended on Cuba."[15] The shot fired at the general, sitting in his Dallas home office after dark, missed his head by a fraction of an inch. So, Marina, who knew her husband better than anyone, was correct: Oswald's purpose for buying the rifle was to adopt the persona of a worthy guerrilla fighter. By killing Walker, he would be aiding Fidel's cause by eliminating a vitriolic enemy of the revolution. He would become one of Fidel's warriors.

From the Soviet Union, Oswald had written his brother Robert that "in the event of war I would kill any American who put a uniform on in defense of the American government—any American." Michael Paine, a young man who knew the assassin in Dallas, told the House committee that it was "Oswald's belief that the only way injustices in this society could be corrected was through a violent revolution." Paine later also said that "Lee wanted to be an active guerrilla in the effort to bring about a new world order.... There's no doubt in my mind that he believed violence was the only effective tool."[16]

Marina snapped photos of her husband in the backyard of a house they rented in Dallas before moving to New Orleans. He is posed as a militant, dressed in black, armed with the Mannlicher-Carcano. A holstered pistol rests on his hip; it is the one he used to kill Dallas policeman J. D. Tippit less than an hour after he murdered Kennedy. He clutches recent issues of the American Communist Party's weekly *The Worker* and *The Militant*, a Trotskyite publication. He had subscribed to both more than a year before; they were his preferred means of keeping up with news from Cuba.

In the photo his face is calm and determined, with the hint of a satisfied smile. In her book on the Oswalds, Priscilla Johnson McMillan described his expression as one of "sublime contentment." He appeared to be a young American equivalent of the thousands of his Latin American contemporaries then enrolled in Cuban guerrilla training schools, eager to take up arms for Fidel. A few days after Kennedy's death, Marina told the Secret Service that Oswald had planned to send a copy of one of the photos to *The Militant* "to show he was ready for anything . . . even if it involved the possible use of arms."[17]

Getting to Cuba was his priority. Oswald told Duran at the consulate in Mexico he wanted to "spend some time" on the island. On the bus trip to the Mexican capital, he had chatted with another passenger and remarked that he planned "to see Castro." The Warren Commission concluded that he most likely "intended to remain in Cuba." Marina thought so too; she testified that, when he left for Mexico City, "He does prefer to go and live in Cuba . . . I honestly did not expect to see him again." To the disturbed twenty-three-year-old, revolutionary Cuba was the utopia he was dreaming of.[18]

LADDIE'S FAMILIARITY WITH THE MEXICO CENTER and what he had learned about Oswald's visits at first came up only in passing with Swenson. Those details did not seem as important to Hal as the operational information he was accumulating about Cuban subversion in Latin America. It would not be long, however, before others began connecting the Mexico City dots. Within about a week of his arrival, Laddie came to the attention of Angleton's Counterintelligence Staff. Ray Rocca, then chief of its Research and Analysis Division—he described it as "a counterintelligence laboratory"—was briefed in on the case.[19]

Rocca and Angleton were backing up Helms, the Agency's chief liaison with the Warren Commission. It was because of their regular dealings with the commission staff that they knew what Swenson at first did not: dissecting Oswald's Mexico sojourn was still a priority. A commission counsel later stated those concerns succinctly. They were focused on whether Oswald was "prompted by, or a part of a conspiracy originating in Cuba, or with supporters of Cuba." There was "some considerable disquiet," he said, about that supremely troubling possibility. With Swenson's early debriefing reports in hand, Angleton's staff began to wonder if the newly arrived defector had fresh information that might implicate Castro.[20]

The hard-line Rocca would have loved nothing more. He was a stocky, gruff professional who joined the Agency at its inception in September 1947. Unlike his boss Angleton, "Rock," as he liked to be called, was not inclined to froth up fantasy conspiracies or lapse into spasms of paranoia imagining KGB moles burrowed in at Langley. But he was loyal to Angleton, quitting the CIA career he loved in solidarity when his chief was compelled to resign in 1974.

On Friday, May 1, Rocca drafted a dozen questions for Swenson to use in a targeted debriefing of the defector. Most important, he wanted answers to these three:

> Was Lee Harvey Oswald known to the Cuban intelligence services before 23 November 1963?

> Were the Cuban services using Oswald in any agent capacity, or in any other manner before 23 November 1963?

> Was any provocative material deliberately fabricated by the Cuban services or others and sent to the United States to confuse the investigation of the Oswald case?[21]

Responses, crafted by Swenson, were in hand within days. Laddie did not know if Oswald had been used by the DGI. With respect to the third question, Hal reported that "the only possible fabrication known by source was the specific denial (by Castro) . . . of any knowledge of Oswald." There was no elaboration, and none was requested.[22]

But tensions within an elite circle in Langley soared over the response to Rocca's first question. Swenson reported that Laddie knew Oswald had visited the consulate and that "before, during, and after the visits he was in contact" with the DGI. This ground-shaking allegation was never adequately clarified. Laddie believed there had been sustained Cuban engagement with Oswald.[23]

If the Warren Commission was informed of that information, it would have been propelled into terrifying new territory. The possibility of a Cuban conspiracy with Oswald would have received much greater attention. Even inconclusive but suggestive evidence—or, as CIA analysts expressed it in a sensitive report, the "imputation" of a Cuban hand in the assassination—would have exploded in Washington like Fourth of July fireworks on the Mall.[24]

It could not possibly stay secret for long. Congress and the American public would know soon enough, and war drums would begin sounding. Punitive military action against Castro might be inevitable. CIA had been reporting regularly about the trip-wire Soviet military force of several thousand that remained on the island. There was no doubt in Washington policy circles that armed conflict with Castro could easily explode into another superpower confrontation.[25]

No one had been more worried in late November 1963 than Cuba's leaders. Laddie told Swenson how his old service went into a virtual lockdown the afternoon of November 22, after news of Oswald's arrest was broadcast. Centers were ordered to package their classified information, separating out top-secret files, and to await further guidance. Travel by headquarters officers and diplomatic pouch deliveries were suspended. Personnel were instructed to stay in or close to their offices "so they could be reached immediately." Piñeiro's deputy held a meeting with National Liberation officers instructing them to prepare a system of coded communications with their agents overseas. A reliable spy in the Cuban government told the Agency that diplomatic missions abroad were ordered to be certain there "were no compromising documents on the premises." Havana was worried that DGI Centers might be targeted by CIA for surreptitious entry.[26]

As was his custom when a crisis was gathering, Fidel took to the airwaves. He delivered three speeches in the days immediately following Kennedy's assassination. (Transcripts of only two have survived outside of Cuba.) The first lasted two hours, delivered from a Havana television studio on Saturday night, November 23, a little more than a day after Kennedy was killed. By then Oswald had been charged with the murders of the president and Officer Tippit.

Fidel was cautious, often eloquent—and profoundly worried. The Monday-morning *CIA Daily Summary*—a sensitive publication devoted solely to Cuba—reported that the speech reflected Castro's "apprehension that US policy toward him may now become even tougher." The *Central Intelligence Bulletin*, a Top Secret global intelligence daily for senior policy readers provided more comprehensive coverage. Fidel had described the assassination as a "dangerous Machiavellian plot against Cuba. . . . We must be cautious and vigilant and alert." He said Kennedy's death could only benefit "ultra rightist and ultra reactionary sectors . . . now breaking loose in the United States."[27]

Che Guevara expressed alarm in a speech on November 24. He warned that "the peace of the world will be threatened for years to come." The most "unscrupulous, ferocious, and warlike" forces were being unleashed. Characteristically lapsing into his signature theme, he stressed that "revolutionary ferment in Latin America is reaching a new climax . . . the people are going to conquer power in whatever manner necessary." *Hoy,* the Cuban Communist Party newspaper at that

time, declared that a "dirty maneuver" was afoot, "aimed at making Cuba the perpetrator of the crime." That summarized the fears of the leadership.[28]

The *CIA Bulletin* reported that "immediately after the news of President
Kennedy's death," Castro ordered an island-wide "defensive military alert." The
analysts knew this from intercepted Cuban military and foreign diplomatic communications. By nightfall on November 22, Cuban army and navy units had been
deployed to strategic positions around Havana and the north coast. According to
one of the intercepts, Fidel was "frightened" that the United States might invade.[29]

When Castro's first speech was broadcast, Oswald was still being interrogated
in Dallas. What might he say that would make matters even worse for Cuba? What
would the Mexican receptionist tell her government when she was interrogated?
What else could emerge? The wiser choice for Fidel might have been to wait a
while longer before speaking, but rambling orations were his lifelong addiction.
And practical reasons compelled him to appear as well.

Until he spoke, Cuban officials and the state media had no idea what to say
about the assassination. Kennedy had been the revolution's most despised and
feared enemy, regularly denounced and reviled. How should the dead president
and his assassin be treated? A CIA analysis of the speech pointed up the dilemma:
"how to react to a crime whose victim had consistently been a prime target of
Havana's vituperation." Until Fidel's appearance, the state-controlled media had
refrained from commenting at all.[30]

The first reaction of some Cubans was to celebrate the president's death. A
JMWAVE source on the island reported spontaneous outbursts at workplaces and
neighborhood defense committees. In Mexico City, DGI agent Luisa Calderon
was heard rejoicing in a telephone conversation secretly recorded by the CIA's
station. When told the news by an unidentified female caller an hour after the assassination, she exclaimed "How great!" Then, mistakenly informed that "Kennedy's brother and his wife were also injured," Calderon laughed and again blurted
"How great!" Kennedy, she said, was "a degenerate, unfortunate, an aggressor."
The caller told her the president had been shot three times in the face. Calderon
thought that was "perfect."[31]

Fidel was not aware of that conversation at the time, but he knew that he
had to go public to establish clear policy and propaganda guidelines. The regime issued orders prohibiting "manifestations of pleasure." On November 23,
Fidel laid out entirely new parameters for a populace that had been taught to

hate Kennedy. He spoke of the deceased president with uncharacteristic defer-
ence, referring to him repeatedly as "President Kennedy." "We always cease our
belligerency at death," he declared, "we always bow with respect at death, even
if it is an enemy." That was not true: Fidel displayed no such forbearance after
the deaths of other enemies, sometimes, as already mentioned, even those that
occurred decades earlier.

In the ensuing nearly fifty years until this writing, Fidel never again spoke or
wrote a disparaging word about Kennedy. Instead, he often praised the president,
sometimes lavishly, sounding like the ebullient sword bearers of Camelot or another court biographer. He became obsessed with Kennedy's memory, inviting a
succession of family members to the island and graciously meeting with them. He
hosted a particularly poignant dinner with John F. Kennedy Jr. in October 1997 in
Havana. "We got together as friends," Castro wrote.[32]

After the assassination, Fidel never openly connected either Kennedy brother
with assassination plots against him. In fact, however, Cuban intelligence had
tracked the three most serious ones from their initial stages. Castro knew he had
been in the Kennedy administration's crosshairs since before the Bay of Pigs and
that he was the target in the fall of 1963 of the murder and coup conspiracy built
around Rolando Cubela. Fidel was aware too that Attorney General Kennedy was
the driving force behind the plot.

But once Kennedy was dead, Castro always put the blame for the conspiracies
squarely on the CIA. His logic was impeccable—and transparent. Accusing the
Kennedy brothers of involvement in conspiracies against him would antagonize
Americans who idolized the fallen young president. And more critically, Fidel
knew that doing so would arouse suspicions that he had been motivated to retaliate in kind.

There was a more urgent priority too when Castro spoke on November 23.
He needed to disassociate himself completely from Oswald. If the grieving American public concluded that the assassin had somehow conspired with Cuba, Fidel
knew the survival of his revolution would be at risk. So he was unequivocal about
not having known anything about Kennedy's assassin.[33]

The commander in chief spoke again about the assassination, at the University of Havana, on November 27. The CIA's *Cuba Daily Summary* reported
two days later that the speech "obviously was a carefully prepared refutation
of charges of complicity between Castro's regime and Oswald." The analysts

added that it "neither proves nor disproves that he had advance knowledge of the plot."[34]

Adopting the position he and Cuban propagandists would push from that moment on, Castro declared categorically that Oswald was not the real culprit. Kennedy's assassin was dead by then, murdered in Dallas police headquarters by small-time mobster Jack Ruby. According to Castro: "This demonstrates that the persons guilty of the death of Kennedy needed and urgently had to eliminate the accused at any cost."[35]

Fidel repeated that he knew nothing of Oswald before the assassination. Referring specifically to the Mexico City consulate visits—visits that by then had been covered extensively by the media—he issued the second of his denials. Meaning himself and the government, he again employed the first-person plural pronoun "we," as was his custom: "We did not know about it."

And then he went farther out on that limb. "We have no other background for the accused . . . other than what has been published in the press."

These and the earlier denial now constituted the official Cuban position. Government leaders and spokesmen would never waver from it. Laddie, however, knew better. He was in Havana when Castro delivered the two speeches and probably heard them live. His desire to expose Fidel's lies to American intelligence may have been among his motives for defecting in the first place.[36]

He told Swenson that when news of the assassination reached the DGI, "it caused much comment concerning the fact that Oswald had been in the Cuban embassy." He also heard Mexico Center chief Manuel Vega speak about Oswald's visit. Vega had been reassigned from Mexico in October 1963, later returning for a second tour in mid-April the next year. After lunch one day soon after the assassination, Vega talked about it with Laddie and about ten of their colleagues at DGI headquarters.[37]

Laddie believed that Vega had seen Kennedy's assassin at the consulate. And he thought that Rodríguez López, the deputy Center chief, had as well. "I feel sure," Laddie told Swenson, that Vega would have requested permission from headquarters to issue a visa. It was standard procedure for DGI officers to screen visa applicants. When Laddie met with representatives of the House committee in 1978, he revealed additional details that had not come up in the debriefings with Swenson: The DGI routinely secretly photographed and recorded visa applicants in Mexico.[38]

Testifying before the House committee in 1978, Ray Rocca had the same impression. He thought Oswald's arguments with the Cubans took place "in the very offices of the DGI, and that the DGI chief must have been in hearing range."[39]

Alas, fourteen years later, unintentional confirmation came from an unlikely source. DGI officer Alfredo Mirabal, the incoming Center chief, admitted to the House committee that he had prepared a report on Oswald for his headquarters. Mirabal said Azcue, the consul who had confronted Oswald, gave him "information" about the visitor. No doubt Mirabal was given the documents, membership cards, and newspaper clippings Oswald had brought with him. Mirabal said that it was "for my report." Apparently, he did not realize he was contradicting what his commander in chief had solemnly claimed years earlier.[40]

Clearly, then, DGI headquarters was informed about the strange young American who presented himself as an adoring friend of the revolution. Moreover, Mirabal's report—probably drafted with Vega's assistance—went directly to Piñeiro's desk via a secure radio link. Laddie knew there was no headquarters desk officer responsible for Mexico, as he had been for El Salvador, so there were no intermediaries between the Center and Redbeard himself. Operations run out of Mexico, affecting as many as a dozen Latin American countries, were that important to Piñeiro and Fidel.[41]

Laddie told Swenson what many other defectors have also reported: Castro buried himself in the minutiae of intelligence operations. He and Interior Minister Ramiro Valdés personally selected most DGI officers dispatched to Latin America. Seemingly routine matters, Laddie said, would "normally . . . be taken up with Castro." Oswald's pleadings and outbursts at the consulate rose well above the ordinary. Mirabal's report would surely have reached Fidel.[42]

LADDIE, IT TURNED OUT, was not the only unimpeachable American intelligence source who reported on Fidel's knowledge of Oswald's visit to the consulate. In late May 1964, a few weeks after Swenson debriefed Rodríguez Lahera, a deep-cover American spy working for the FBI met with Castro in Havana. Fidel told him that he had indeed been informed about Oswald's visit.

"Our people in Mexico gave us the details in a full report of how he acted when he came to our embassy." Oswald had not just berated the Cubans when they refused him a visa. He had not just stormed out slamming the consulate door behind him.

According to Fidel, he threatened Kennedy's life.[43]

Castro never imagined he was confiding that spring day in one of the most remarkable American spies of the cold war. Jack Childs was, in fact, the junior partner with his brother Morris in espionage operations run for twenty-three years against the uppermost leadership of the Soviet Union and its communist allies. Beginning in the early 1950s, Morris, the more intellectual and sophisticated of the brothers, ingratiated himself with Khrushchev, his successors Leonid Brezhnev and Yuri Andropov, and other members of the Soviet Politburo. As protégés of those communist titans, the Childses developed trusting relationships with Fidel, Ho Chi Minh, and eastern European communist chiefs. With their wives as accomplices, the brothers' family spy network was known as Operation SOLO.

Born in czarist Russia, Morris and Jack emigrated in 1911 as children with their family to Chicago where, in their twenties, they joined the American Communist Party. Morris rose quickly and was selected to study subversion and covert tradecraft at the Lenin School in Moscow. It was there he was recruited by Soviet intelligence. Then he served for years essentially as the "secretary of state" of the American party, respected and welcomed by leaders of ruling Communist parties. Morris traveled fifty-two times to Cuba, the Soviet Union, and its satellite nations, returning with valuable information he shared with his FBI handlers. He ran as the Communist Party's candidate for the United States Senate from Illinois in 1938.

But it was the younger brother, Jack, who first became an American agent. He was cold-pitched by FBI officers on a New York City street in 1951. He smiled sardonically when approached, according to John Barron's definitive study. "Where in the hell have you guys been all these years?" He was easily recruited. "I never really believed in any of that communist bullshit," he told them. For his efforts, the Soviet leadership awarded Jack the Order of the Red Banner in 1975, one of its highest distinctions for dangerous duty. Not to be outdone, the United States posthumously honored him with the National Security medal in 1988.[44]

Jack was flamboyant, a risk taker, and it was probably because of their similar personalities that he and Fidel got along so well. He told his Bureau handlers: "I am basically a con man. If I had a choice between entering a house by walking through the front door or crawling through a back window, I'd go through the window because that's more exciting." Soviet leaders used Jack as a trusted intermediary with Castro. They contrived a dinner meeting in Moscow to introduce the men in May 1963 during Fidel's first journey to the Soviet Union. It went so well that Jack was invited to meet with him again.

A year later, during another trip to Moscow, Jack planned his first journey to Cuba. Before leaving, he was briefed extensively by a Soviet party official. Don't trust Raúl Roa, he was told. "When he became foreign minister we were almost sure he would go straight to the State Department." The KGB was well informed: The CIA had indeed attempted to recruit Roa in October 1962, at the time of the missile crisis, but he rejected the overtures. Jack was advised to deal instead with two other Cuban officials, reliable pro-Soviet communists in Fidel's inner circle. He was also given sage advice about dealing with Castro. By then, Kremlin leaders had learned the hard way.[45]

"Comrade Fidel is a very sensitive comrade. Our experience with him has been to talk to him most carefully . . . we have learned there are times not to speak to him, because he is a man of many moods. If his mood is good, he will listen, he will agree with you. But should it be bad, he would pout and shout." Memories of Castro's Armageddon letter were still vivid in the Kremlin. Jack later wrote that "they were depending on me to go there to talk sense to Castro.[46]

He left Moscow on May 18, 1964, on a direct Aeroflot flight to Havana. "When I first arrived, my request was to see Fidel first," Jack recorded in a long letter to Gus Hall, the head of the American Communist Party. But as with even the most distinguished guests, he would be kept waiting. It was standard practice for Fidel; he manipulated visitors this way, keeping them on tenterhooks, not knowing if he would deign to meet with them at all. Often in the end, he arrived unannounced at midnight or later. "I didn't dare leave the house for fear that I would miss Fidel," Jack recorded.

Finally, "On the tenth night, several hours before my leaving, he came to see me. I was received very well, greeted very warmly." Rene Vallejo, an American-trained doctor who was Fidel's personal physician, interpreter, and aide, accompanied him. Jack wrote Hall: "My regards and greetings to Castro were very dramatic and effective. He liked them." He gave Fidel an expensive fishing rod and equipment, gifts from Hall. They were getting along famously.[47]

Castro wanted to know how to establish better communications between Havana and the American party. He asked Jack what he and his communist associates knew about the Cuban exile community. "I told him we know very little . . .

they are running around the streets gossiping and spreading false rumors." Castro agreed, using his favorite term of derision: "they are nothing but a bunch of worms."[48]

Then, seemingly out of the blue, Fidel asked Jack: "Do you think Oswald killed President Kennedy?"

Jack wrote: "Before I could answer, he said, 'he could not have done it alone. I am sure of that. It was at least two or three men who did it, most likely three.'"

Castro explained that "soon after the president was assassinated," he and a number of Cuban sharpshooters reenacted the scene. They used rifles similar to the Mannlicher-Carcano with telescopic sights and, according to Jack's account, "shot at the target under the same conditions, same distance, same height." Quoting Castro, Jack wrote that "after having aimed and set the sights and squeezed the trigger and the shot was fired, then the marksman must reset the telescopic sight again, reload the rifle again, by that time having lost many valuable seconds." Fidel concluded that "it was impossible" for one man to have fired three times in such short succession.[49]

He had made similar points in his November 27 speech, boasting of his own expertise as a marksman who used telescopic sights. He organized the firing range exercise with obvious urgency within five days of Kennedy's assassination and convinced himself that Oswald could not have rapidly fired three shots, two accurately, from the window of the Texas Book Depository. It was a self-fulfilling wish; he needed to rid himself of the Oswald albatross by whatever means. But the sharpshooter exercise bore no resemblance to what really happened the day of the shooting in Dallas.

FBI Director J. Edgar Hoover informed the Warren Commission that his firearms experts also conducted tests and "determined that three shots could be fired with the same kind of rifle and sight used by Oswald in the five to six seconds which were available." That became the commission's conclusion too and led to the controversial "single-bullet" judgment about the assassination. Later, author Gerald Posner interviewed an FBI firearms expert who confirmed that it "required no training at all to shoot a weapon with a telescopic sight." Adjustments after each shot are not necessary. Fidel was wrong, or lying, but to this day he has not abandoned his position.[50]

He was not finished with his monologue with Jack. Castro went on to tell the American what Oswald shouted as he bolted from the Cuban consulate.

Presumably that had been included in the report cabled to Piñeiro by Mirabal and Vega. Fidel said that Oswald "[s]tormed into the embassy, demanded the visa and when it was refused to him headed out saying, 'I'm going to kill Kennedy for this.'"[51]

Jack's letter to Hall contains only that much information. John Barron's book about Operation SOLO goes no further either. I have reviewed the Morris Childs and John Barron collections at the Hoover Archives at Stanford University but found no more details.

But recently I discovered a newly declassified FBI document at the National Archives. A Top Secret report from the FBI office in New York to Hoover on June 12, 1964, it included additional information provided by Jack. He said that Castro had been "in a very good mood" and was not under "the influence of liquor" when they met. Fidel had spoken "in broken English" and Hoover was told "there is no question as to the accuracy of what he said (because) the informant indicated that he had made notes at the time Castro was talking and he had scribbled down what he considered was important."[52] Seemingly unaware that Fidel had denied knowing anything about Oswald before the assassination, Jack reported that "Castro received the information about Oswald's appearances at the Cuban embassy in Mexico in an oral report from 'his people' in the embassy, because he, Castro, was told about it immediately." The FBI's field report added that "Castro was neither engaging in dramatics nor oratory," and reiterated that he "was speaking on the basis of facts given to him by his embassy personnel who dealt with Oswald, and apparently made a full, detailed report."[53]

That Jack repeated the story accurately cannot reasonably be disputed. I. C. Smith, a retired senior FBI official involved in Operation SOLO, told me that Jack "was an extreme risk taker, but it did not detract from his reporting," and that "no one in the FBI ever accused him of embellishing." Although there has never been any doubt about the veracity of the Childs brothers' reporting, Jack's recollections of the meeting with Fidel have received scant attention in the nearly 50 years since. Yet they provide conclusive evidence that Fidel has been lying about Oswald since November 23, 1963.

On June 17, 1964, Hoover summarized Jack's meeting with Castro in a Top Secret letter to the Warren Commission's chief counsel. But he conveyed only the minimal essence of Jack's story. The FBI director—who from the start of his investigation was wedded to the conclusion that Kennedy's death did *not* result from a conspiracy—trivialized what Jack reported.

According to the letter, Fidel had merely repeated what he had said in public on November 27. But, in truth, that speech and what Jack heard were substantially different. Castro had said nothing publicly about Oswald's threat or the firing range exercise. Hoover described Jack as "a confidential source who has provided reliable information," not an American superspy who had been reporting valuable strategic insights for years. Jack's report was made to sound like hearsay in Hoover's telling, and he included none of the substantiating information the New York field office had provided him days earlier.

No wonder the commission paid no attention to his letter. Later two senior staffers said that they could not recall ever seeing it, and former CIA director McCone told a journalist in November 1976 that he had never seen it either. In essence, Hoover marginalized the best evidence that Castro was lying and hiding information of critical importance to the investigation. Had the FBI been more forthcoming, Fidel's lies might have become apparent to assassination investigators and raised doubts about what else he was concealing.[54]

Author Jean Davison, whose 1983 book on Oswald was a major contribution to the Kennedy assassination literature, cited a corroborating source, a British journalist named Comer Clark. He claimed to have heard an account nearly identical to Jack's from Castro in July 1967.

In this version, Fidel is quoted saying that when Oswald was at the consulate, he declared that "he wanted to work for us" and to "free Cuba from American imperialism." And then, Fidel said, Oswald threatened to kill Kennedy. Some historians have discounted this reporter because he published his account in a sensationalist paper and wrote purple-tinged exposés for others. Davison concluded, nonetheless, that there are "several good reasons" for believing that the reports of the two sources were reliable. Not least was their near-perfect symmetry.[55]

Representatives of the House committee asked Fidel about the journalist's account in April 1978 in Havana. That story was considerably easier to refute than the Operation SOLO report would have been, but the Childs brothers were still providing valuable information from inside the communist bloc and remained under the deepest cover. Hoover's letter to the Warren Commission, not fully declassified until November 1993, could not be used. The congressional investigators had no choice but to rely solely on the shakier of the two reports.

Never at a loss for words, Fidel denied ever quoting Oswald or meeting with the British reporter. "I am absolutely certain that interview never took place. This is absurd. I didn't say that. It's a lie from head to toe." There was no way to refute Fidel; by that time, the journalist had died.[56]

The meeting with House committee members and staff was conducted in Fidel's offices in Havana, at his pleasure. The Americans were deferential. They did not follow up with tough questions or press him as they do in hearings in Washington with sitting-duck witnesses arrayed before them. Fidel sat with a claque of his DGI assassination experts who helped him with his responses. One of them appeared to be as well informed about Kennedy assassination trivia and lore as any American conspiracy buff. Since that meeting, no one has questioned Fidel again on the record about Oswald's parting words at the consulate.

Azcue and Mirabal, the two Cubans who admitted dealing with Oswald, were also strident in their denials. Mirabal said the allegation was "totally absurd . . . incredible." Referring to the United States, Azcue said, it is "ridiculous that we should attempt to walk into the mouth of the lion." The faithful Mexican receptionist hewed to the official Cuban line too, claiming not to remember any threatening comments from Oswald.

But they should not be considered more credible than Jack Childs. Mirabal—known to his colleagues as "Eulogio"—was an experienced DGI officer. Laddie had plotted Cuban subversive operations in El Salvador with him when visiting the Mexico Center. Azcue was described in a CIA agent report in 1960 as "blindly antagonistic to the United States," and his testimony was suspect for another reason. He insisted that the man he argued with at the consulate was not Oswald but a double, an imposter. And he expressed "absolute certainty" about it. Azcue was doing the regime's bidding by propounding another of the canards its propagandists have repeated endlessly.[57]

J. EDGAR HOOVER HAD DONE his best to bring down the curtain on the assassination investigation. By June 1964 in his view, the Warren Commission's production had to be brought to a close. Richard Helms, the "man who kept the secrets," as his biographer Thomas Powers aptly described him, made sure the house lights were turned off.

It appears that within the CIA, Laddie's belief that Fidel had lied about Oswald was deemed of no consequence. His reporting was filtered and minimized for the Warren Commission staff. The brazen, Kennedy-hating Luisa Calderon was also passed over lightly. The Warren Commission was told she was a DGI officer, but it was given no other information about her. She might have attracted more investigative interest had the commission been provided transcripts of her phone conversations. Some students of the assassination consider one, with an unidentified male caller about four hours after Kennedy died, as a smoking gun pointing straight at a Cuban conspiracy. The caller asked Calderon if she knew what had happened in Dallas.

"Yes, of course," she replied. "I learned of it almost before Kennedy."[58]

That could suggest she had foreknowledge of the assassination. House investigators later pursued the possibility vigorously, but to no end. Calderon was not made available to meet with the committee in Havana but denied any prior knowledge of Oswald in the written statement the Cuban government provided. Her strange remark, of course, can be interpreted in a variety of ways. Nonetheless, in its concluding report, the committee criticized CIA for withholding the transcripts from the Warren Commission.[59]

There was another exchange between Calderon during the same conversation that, surprisingly, has not drawn attention before. Speaking of Oswald, the unidentified person told Calderon:

"Oh yes, he knows Russian well, and also this fellow went with Fidel's forces into the mountains, or wanted to go, something like that."[60]

Calderon did not appear to be surprised, and the caller quickly changed the subject. The reference appeared, however, to recall Oswald's Marine Corps service in southern California. It will be recalled that he allegedly met with Cuban diplomats—or, more likely, intelligence officers—in Los Angeles in 1959, when he first hoped to volunteer as a guerrilla fighter for Fidel. Calderon's caller was probably also DGI and, by the time of the conversation, probably had reviewed Oswald's records in Havana. But, this Calderon exchange also was not presented to the Warren Commission.

These and other omissions turned out to be the least of what Helms and CIA concealed. The commission was never told about the Kennedy-era assassination plots against Castro or the brutal secret war against Cuba waged out of JMWAVE. Worst of all, also kept under tight wraps was the ultra-secret plot with Rolando Cubela that coincided with Kennedy's death.

How different the assassination investigation might have been if Helms had told the Warren Commission what he and Des and Bobby Kennedy knew better than anyone: that Castro had a compelling motive to conspire against John F. Kennedy's life.

Lee Harvey Oswald had wanted since his Marine Corps days in the late 1950s to bear arms for Fidel and the Cuban revolution. Castro "was his hero . . . he would be happy to work for [his] causes," recalled his wife Marina. Oswald posed as a militant in this photo Marina took in the backyard of their rented apartment in Dallas in 1963. He killed Dallas police officer J. D. Tippit with the pistol on his hip. The rifle is the one he used to assassinate President Kennedy.

The "Tourist" shortwave radio Oswald acquired in the Soviet Union was found in his rented room in Dallas after his arrest. He is believed to have regularly listened to incendiary Radio Havana broadcasts in English. Among others, he may well have heard coverage of Fidel's tirade on October 30, 1963, condemning the CIA for plotting "subversion, espionage, and coups."

Photo courtesy of the National Archives

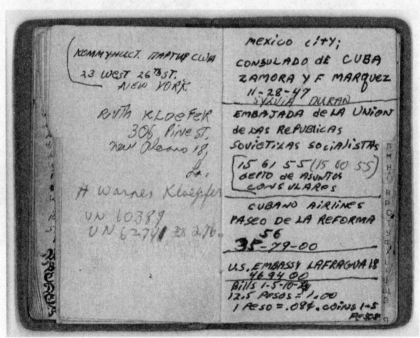

Oswald's pocket-sized address book was also found among his belongings. These pages show that he kept the phone number of Silvia Duran, the receptionist at the Cuban consulate in Mexico City. If he called her number in the days just before the assassination, he may actually have spoken to Cuban intelligence officer Luisa Calderon, who has never been questioned about Oswald.

Photo courtesy of the National Archives

New Yorker Samuel Halpern joined CIA at its inception in 1947 after serving in Ceylon during his wartime OSS service. An indispensable aide to Bill Harvey, Richard Helms, and Des FitzGerald, he never hedged when testifying about the Cuba wars of the early 1960s. Asked under oath, "When you said get rid of [Castro], you meant kill him?" he answered, "Yes, sir."

Photo courtesy of the Halpern Family

Harold "Hal" Swenson joined Bill Harvey's Task Force W in October 1962, about a year after this photo was taken. Later, as chief of Des FitzGerald's counterintelligence staff he clashed with his boss. In 1976 he testified that he considered the Cubela plot "dangerous and stupid . . . a lot of nonsense." There was good reason, he realized, "to doubt AMLASH's reliability."

Photo courtesy of Sally Swenson Cascio

Richard McGarrah Helms avoided the taint of the Bay of Pigs calamity of April 1961, but he was reluctantly inducted to manage the second and third phases of the covert campaigns against Cuba. He testified that "almost the entire energy" of the CIA clandestine service he headed from 1962 to 1965 was devoted to ousting Castro. "The Kennedy brothers" he said, "wanted to unseat Castro by whatever means."

The Groza "Thunderstorm" miniature assassination pistol is double-barreled and silent when fired, small enough to be held in the palm of one hand. In September 1988 Fidel ordered his intelligence operatives to acquire one from the KGB to be used in the planned assassination of Florentino Aspillaga. Castro then personally managed that unsuccessful operation, directing most of its details.

Photo courtesy Maxim Popnicer photo collection

EIGHT

WHIPLASH

TO CIA, ROLANDO CUBELA SEEMED THE PERFECT PROSPECT TO assassinate Fidel Castro. Young and fit, a battle-tested conspirator, he had killed in cold blood before. Unlike most Cuban officials who toiled under the suspicious gaze of the security services, he was allowed to travel abroad freely where illicit meetings with his Agency handlers were easy to arrange. He used a beach house adjacent to one reserved for Fidel at Varadero, a resort a couple of hours east of Havana. There it could be a simple hit, on the sand or in the surf where the Cuban leader and his security would least expect it.

A medical doctor and wounded revolutionary hero, Cubela circulated in the top ranks of the civilian and military hierarchies. When I met him in Miami in the summer of 2009 to talk about his exploits, he proudly showed me the long curving scar that ran from his right shoulder down the length of his bicep. It was acquired in combat during one of the watershed battles in the last months of the guerrilla war. He told me that he had lost faith in Fidel during those days. Declassified CIA files show that as early as March 1959—three months after the victory—Cubela was already confiding in friends a desire to kill Castro.[1]

Cubela was one of the top two leaders of the Revolutionary Student Directorate, originally a rival of the Castros' 26th of July Movement. The two forces were integrated after Batista fell, and a few leaders of the Directorate won important posts in the new regime, though tensions between the groups would always fester. Cubela served as the revolution's first university federation president but was never given a position of greater responsibility or trust, neither commanding troops nor managing a government agency.

He knew the Castros well, especially Raúl. The brothers respected his heroic record but were wary of his charm, dashing good looks, and cavalier nature. When flashing a capricious smile and swaggering, he was for all appearances an unpredictable rogue and seducer. Cubela was "a strange man," according to his first CIA case officer, temperamental and often exasperating. Nestor Sanchez, his last handler and the one who knew him best, remembered he was "moody, sensitive, mercurial."

An Agency biographic and psychological profile oddly described his "almost petulant mouth." A handwriting analysis characterized him as "shrewd, clever, a role player, self-centered, and vain." It also held that "he can exercise various deceptive mechanisms in the most adroit fashion" and "has not yet found his proper course." Some Agency case officers in the 1960s and 1970s believed graphology could help in agent assessment. This report turned out to be close to the mark.[2]

Carlos Tepedino, a Cuban émigré jeweler and Cubela's co-conspirator with CIA, told me in Miami that his lifelong friend never trusted Fidel but that the Cuban leader "had great sympathy for him." Maybe, Tepedino offered, it was because "Rolando always spoke directly; and Fidel liked that." That may have been so, but modern Cuban history is littered with disgraced officials more clever than Cubela who talked too candidly to their commander in chief. Seven years younger than Castro, Cubela was his favorite in the Student Directorate, but that could have been because he was the most malleable, the most vulnerable to Fidel's charms and suasion. To be sure, they shared many unfathomable affinities, not least, similar violent pathologies.

In October 1956, Cubela carried out one of the most notorious assassinations in Cuban history in the predawn hours on a quiet Sunday. A group of police and army officers, some accompanied by their wives, had been drinking and gambling at the Montmartre, an elegant Havana nightclub. As they left the club, they were drenched in a merciless barrage of gunfire. A colonel, Batista's military intelligence chief, died instantly. A second colonel, his wife, and another woman were severely wounded. "The bleeding and bewildered women reeled into mirrors in the foyer, which in their fright, they took for open space," according to a prominent historian. Amid the mayhem, Cubela and his main accomplice fled through the casino to safety.[3]

In 1963, he was easily the best candidate the Agency ever had to complete another murder mission, one that had failed many times. The inspector general's report commissioned by Helms in 1967, and now fully declassified, cataloged the sordid history of CIA assassination plotting against Castro. The first of the attempts, mounted during the last months of the Eisenhower administration, never got much beyond a secret laboratory. A CIA medical doctor, Edward "Manny" Gunn, taking leave of his Hippocratic Oath, concocted the murder weapon—half a dozen lethal pills.

The poison had to meet stringent requirements: safe to handle, stable, soluble, undetectable, and acting immediately. Shellfish toxin—used in the "L," or suicide pills, sometimes given to highly placed spies—was considered. So was liquefied bacteria. But after being successfully tested on guinea pigs and monkeys, botulism was the choice.[4]

When interviewed years later, Gunn remembered another plot that centered on fifty expensive cigars laced with the same deadly toxin. They were carefully resealed in cellophane wrappers and nestled in the ornate box of a world-famous brand, the one believed to be Fidel's favorite. But no way could be found to get them directly into his hands without risking the poisoning of any number of innocents. Seven years later Gunn came across one of the cigars in his office safe, a strange souvenir. It was still potent enough to kill a person who might clasp it between moist lips.[5]

Two other murder schemes—developed with Mafia co-conspirators—were initiated during the early Kennedy years. One was planned to coincide with the Bay of Pigs invasion in order to decapitate the regime and sow chaos as the exile brigade stormed the beaches. The second, about a year later, brought together a cast of colorful characters straight out of a Prohibition-era gangster film, none of them more fascinating than legendary CIA operative Bill Harvey. The attempt he masterminded was plotted around a hotel restaurant Fidel was known to frequent and where he favored its specialty, thick *batidos*, Cuban-style milkshakes.

Twenty-two years later Ramiro Valdés, whose first tour as interior minister extended from 1961 until 1968, revealed more about the plot. The pills, he told an American journalist, were stored in a freezer, to be retrieved by a restaurant worker. Supposedly a trusted Mafia asset, he was to slip them into Castro's drink when he visited. But they disintegrated or burst when the Mafia's man retrieved them. He lost his nerve and the conspiracy evaporated. Still, Valdés said the plot was the closest Fidel ever came to death at the hands of a CIA assassination team.[6]

Valdés did not reveal more about the caper, but it is clear from his unguarded recollections that Cuban security had been tracking it, probably with the help of a double agent. They knew more about the conspiracy than CIA itself did. Valdés commented that Fidel, the leader he worshipped, was preternaturally gifted at sniffing out such threats, that he had been born, as it were, with finely tuned counterintelligence sensors. "He has a nose for risks and dangers." Valdés seemed to be saying that Fidel himself had somehow become aware of the plot and defeated it.

Bill Harvey, similarly attuned, had sensed the invisible hand of Cuban intelligence in the foiling of his milkshake plot. When interviewed by Senate staffers at his retirement home in Indianapolis in 1975, he said, "Given the capabilities of Castro's security apparatus . . . I think—and I thought at the time—it was quite conceivable it had been penetrated." His judgment has to be taken seriously.[7]

There were other plots and bizarre schemes, some of which were not discovered until years later. Larry Houston, the Agency's legal counsel, remembered that a high-powered sniper rifle had been left behind in the American embassy in Havana after diplomatic relations were broken. It was intended, he thought, for an assassination attempt on Fidel. The Swiss government had taken over responsibility for the embassy building, causing Houston wryly to muse, "If they go through the attic, they are going to find it." Cuban exiles working out of JMWAVE tell of still other plots undertaken with what they believed was full Agency sponsorship. All failed because no assassin could get close enough to the well-protected target.[8]

The authors of the assassination report could not determine at what level the plots had been authorized. They felt compelled to emphasize, nonetheless, "the extent to which responsible Agency officers felt themselves subject to the Kennedy administration's severe pressures to do something about Castro and his regime." Harvey was not as circumspect in Senate testimony. He was sure the milkshake plot "had been fully approved, at least in principle, by the Kennedy White House," insisting he would not have pursued it otherwise. After all, he said under oath:

"One of the very top-most priorities of the administration was the overthrow, the destruction of the Castro regime."[9]

The flamboyant Harvey, a former FBI agent, was one of the best counterintelligence officers the Agency ever had. He looked and lived the part, although his interpretation of it bore no resemblance to the taciturn, cerebral Angleton's. Sporting a thin dash of a mustache, Harvey was always armed and voluble. Sam Halpern, who was his chief of staff, said he "was a wonderful guy to work for . . . if you didn't mind having a loaded gun pointed at you!"[10]

Harvey was so accustomed to carrying a concealed sidearm that he once entered the White House with one, although he later clarified that he had had the good sense to check it with the Secret Service before meeting with President Kennedy in the Oval Office. One of his contemporaries reminisced with me about Harvey, remembering his booming, reckless energy; how he was "always rampaging about." For Helms, who knew him well, Harvey was "deliberately blunt and loudly outspoken" . . . never pretending to be a "man for all seasons."[11]

He ran Cuba operations for about a year until the missile crisis and was sufficiently senior to choose his own alias. It was William Walker; and he called his large staff Task Force W, fancying himself after the mid-nineteenth century Tennessee dreamer and freebooter he admired. Walker had invaded and briefly ruled Nicaragua, sporting his own invented regalia as its self-appointed president, before being executed by a firing squad.

It was not Harvey's ambition to lead a free Cuba, far from it; but overthrowing Castro was the assignment he pursued with fevered determination until he crashed headlong into Bobby Kennedy. Harvey deplored the Kennedy brothers and could not conceal his contempt. The final confrontation with the attorney general was so explosive that Helms forced Harvey to take a foreign assignment, a good one, but nearly as far from Washington as was possible.[12]

WHEN DES FITZGERALD SUCCEEDED HARVEY in January 1963 and renamed the staff, plans for Castro's death were renewed and soon focused on Rolando Cubela. Unlike the Mafia hit men and querulous Miami exiles who had been enlisted in the earlier conspiracies, he volunteered for the job. At times he eagerly pressed his Agency handlers to get on with it. By the summer and fall of 1963, he seemed resolute: He would assassinate Castro with or without American support.[13]

His friend Tepedino had arranged Cubela's first meeting with a CIA case officer, in March 1961. Declassified Agency records show the jeweler was "a longtime contact"; he had known the undercover officer in Havana before going into exile. For several more years he continued as the often-indispensable link between Cubela and the Agency. In 2009, then eighty-four years old, Tepedino performed the same service for me, arranging a meeting with Cubela in his swank jewelry store in the Coral Gables area of Miami.

In 1961, the jeweler had a score to settle with Fidel's revolution: His fashionable shop in Havana—and presumably all of its valuable contents—had been seized by the regime. He hoped to coax his old friend Cubela to join him in opposition, either as a defector or a conspirator in place. The two Cubans met with the CIA case officer late one night in the Skyroom bar of the Hilton Continental hotel in Mexico City. The CIA man employed a classic recruitment approach, one that had already worked with hundreds of Cubans. He warned how rapidly Castro was imposing Marxist ideology and lashing Cuba to the Soviet Union. "He told me that in Cuba there was a great communist infiltration and that the Cuban people were headed toward the installation of a communist system," Cubela later recalled. But he was unreceptive, responding with hard-line, pro-revolutionary positions. It was an inauspicious start and there would be no further contact for another fifteen months.[14]

The Agency's biographical file on the *comandante*, much of it now declassified, shows there were unresolved doubts about Cubela from the start. It was impossible to chart a straight line through his contradictory past. There were reports of inconsistencies and indiscretions in his private life. He was headstrong, intractable, unpredictable. Helms, who was kept fully informed of the Cubela operation and approved of every important step it took forward, admitted in his memoirs that the Cuban "was something of an unknown quantity."

He seemed to be simultaneously for and against Fidel, a friend and a foe of the Americans, a merciless killer yet a compliant follower. There were plentiful indications he was in serious disagreement with Castro and Che Guevara. Yet after taking over the student federation, he traveled in Latin America encouraging radical groups. In May 1960 the U.S. Embassy reported he was being "skillfully maneuvered" by the regime, inciting a "vicious anti-American display" at the University of Havana while intimidating anticommunist students. He went about the campus armed, a faithful *barbudo*—a bearded revolutionary loyalist. He won strangely baroque praise from the regime for his "thousand times glorious" behavior. The Miami station wanted nothing to do with him, commenting on his "unsavory reputation."[15]

But obviously, spies and candidate agents are recruited for what and who they know, their access to secrets and leaders. So, encouraged again by Tepedino, contact was renewed. A new case officer, still known only by the alias "Weatherby," took over. Tepedino described him to me as young, very agreeable, a redhead, and revealed another name the man used. During the summer of 1962, Weatherby arranged a series of meetings with Cubela in Paris and three Scandinavian capitals. They huddled in hotel rooms and parked cars, often with Tepedino translating. In Helsinki, "we used countersurveillance," Weatherby told the Church committee. "There were no indications we were being followed."[16]

It was different two weeks later in Paris, where French security had Cubela under surveillance. It may have been because he had been talking too loosely, acting suspiciously, or his name had come up on a watch list. Weatherby was sure it was not a freak coincidence. The CIA's Paris station assuaged their French counterparts, explaining that the contacts with Cubela were to help him defect. No harm was done, but the incident indicated that DGI surveillants could just as easily have been tracking Cubela. Almost every Cuban accredited to their Paris embassy was an intelligence officer.[17]

In meetings with Weatherby Cubela expressed interest in defecting but, incongruously, also tried to impress him with the need for lethal action against Castro. He meant that he was the man for that job. Headquarters was informed that he was not interested in "risking his life for any small undertaking" but rather sought a "really large part to play. He prefers violent action." Cuba's plight could be solved "in one master stroke." Cubela said unequivocally that he wanted to overthrow the regime. He told the case officer he felt "a sense of urgency" to begin plotting Castro's demise.[18]

Weatherby cabled headquarters that Cubela was "extremely intense, emotional, very temperamental, not trustworthy yet." He had contemplated suicide a year earlier. A polygraph exam was recommended "before using the subject . . . Paris the best opportunity." But Cubela recoiled, refusing indignantly to be strapped into the device. That is a normal reaction to what in the Agency was poetically code-named the "flutter," but rarely does such a refusal go un-challenged. In this unusual case, however, Cubela prevailed. The matter appar-ently was never raised again. He was considered far too promising a prospect to antagonize.[19]

Weatherby knew the Cuban would "present difficult control problems in any operational situation." We often worried, he testified years later, "about his appar-ent lack of a sense of security in the classic agent sense." He was concerned the brooding Cubela might already have come to the attention of Cuban intelligence. He had been "allowed a lot of idiosyncrasies and indiscretions that normally would not be afforded a newcomer." Those were serious concerns, the sort that normally would cause an operation to be suspended or shut down. Without poly-graph results, the Agency could not determine whether Cubela was trustworthy. There was no way to be sure of who was really in charge of the three-sided covert relationship: Cubela, Weatherby, or the ubiquitous Tepedino.

Yet, despite the many legitimate concerns, and only a day after Cubela's first meeting with Weatherby, a provisional operational approval was issued on Au-gust 2, 1962. Cubela's recruitment as a designated CIA asset was official. He be-came AMLASH.[20]

Remaining for an extended stay in France that summer, he received special-ized agent training. It was in part an initiation rite, an induction into the clandes-tine fold. At an American military base a few hours south of Paris, he was given a brief course in plastic explosives. He set off one small charge and did it well. He had told Weatherby that he wanted to blow up a Cuban oil refinery; headquarters may also have thought that he could be trained to kill Fidel with a well-placed bomb. Indeed, he expressed interest in smaller explosives and remote controls for detonating them.[21]

In Paris, Cubela was instructed for about five hours in secret writing and given the materials to communicate covertly when back on the island. Station of-ficers noted he "was an interested pupil and it's believed he will carry out instruc-tions in a proper manner." They were mistaken. He later complained the system was too cumbersome and sent only a single message. Absurdly, he claimed there had been nothing important to report.[22]

Helms acknowledged that Cubela never amounted to much as an insider source of valuable information. His reports "were of interest" but "not very re-vealing." Cubela knew, for instance, from Fidel himself, fifteen days in advance, that in the spring of 1963 the Cuban leader would be traveling to the Soviet Union for the first time. Yet Cubela did not inform the Agency. It was exactly the kind of news the CIA wanted and had encouraged him to report. Fearing an assassination attempt, Castro had kept his plans secret from all but a few. Both legs of the long flights across the Atlantic were completed in strict secrecy. It was because "we live 90 miles from Yankee imperialism," Fidel said after his return. He was worried about assassination plots, and Cubela, apparently, was protecting him, although no one in the CIA thought so at the time.[23]

Other developments should also have raised warning flags at Langley. Cubela lived extravagantly at a time when the Cuban economy was spiraling downward, and it was not clear how he acquired his money. An on-island agent reported by secret writing in October 1962 that Cubela was spending a great deal. Working for minimum wage at a Havana hospital, he had no private medical practice. Some who knew him concluded he had a secret source of income. He traveled on four continents while in the Agency's unpaid embrace—lodging in upscale hotels, vacationing at European resorts, socializing like a bourgeois businessman at every stop. Tepedino told Weatherby that Cubela loved to go nightclubbing. While other Cubans with similar revolutionary experience were scuttling off secretly to fight with foreign revolutionaries, he was living the high life of an itinerant dilettante.[24]

It was an unusual case to be sure, and one that normally would not have been tolerated by CIA agent handlers. And it was not getting the attention it deserved. Weatherby said he doubted Bill Harvey had even read his contact reports about the Helsinki meetings, though surely the hard-charging Task Force W chief was briefed. Harvey had long been fully engaged in every promising Cuba operation and was under too much pressure from Bobby Kennedy to have missed any opportunity. His reticence must have been due to powerful doubts about Cubela's bona fides. Harvey was reluctant to make more use of him but was under too much political pressure to abandon the case.[25]

The solution was to let it languish. Weatherby was working about thirty other agents simultaneously, and he was a lower-ranking officer without the standing to make recommendations stick. He spoke only a few words of Spanish, and Cubela's English was about as good. Paradoxically nonetheless, the overworked young case officer considered the Cubela operation "one of the most promising . . . if it could ever jell."[26]

IT WOULD BE UP TO Des FitzGerald to make that happen. When he took over Cuba operations, planning for Fidel's death took on greater urgency. Sam Halpern testified it was then, "in early 1963," that they were ordered "to come up with some ideas to kill Castro." Pressed by a senator in a hearing room and speaking under oath, Halpern was confident that the demand originated in the Oval Office. "In my opinion, that came from higher authorities. . . . I don't think Mr. FitzGerald would have come up with this out of his own head . . . he is just not the kind of man to move on any activity, particularly something as sensitive as that, without orders from on high."[27]

Des knew the president well and was on a first-name basis with the attorney general. They saw each other on weekends in the Virginia horse country, and FitzGerald often came into the office on Monday mornings "all charged up," according to Halpern, itching to start some new operation against Castro. He would announce to his senior staff, "I saw Bobby in Middleburg. Here's what we've got to crank up for next month." Halpern concluded that Bobby was a bad influence on Des, reinforcing his worst instincts. Des never doubted the critical importance of his assignment: Ridding Cuba of Castro was an overriding administration priority.

The president was not about to resign himself to peaceful coexistence with Cuba. Nor was Fidel interested in ending violent support for regional revolutionaries, his venomous anti-Americanism, or his military alliance with the Kremlin. Enmity between the two men dated from the 1960 presidential campaign, when each hurled scathing rhetoric at the other. The Bay of Pigs fiasco had been the previous low point, but relations were approaching a new nadir. In a speech at the Orange Bowl in Miami a few days after Christmas in 1962, Kennedy gave a hint of the more militant policies he would pursue.

Speaking to a festive crowd honoring the fifteen hundred Bay of Pigs veterans just released from Cuban prisons, the president waved the battle flag they had held aloft as they waded onto a Cuban beach. He shouted, "I can assure you that this flag will be returned to this brigade in a free Havana." The crowd cheered him thunderously, and Jackie Kennedy delivered a warm speech in lilting Spanish.

It was an electrifying event for the exile community, and it enraged Fidel. A week later he staged a trumping event in Havana's Revolutionary Plaza. Haranguing a cheering crowd of tens of thousands, he denounced Kennedy as a "pirate and filibusterer. . . . I have no love for him; we do not trust the imperialists."

Rancor between the two men had reached a new intensity. Rapprochement was a more distant possibility than ever. Ridding Cuba of Castro was the overriding American priority; spreading violent revolution throughout Latin America was Fidel's. The pressure on FitzGerald was mounting.

There had been no contact with the elusive Cubela since the previous summer, so Des did his best to concoct elimination schemes that proved even zanier than the poisoned cigars and milkshake plots. His most notorious idea, quickly discarded, seemed to his staff like a three-martini idea, except that it occurred to him one morning while shaving. He wanted the Agency's "dirty tricks department"—the technical services staff—to devise a waterproof explosive seashell.

Castro was an avid skin diver. The shell—it would have to be an exceptionally attractive one to catch his attention—would be planted somewhere in the waters off Cuba's north coast where he might just discover it. When he plucked it off the ocean floor, "it would blow up in his face," as Halpern remembered it. Des was so taken with his idea that he arrived at the office one day with books about Caribbean mollusks and insisted Agency technicians work up a prototype. Halpern and others considered the explosive shell a ridiculous idea, even if such an improbable devise could be fabricated, and persuaded him to drop it.

Undeterred, Des had another brainstorm. He thought of lacing the inside of a diver's wet suit with toxins and arranging for it to be delivered to Fidel. One of the authors of the inspector general report testified: "I think it was fungus that would result in a debilitating disease . . . they acquired a suit and did impregnate it." Helms remembered some of the odder details. He thought tuberculosis pathogens would be introduced into the "breathing apparatus" and fungus to produce "madura foot" smeared on the inside of the suit. "They came up every day with some harebrained idea," he later testified, "but they were never approved." This one in any case was overtaken by events. An American lawyer who negotiated the release of the Bay of Pigs prisoners decided on his own to give Fidel a perfectly sanitary wet suit. To impress Castro, he lied and told him he had bought it at Abercrombie & Fitch.[28]

On April 3, FitzGerald got marching orders from the White House. The president and the attorney general instructed CIA "to survey all possibilities for aggressive action" against Cuba. It was the beginning of the third and, it was thought, culminating act of the American clandestine war. The president requested a new covert action program that assumed "unlimited policy and funds." Des was now in frequent touch with the Kennedy brothers; he was their new best hope to rid them of Castro.[29]

Cubela soon vaulted to much greater prominence, becoming the linchpin in Des's secret plan to promote a military uprising against the Castro brothers. The Cuban would be tasked with enlisting other prestigious officers in a conspiracy. With CIA backing, they would assassinate Fidel and spark a coup. SAS was working simultaneously on a parallel track with a few other supposedly disaffected military; this was known as the AMTRUNK operation. Consensus quickly formed around the new plan in the spring, and by late June, with presidential approval, nearly everything else in the SAS and JMWAVE arsenal was supporting it.

Nothing else had worked. Coastal sabotage attacks and economic denial programs, no matter how aggressive, were still just counterproductive pinpricks that reinforced the Kremlin's commitment to provide billions of dollars of annual subsidies and strengthened Fidel with his hardcore base. The earlier assassination attempts had been ludicrous. Propaganda and covert actions, however imaginative, had no enduring impact. Exile groups were disorganized, penetrated by the DGI, and proliferating into warring factions. A national intelligence estimate summed it up: Neither internal opposition nor economic difficulties would cause Fidel's regime to collapse. With his larger and more muscular military, by early 1963 Castro was stronger and more brazen and entrenched than ever.[30]

What the Americans had not tried before was promoting a military coup led by a genuine hero of the revolution. Until Cubela was anointed as AMLASH, there had been no candidates, not even lower-ranking, unpromising ones. Des was confident that he was on the right track, that he would succeed where Bill Harvey and Dick Bissell, the flawed mastermind of the Bay of Pigs invasion, had failed. He would be Castro's nemesis, the Kennedy administration's commanding officer in an invigorated secret war. Des had inherited a large, prestigious organization from Harvey, and he was in a hurry to put his own brand on it and to move forward quickly.

He assembled a first-rate senior staff. Bruce Cheever remained as deputy. Ed Marelius was brought in as FI chief, responsible for foreign intelligence, or covert information collection. Seymour Bolten—rumored among admiring younger officers to have virtually created the West German Christian Democratic Party from scratch after World War II—headed the large covert action and psychological warfare branch. Art Maloney took over the paramilitary branch, coordinating sabotage and other commando operations with JMWAVE. Hal Swenson led a counterintelligence branch of twenty-five or thirty. From Chief of Staff Sam Halpern's perspective, "These were all very senior guys who were well regarded by everyone . . . they wouldn't take horseshit from anybody, and ran a very tight ship."[31]

Together, they were responsible for many espionage successes against the Cubans, even penetrations into the Castro brothers' family circle. Juanita, one of their sisters, worked covertly for the CIA in Havana before defecting to the United States in 1964. According to her own published account, she was recruited by the wife of the Brazilian ambassador in Havana, acting as a cut-out for the CIA. Another Castro sibling, elder brother Ramón, was also in touch with the Agency at least five or six times and was thought by Ted Shackley to have been close to defecting too.[32]

The longtime personal physician of the Castros' mother and some of her daughters was a reporting source. Bernardo Milanes, known in the Agency by his cryptonym AMCROAK, was recruited in December 1963 in Madrid. At the time he and others were plotting an assassination attempt against Castro. He had known Fidel and Raúl since their childhoods and provided some of the earliest and most revealing insights into their characters and psychologies.

Suspicious of everyone, Fidel appears not even to have trusted his own mother, Lina Ruz González, and perhaps with good reason. She told Milanes that she considered Fidel responsible for "the wholesale murder and repression being carried out" in Cuba. Shortly before her death in July 1963, Lina also confided that her personal bodyguards were under orders to report to Fidel about everyone who visited her and everything that was said.[33]

Dr. Milanes told his handlers of Fidel's seething hatred of President Kennedy. In January 1963 he encountered Castro at Lina's home while providing her medical care after she had suffered two heart attacks. The account of that meeting is contained in a lengthy CIA dispatch. "With a sarcastic smile on his face," Fidel asked Milanes "'what he thought'" of Kennedy. The doctor responded that Castro was probably underestimating his adversary and that Kennedy was certainly not "an illiterate and an imbecile as Fidel often described him." Fidel laughed, mocking the doctor, saying he "would be the one who would ruin Kennedy." Castro then made an obscene gesture demeaning the president.[34]

Audacity was the norm in Cuba operations. Agents made cold recruitment pitches to some of the most senior officials in Castro's government. Even if the chances of success were remote, the officials might be compromised in the process; at least they would be rattled and perhaps made to appear suspicious to their own counterintelligence. Figurehead president Osvaldo Dorticós was approached in New York in October 1962. He became enraged, causing a raucous scene, according to a CIA record, and had "the agent who pitched him forcibly removed from his hotel." The mayor of Havana and other prominent leaders rejected similar gambits. But many others assigned cryptonyms in the AM series were recruited as working CIA spies.[35]

AFTER HIS RETIREMENT, Sam Halpern became the unofficial historian of the early 1960s Cuba wars. Brooklyn-born, a City College of New York graduate, he was a World War II veteran of the OSS. Working with FitzGerald, he was one of just four men fully informed of the Cubela plan. Halpern was valued for his street-smart realism and irrepressible candor, always willing to gently reproach his bosses when they crossed over into the absurd. His sworn congressional testimonies about Cubela are the most honest and reliable accounts of what actually happened. In three lengthy oral history interviews, all now declassified, he later provided even more detail and texture about SAS operations.[36]

Halpern put SAS junior staffers to work with analysts at the Defense Intelligence Agency studying Cuba's military leadership. Des wanted lists of all those who might be dissatisfied or opposed to the Castros. He hoped to learn of any weak links in the chain of command, rivalries and tensions among commanders. By early November detailed biographic studies of 150 officers were compiled, 45 of whom were of special interest as potential coup leaders.[37]

Des was pleased with the progress, but little was actually known about Raúl Castro's military. Easily the most powerful institution on the island, it was nearly as shrouded in revolutionary mist as the DGI. The armed forces were then, and remain, heavily insulated from outside scrutiny and influence. Using U-2 imagery and other technical means of data collection, American analysts could assess the Cuban order of battle. They were able to count Raúl's tanks and armored personnel vehicles, keep track of the air force and growing navy, judge the number of men in uniform. But in 1963 there was hardly any reliable information about attitudes and relationships in the high command. No ranking officer had defected since the first months of the revolution, and none would do so for twenty-four more years.

The Americans underestimated Raúl's leadership and organizational abilities, and there were some in SAS—Des among them—who mistakenly believed that the Cuban military was an easy mark. Most commanders were guerrilla veterans, simple, uneducated men, thought to be feckless. But nearly all were devoted to the Castros, and they were battle-tested warriors with no love for the Americans. Cuban military counterintelligence was pervasive and proficient at ferreting out weaklings and doubters. It would not be easy to create a murderous cabal from within the ranks of the Castros' officer corps. Despite all the studies and wishful thinking in Langley, the Agency simply did not appreciate the formidable strengths of the Cuban military machine.

Even less was known about intentions and advanced capabilities. In December CIA military analysts completed a comprehensive assessment of Castro's armed forces. Among the key judgments was that "the Cubans lack either the sea or airlift capability necessary for conducting overseas military operations." That must have been reassuring for downtown policy makers. But, three months earlier, unbeknownst to the analysts, a large Cuban expeditionary force, including a tank battalion, senior officers, and about seven hundred foot soldier volunteers, had arrived by sea in Algeria ready to fight against neighboring Morocco. The Cuban commanding officer, a tough veteran who was bristling to get his men into battle in the North African sands, was one of those on the short list of supposed coup collaborators with Cubela.[38]

Within an hour of being asked by Algeria's revolutionary president to provide that military assistance, Fidel had agreed, and with characteristic decisiveness. He instructed his field commander to put himself at the disposal of the Algerians, "to go wherever they wanted, whenever they wanted." It was the first of many audacious Cuban adventures in Africa. In this instance, unlike several others, the Cubans did no fighting; Algeria concluded an armistice with the Moroccan king.[39]

Whatever could be gleaned by headquarters analysts about the military appeared in the pages of the *Cuba Daily Summary*. The prestigious Office of National Estimates was repeatedly tasked as well, producing more forecasts about Cuba during the second half of 1963 than in any comparable period. A standard theme in all of the reports was how dependent the regime was on "the person of Castro" and therefore how vulnerable it was. "Cuba Without Castro" was the title of one of several forward-looking assessments that grappled with the question highest on Des FitzGerald's agenda. The most likely eventuality, the estimators judged, was that, after Fidel, Cuban leaders would rally around Raúl Castro, the designated successor. They had it right, of course. That is what happened forty-three years later.[40]

In mid-April they prepared a highly restricted, EYES-ONLY report for the director. Four senior experts were tasked to comment on Des's emerging plan to provoke a military coup. All Soviet specialists, they worried about how the Kremlin would respond to the aggressively stepped-up clandestine pressures on Cuba that were in the works. Soviet leaders realize, they wrote, that "the US is un-reconciled" to the Castro regime and "as incidents mounted" would increasingly believe the administration "could not be induced" to let it survive.[41]

Khrushchev's first step, they thought, would probably be to communicate di-rectly with Kennedy—perhaps through the emergency "hot line" set up after the missile crisis—to threaten tough responses in defense of Cuba. As the Soviet pre-mier had once said, the imperialists were trying to strangle the Marxist infant in its crib. "To dramatize their rage," the analysts observed, the Soviets "might shoot down a U-2" reconnaissance aircraft over Cuba, despite the high likelihood of an American military retaliation. These were grim reminders of just how volatile the stand-off with Castro remained six months after the October 1962 nuclear show-down. McCone surely would have shared those bleak warnings with the White House and the national security team.[42]

A companion forecast prepared a few days later looked out a year into Cuba's future. It concluded that by then the "regime is likely to be more firmly estab-lished than ever." But other judgments must have buoyed FitzGerald's determina-tion to proceed with his program. The analysts believed that "considerably less than half the Cuban people" positively supported the regime. And even more to Des's liking, the analysts speculated about how popular resistance could provoke factionalism in the leadership. Although still unlikely, there could be "a disrup-tion of the security apparatus and the defection of armed elements." However qualified—and perhaps induced—that judgment was, it would have helped to win higher-level approvals for Des's war plan.[43]

He had broached it in a memorandum to Helms and McCone in mid-March. A new file folder was opened in SAS, titled "Split the Regime." "The real pay-off will come," Des wrote, "when we are able to gain access to . . . key military personalities [prepared] to dispose of Castro and his immediate entourage." The idea that was to come to a head in November in a Paris safe house was taking shape. There was no intent, however, to restore a regime anything like the old Batista dictatorship. The new post-Castro one should be economically and socially progressive but anti-*fidelista* and anticommunist. A new government, Des wrote, would not be expected to "turn the clock back." He knew President Kennedy was adamant about that.[44]

Cubela and his co-conspirators would require high-level American assurances. If their coup attempt bogged down or if Soviet forces on the island threatened to get involved, the rebels would receive American recognition and possibly military support. Coup leaders would be embraced even if they had originally been Castro loyalists with blood on their hands. As the plans evolved, provisions were made for a "special team" to be inserted "black" to link up with the coup leaders. CIA and military operatives would remain in Cuba to coordinate a military intervention if that were necessary to finish off Castro.[45]

Des also told McCone and Helms that SAS was brainstorming ideas for "using the full gamut of sophisticated technical, black, and deception operations" to increase the chances of a successful coup. According to declassified CIA documents, "a number of non-violent operations were carried out." One targeted the Cuban military, judging at least from a proclamation issued by Raúl Castro in early April. In an unusual, widely publicized order to all Cuban military personnel, they were warned not to be fooled if they received orders to steal arms and ammunition from military depots "with the apparently noble pretext" of supplying them to Latin American revolutionaries. CIA was under mounting pressure from the attorney general to come up with smoking-gun evidence of Cuban arms smuggling. Raúl blamed the Agency and the Pentagon for trying to create an incriminating incident that could be used as a pretext for punitive military action.[46]

During his first six months in charge at SAS, FitzGerald attended numerous meetings of the senior White House council that approved covert actions. Bobby Kennedy attended frequently, and sometimes the president—euphemistically referred to in the meeting minutes as "Higher Authority"—did as well. Whether present or not, he was always fully engaged in the details of covert planning against Cuba. In an oral history, Sam Halpern recalled, "Kennedy was awful on minutiae." Exaggerating to make his point, Halpern complained that both Kennedys were always so involved in planning for JMWAVE sabotage operations that they would want to know "what kind of shoelaces are the men going to wear? . . . what's the gradient on the beach? . . . what kind of sand is there?" In fact, the president approved in advance virtually every sabotage operation. He sometimes reviewed charts and maps of what was planned and kept track of the results. In a few meetings he pushed for more and more damaging attacks. Kennedy had prevailed in the missile crisis by directing every move of American policy, supervising all details; he would defeat Castro the same way.[47]

Kennedy was not reluctant to approve other bold initiatives even if they antagonized the Kremlin. On April 9, for example, he signed off on a propaganda plan—one of two similar ones—to incite Cubans on the island to attack Soviet troops.[48]

BY MID-JUNE KENNEDY had approved most of SAS's action plan. It included the same six line items that Des later reviewed with him on November 12 in the Cabinet Room. The keystone of the plan was the use of Cubela to stimulate rebellion in the Cuban military.

But there had been no contact with Cubela since Weatherby's meetings with him in Europe the year before. All that was known about his current thinking was being filtered through Tepedino from his jewelry factory and showroom in midtown Manhattan. Known then by his complementary cryptonym AMWHIP, Tepedino was eager to get Cubela back in touch with the Agency. FitzGerald and Helms realized that once it could be arranged, a more experienced, higher-ranking case officer than Weatherby would have to take over.

Nestor Sanchez, a Spanish speaker who had served in Korea and Middle Eastern affairs, was reading in on Cubela. He had few opportunities to use his native Spanish until joining SAS in February 1963. It was not sheer luck that had helped him avoid all association with the Bay of Pigs. Helms, who had taken a liking to Sanchez, had discreetly advised him to steer clear of what he expected to be a disaster. He considered Sanchez one of the Agency's young fast-trackers and correctly viewed him as a future chief of Latin American operations.[49]

Until I corrected them, Cubela and Tepedino had always believed that Sanchez was Puerto Rican. In fact, he had been born in little Magdalena, New Mexico,
and grew up on a large, isolated ranch. His father was one of ten children, all
boys, descended from the early Spaniards and Basques who had settled the area.
Sanchez studied at Georgetown University and joined the four-year-old CIA in
1951. Cubela and Tepedino did not like him, although they spoke to me warmly
about Weatherby and two other case officers. It may have been because Sanchez
was more demanding, pressing Cubela hard to make up his mind and come to
closure about his intentions.

They met for the first time on September 5, 1963, in Porto Alegre, the most
European of large Brazilian cities, on a spacious lagoon in the southern state of Rio
Grande do Sul. Cubela was there as the official Cuban representative at an athletic
competition. Weatherby introduced them in a safe house and tried to be sure the
hand-off went smoothly. Then he stood as look-out while Sanchez took over.[50]

Cubela revealed that he had recently completed nine months of military
training and then vacationed with Fidel in adjoining beach houses at Varadero.
Raúl had offered him a trifling position as a provincial army information officer,
which he declined. There was still no chance he would be entrusted with a troop
command. But at least he had access to the Castros and top military officers and
was legitimately wearing the army uniform. The regime later claimed he had been
discharged at about that time "for lack of discipline." But it was disinformation.
Cubela was pictured smiling broadly, in uniform, with three other well-known
comandantes, during the 1963 May Day parade in Havana.[51]

Sanchez was at best ambivalent about his new charge. From the Agency's
Porto Alegre base, he cabled Des that "AMLASH cocky, totally spoiled brat who
will always be control problem." But with an eye more on Cubela's potential than
his deficiencies, he concluded that his "feelings against regime sincere and he basically honest." Far from an unequivocal endorsement, it was a motion to proceed despite serious reservations. Under enormous pressure from Des, he tamped
down his concerns. The mission was just too important and the opportunity
Cubela provided so unprecedented that the case could not be whittled away by
unsubstantiated doubts.

Still, there was no possibility that Cubela could be disciplined enough ever to
communicate using OWVL or the secret writing he had already rejected. When

he was in Cuba, clandestine contact would be nearly impossible without interme-diaries. He would need help, Sanchez reported, a support agent who could bolster and keep him organized, someone who would be a "strong confidant inside who will push him and serve as chaplain." It was a stunning acknowledgment of just how little the Americans could depend on Cubela. But the incentive to believe in him was high.[52]

Sanchez cabled that Cubela told him there were only two ways "to accom-plish change" in Cuba: either by an "inside job" or an American invasion. Yet Sanchez testified in 1975 that there had been no discussion of assassination. Un-der persistent questioning by the Senate committee, he stood his ground; he had peppered Cubela with questions about attitudes in the military and which officers might be ready to join in a conspiracy. "I was interested in who he knew and what they thought of the regime." He never explained the reference to an "inside job."[53]

In this and his other declassified reports about Cubela, Sanchez resorted to euphemisms or simply omitted the most incendiary material. He was doing what Des FitzGerald wanted: leaving virtually no paper trail, no incriminating record of assassination planning. When we met at his retirement home in the shadow of the Camp David presidential retreat in August 2008, Sanchez told me that he talked only to his boss about the case, "not with anyone else." He said "hardly anyone else was even informed. Des always told me 'Just you and me. Don't talk to anyone!'" FitzGerald also instructed him to eschew any explicit written record of plotting Fidel's death. Reports of Sanchez's meetings with Cubela are, therefore, meager and innocuous.

Sanchez always insisted that the man he worked so closely with was reliable; Cubela was not a double or a dangle, and the operation was not penetrated by Cuban intelligence. Sanchez told me he never doubted Cubela's bona fides. When I pressed him, he was offended.

"I *never* suspected Cubela was bad." Raising his voice and leaning toward me, he glowered. *"And he was not."*

Weatherby, Helms, FitzGerald, and Halpern all agreed. I discussed the case many times with Halpern, and he was consistent. There were no valid reasons, he believed, to have suspected Cubela was under DGI control or that the operation was compromised. "AMLASH was never a double agent by anybody's stretch of the imagination," he told me.[54]

As usual, Helms was the most nuanced. In his memoirs, he hinted at doubts about Cubela by describing the dilemma that weighed so heavily on him: "Given the relentless, blistering heat from the White House, I was scarcely of a mind to drop anyone whom we were satisfied had reasonable access to Castro and was apparently determined to turn him out of office."[55]

However nagging his doubts may have been, the savvy spymaster felt he had no choice but to remain silent and faithful to the Kennedys' demands. He told the Senate committee that Cubela would "fit like a hand in a glove" for the administration's purposes.[56]

NINE

THE BIG JOB

NESTOR SANCHEZ AND ROLANDO CUBELA CONTINUED MEETING in Porto Alegre on and off over four days in early September. They were getting to know each other, though awkwardly. Sanchez was not in disguise but used the alias Nicholas Sanson. He encouraged Cubela to call him Nick. Still, the Cuban was never able to relax with his new case officer, as he had with Weatherby, or to develop genuine rapport.[1]

They concentrated on Des FitzGerald's gnawing priority: the need to identify senior Cuban officers who might rally to a coup. Cubela provided the names of a dozen candidates, but as a rogues' gallery of potential conspirators, not one among them qualified. They were loyal to the Castros, had little in common, and there was no Cubela sidekick among them prepared to do his bidding. Almost all were desk-bound staff officers. One tough young troop commander, a drinking and carousing friend of Cubela's, might eventually turn against Fidel. But not yet. He was the same *comandante* who a month later would eagerly lead the Cuban expeditionary force in Algeria.[2]

Cubela thought several others were unhappy with the revolution but unwilling to speak up or take confrontational action. Fidel was so feared, Cubela said, it was as if he had supernatural powers. Another unlikely candidate lived in isolation at a ranch where he stayed busy with a kennel of fighting dogs, hoping to avoid politics altogether. One of the better known, José Ramón Fernández, was mistakenly described as anti-communist. But nearly half a century later he was still locked in the Castros' embrace, serving as a leading member of the Communist Party and a vice president of the council of ministers.

In his debut performance with Sanchez, Cubela had been a disappointment both as prospective coup leader and source of useful intelligence. But those were not the qualities most in demand in Langley because there was no doubt about his credentials as a brutal assassin. Given the pressures to get on with a plan to topple Castro, Cubela still seemed to be the ideal candidate, the first recruit in the sprawling network of Cuban agents who retained senior military rank and was an authentic revolutionary hero. If his promise was greater than what he had delivered so far, it would be up to Sanchez to mold and motivate him.[3]

The last of their meetings in Brazil was on Sunday, September 8. Unknown to anyone at CIA, by then Fidel knew nearly everything that had taken place between the men. DGI agents were informing headquarters that Cubela was in and out of CIA's grip, meeting in a safe house, talking about which military officers might be tempted away. Fidel knew the Americans were stalking him again. Just as he had learned of the earlier plots, counterintelligence was advising him of the latest threat. He revealed this himself in April 1978 when he met in Havana with a delegation from the House assassinations committee.

"For three years we had known there were plots against us."[4]

He did not specify exactly what he meant. But it made no difference to him if the Americans were plotting his assassination or a coup. It was a distinction without a difference. His fate would be the same in either event. Anyone with the least understanding of Cuba's experience understood that Fidel Castro was synonymous with the revolution. Umbilically connected, they live or perish as one. It had been that way since the first shots were fired against the Batista dictatorship in July 1953. Since he won power no Cuban had ever challenged Fidel's hegemony and gotten away with it.

If he survived the initial treachery of a Yankee-sponsored coup attempt, even one that resulted in numerous casualties, he would never surrender. He would rally as many followers as possible, retreat to the same mountains in Oriente where he had waged his guerrilla war, and counterattack until either he triumphed again or was killed in the effort. Martyrdom was far preferable to the shame of exile or captivity.

Fidel had no intention, though, of meeting any of those fates. Since his troubled childhood, Castro had always battled his enemies, conspired against them,
manipulated and undermined them in every way possible. He would seize the
initiative, take advantage of any opportunity, artfully dodge and dissemble. He
calculated every move with an accomplished gambler's take on the odds and a
sharpie's eye on risks and benefits. He gave no quarter and kept his foreign enemies in the dark. During nearly five decades in power, Fidel rarely ever threatened any of them in concrete and specific terms. Warnings and threats would only
alert them, yield them advantages, and reduce his chances of being able to spring
surprises.

But the news he was receiving from Porto Alegre alarmed and enraged him.
He understood now more conclusively than ever that the Kennedys would never
reconcile with him. Washington always ignored the feelers he put out suggesting he was amenable to bilateral talks that might reduce tensions. He shared his
brooding true feelings about what he confronted in Havana with a visiting former American congressman in early October, soon after Sanchez's meetings with
Cubela in Porto Alegre. "We don't trust President Kennedy . . . we know of the
plans the CIA is carrying out."[5]

In public he had said something similar only once before. In a speech in April
1963 on the anniversary of the Bay of Pigs, he shouted to a crowd of tens of thousands in Havana's Revolutionary Plaza: "Recently, they have been emphasizing the
need to murder the leaders of the revolution." This was just as CIA started gearing
up its arsenal of covert programs and after Cubela's meetings with Weatherby in
Europe. Cuban doubles, illegals, and penetration agents were keeping Fidel well
informed. He may also have been hearing from a supermole somewhere in the
upper reaches of the Kennedy administration. Duly warned and fearing for his
life more than at any time since the eve of the Bay of Pigs, he decided to do something unprecedented.

On Saturday evening, September 7, he showed up at an independence day
reception at the Brazilian embassy in Havana. It was not the kind of event he
usually bothered with, and relations with Brazil were not particularly close,
but there were things he meant to put on the public record. Beckoning Daniel
Harker, a favorite wire service reporter, Fidel leaned forward and spoke rapidly
in a long, impassioned monologue. An unidentified reporter with the UPI news

service also participated, describing Fidel as "puffing on a cigar and leaning back in an easy chair."[6]

Colombian-born, fluent in Spanish, and reporting for the Associated Press, Harker's story got the widest circulation. It reached New York the next day and was published in different versions in major American dailies on Monday morning, September 9. Many of the headlines began the same way—"Castro Warns U.S."[7]

The front page of the *Miami Herald* read: "We'll Fight Back, Fidel Warns U.S." The *Los Angeles Times* said: "Castro Warns U.S. on Meddling with Cuba." The *Chicago Tribune:* "Castro Warns U.S. Not to Aid His Foes." In New Orleans, where Lee Harvey Oswald was a regular newspaper reader, the *Times Picayune* carried the story on page 7. Its headline was: "Castro Blasts Raids on Cuba; Says US Leaders Imperiled by Aid to Rebels."

Most of the papers quoted Fidel's saber-rattling threats: "We are prepared to fight them and answer in kind. US leaders should think that if they are aiding terrorist plans to eliminate Cuban leaders, they themselves will not be safe ... United States leaders would be in danger if they helped in any attempt to do away with leaders of Cuba."

Fidel's words were inflammatory, unprecedented. The Cuban leader was signaling that he knew what Sanchez and Cubela were discussing. They may in fact have been meeting in Brazil just when Castro was at the Brazilian embassy in Cuba. That he chose to level his blast there could not have been coincidental.

Fidel probably thought that once alerted this way, Kennedy and CIA might be deterred from proceeding with their plot against him. He calculated too that it could be worth showing his hand on the chance he might gain some relief from the intensifying covert onslaught. His enemies might even fear that he had the motive and capability to spawn retaliatory plots against American leaders.

Harker quoted Castro saying: "The CIA and other dreamers believe in their hopes of an insurrection ... [but] they can go on dreaming forever." He was more than usually acrimonious when describing Kennedy. The president was "double-crossing," following "shifting policies" toward Cuba. He is a "cretin ... the Batista of his times." Kennedy and Republican senator Barry Goldwater, a main aspirant for his party's presidential nomination the following year, were ridiculed as "cheap, crooked politicians."

Ray Rocca was correct when he later concluded that the interview "repre-sented a more-than-ordinary attempt" by Castro "to get a message on the record in the United States." Fidel had condemned and ridiculed Kennedy many times before, although never with as much venom and pugnacity. It was the first—and as far as I know, the only—time he ever explicitly threatened American leaders. Because he reiterated the threats, in different ways, they could not have been slips of the tongue.[8]

Remarkably, however, his harsh words had little or no resonance in American policy circles. The *Washington Post,* the most widely circulated daily in the capital, did not carry the story. The *New York Times,* read by most Washington govern-ment officials, carried an abbreviated UPI account on page 9. But the threats were not mentioned. The smaller-circulation *Washington Evening Star* carried much of Harker's account but buried Fidel's threat in the last third of its treatment on a back page. Fidel's intended audiences had no ready access to his shots across their bow.

Only four men in CIA—Helms, FitzGerald, Halpern, and Sanchez—were fully in the know about the Cubela conspiracy. Only they would have been able to connect the dots. Sanchez said he was not aware of the Harker article until long after. Apparently it did not come to Helms's attention either. Sam Halpern, in contrast, said he knew what Fidel said at the time: "We heard his threats against the president." So it can be assumed that Des FitzGerald was informed as well. Even so, Halpern said it never occurred to anyone in the Agency that there could have been a connection between Fidel's outburst on September 7 and Kennedy's assassination in Dallas eleven weeks later. No one in CIA ever investigated that possibility. Still, as Halpern also observed, "[I]t may have been we just never gave Castro that much credit."[9]

Beyond SAS, almost no one could have appreciated the enormity of what Fidel said. Most newspaper readers would have viewed Harker's interview simply as more overheated hyperbole, the normal Castro fare. As they did not know of the assassination plots, CIA desk analysts had no reason to consider the story sig-nificant. Nor did propaganda specialists who followed Cuban rhetoric in another Agency component. There was no mention of Harker in the otherwise compre-hensive CIA inspector general's report. The Secret Service apparently was not told of the threats against the president. I do not believe that the Warren Commission was informed of them when it began its investigation a few months after the assassination.[10]

The only time Fidel was asked on the record about the interview was in 1978, during his meeting with a delegation from the House assassinations committee. The Harker interview was one of the first issues raised. Fidel was masterful in self-defense:

"I remember my intention . . . was to warn the government that we knew about the plots against our lives . . . that they could become a boomerang against the authors of those actions, but I did not mean to threaten."[11]

Whether a warning, a threat, or a plea—and, in reality, it was all three—Fidel wanted relief from the ever more encroaching American aggression. He did not worry much about an organized coup as such. He and Raul had hand-picked their troop commanders and senior defense ministry staffers. All were hardcore loyalists. Fidel knew Cubela well and was confident he could not organize and lead a military revolt. His standing as a *comandante* was really honorific. He was peripheral in the leadership, too odd and indecisive.

Assassination, however, was something else. A coup would have a chance at success only if the Castro brothers were killed in an initial lightning strike. Fidel worried about such a scenario all the time. Even in 1963, as perhaps the world's best-protected head of state, he could not be sure he would be warned in time of the next assassin. He knew that some of the CIA plots against him had been ingenious, even if they had all been foiled. What he feared most was the unexpected ploy, some bolt from the blue they might try next. How many others were out there intent on murdering him? Quite a few, as it later became clear.

Among them was Mario Salabarria, an exile asset known in the Agency as AMTURVY–13. A formidable enemy of Fidel's since the university gang wars of the late 1940s, he had served a stint as secret police chief before fleeing to Miami. By the summer of 1963 he was seeking weapons and support from JMWAVE to assassinate his old nemesis. A declassified Agency dossier explains that in October he was given "a few pistols, revolvers, and sabotage materials." Another document adds, however, that "Salabarria's case presents certain CI [counterintelligence] considerations." CIA analysts later judged that it appeared likely the DGI had been tracking the AMTURVY plot, and others, from the start. It seemed as if half of the Miami exile community was plotting how to eliminate Castro.[12]

By the fall of 1963, Fidel was certain he was facing a proliferating and truly existential threat. A Soviet defector referred to it in his memoirs. The high-level Kremlin officials he worked with all believed Castro was "terrified" of Kennedy. That may have been an exaggeration, though not by much. In April 2009, a year after he retired from the Cuban presidency, Fidel published an editorial stating that, of the ten American presidents he had confronted, he had feared Kennedy the most. The remark accurately reflected the forebodings he felt in 1963.[13]

Kennedy was indeed a formidable enemy. Jack Bell, a journalist friend of the president's, remarked in an oral history interview that Kennedy "had the feeling he could cope with anybody on earth." That was precisely what preoccupied Fidel. He understood that because of Kennedy's humiliation at the Bay of Pigs and the brinksmanship of the missile crisis, he would remain the president's implacable foe. And he was convinced that the Kennedys were capable of almost anything as they endeavored to topple him from power.[14]

DES FITZGERALD WAS IN A HURRY, as usual. The Pentagon is about a fifteen-mile drive from Langley, downriver along the Potomac on the scenic George Washington Parkway. His driver, hugging the left lane all the way, knew to stay well above the speed limit. Des liked to drive that way when going to work after weekends at his country place. Halpern remembered that his foot was always pressed "through the floorboards" as he raced in his Volkswagen Beetle. "When he got on those highways, he was murder." (Des also drove a Jaguar, but it was often in the shop.)[15]

The meeting with the Joint Chiefs of Staff began at two P.M. on September 25. Two months earlier FitzGerald had also consulted with the nation's top four-star generals and admirals for the same purpose: to review the Cuba covert action program, particularly the plan for a military uprising. In that first meeting he had wanted the officers to be aware that once the coup was ignited, American military intervention might be required to reinforce it. The Pentagon needed to begin working with SAS on contingency plans. Des returned to brief the chiefs again as the prospects for overthrowing Castro seemed to be brightening.[16]

FitzGerald was a showman, utterly convincing in the role of debonair super-spy, his booming, patrician-inflected voice reverberating in the paneled conference room. Rarely, perhaps never before, had the Pentagon's top brass convened to meet with a CIA executive. It was not within their normal span of responsibilities. But Des sat down with them twice, as the president's representative in charge of the Cuba war that they knew to be a White House priority.

Des said that he had a stronger mandate than ever before to proceed with the gamut of covert operations. The prospects for success were steadily improving. He told them—with more hope than conviction—that Fidel's hold on power had been slipping since their last meeting. The JMWAVE sabotage attacks, and others mounted independently by dissidents on the island, were beginning to take a real toll. He mentioned raids by light aircraft on Cuban targets, something that Ted Shackley denied ever happened. Unrest was growing, Des was sure. Fidel would fall in the not-distant future.[17]

None of that was remotely what the analysts were writing, nor did it resemble the talking points FitzGerald shared with the National Security Council six days later at the White House. With the attorney general present that day, Des was more cautious, reluctant to raise expectations for Castro's imminent demise too high. He had been bullish, maybe a bit bombastic with the Joint Chiefs. He may have wanted to lord it over that roomful of the nation's most senior officers. Author Evan Thomas wrote that even at White House policy meetings, FitzGerald was often "outgoing, cocky, and confident." He treated the president's most senior national security advisors as his equals "and bluffed the rest."[18]

Des was buoyant, on some matters prescient with the Chiefs. He warned that Castro would "probably take desperate measures" as his situation deteriorated. Specifically, he meant that violent subversion in Latin America would intensify. He also worried that Cuban air and naval forces had gained so much strength with Soviet assistance that CIA ships ferrying exile commandos and saboteurs from Florida were in increasing peril. The Kremlin had provided Cuba with six sub chasers and a dozen motor torpedo boats. Hundreds of naval personnel had been trained in the Soviet Union to man them. JMWAVE might need emergency military backup if the Cubans tried to commandeer the *Rex*, the *Leda*, or other large ships in Shackley's navy.[19]

Des could have added that Fidel would also crack down more cruelly on domestic opposition if he feared that his position was weakening. No one in Washington knew about the bizarre October 1962 Armageddon letter, but there were plenty of other well-known examples of Castro's truculence and brutality. If Des was in fact aware of the Harker interview, he was undeterred, proceeding at full throttle with the AMLASH plot and a number of others, though possibly with a more wary eye on the unpredictable and vengeful Fidel.

At the Pentagon, Des told his audience that he was having "great success getting closer to military personnel who might break with Castro." There were at least ten high-level military commanders "talking with the CIA," he claimed. Declassified CIA records suggest he was exaggerating at least by half. It is not clear if he included some of the dozen officers Cubela had told Sanchez about in Porto Alegre, but if so, Des was ignoring how useless that report had been. He admitted that the potential coup members were not yet talking to each other. Cubela, the magic missing link to make that happen, could not be unveiled. No one at the Defense Department knew he was talking to the Agency.

Yet something else Des revealed that afternoon could not have been misunderstood. He told them he had been studying "in detail" the 1944 Valkyrie assassination attempt against Hitler by dissident German military officers. He was looking for precedents, hoping, he said, "to develop an approach." That plot failed when a bomb placed by a conspirator blew up close to the Führer, injuring him only slightly. Des wanted to learn from the mistakes made there so that a similar operation against Castro could succeed. The only record of this discussion that I have been able to find is in the minutes of the Pentagon meeting recorded by an officer there. Whatever else may have been collected in SAS about plans to mimic the Hitler plot has disappeared or remains locked away in CIA vaults.[20]

However much Agency officers later tried to downplay the assassination part of the plot, Des had confirmed it was to be the trigger for a military coup. In their congressional testimonies, Helms and Sanchez insisted that with Cubela, they were only promoting a coup, not an assassination conspiracy. The first, they admitted, might easily result in the second, but regime change was the objective, not Castro's death. Sanchez admitted when pressed that a coup would undoubtedly be messy: There would be gunfire and bloodshed, people would die. But murder, he insisted, was not the goal. In his memoirs Helms agreed.[21]

Halpern, who knew the AMLASH case as well as anyone, never tried to hide its true purpose. Cubela, he admitted on different occasions, was meant to assassinate Fidel. In an oral history interview in 1988, he said it was the only assassination operation "I was directly involved in." During other confessional moments—in congressional testimonies and a signed affidavit—he stripped the story of any pretense. A senator asked him in 1975 if CIA had "carte blanche authority to remove Mr. Castro in any way, either overthrow him, or kill him?" Under oath, Sam responded: "Yes sir." The authors of the 1967 inspector general's assassination report, who interviewed Halpern, FitzGerald, Sanchez, and others, also concluded that assassination was the goal.[22]

Des's draft coup plan, elaborately detailed, was circulating in policy circles in October. Classified TOP SECRET-SENSITIVE, it would have been seen by fewer than two dozen officials. The objective was to guarantee that an acceptable anti-communist government would emerge after Fidel, even if a massive American military intervention was required. That possibility was described as "rescue of a revolt." Cubela and his presumed co-conspirators were expected to proclaim a provisional government as soon as Fidel and "the top echelon of the Cuban leadership" were dead or deposed. The euphemism employed was "neutralize." Nothing in the plan allowed for Fidel's capture alive. Once the rebels gained momentum and controlled some territory, American diplomatic recognition and support would follow.[23]

The CIA estimates office was tasked with scoping out how the Kremlin might react. Naturally, there was concern that another superpower showdown could erupt in Cuba, especially if American troops got involved. Des was encouraged by the analysts' response. They concluded that "there is almost nothing the Soviets could do in Cuba itself to influence the course of events." Relations with the United States would suffer a shuddering blow, because Marxist Cuba was such an important Soviet lodgment on the American doorstep, but there would be no truly dire consequences.

Even if the coup attempt faltered in the face of fierce resistance from Castro loyalists, most likely the several thousand Soviet military on the island would stay out of the fray. Sherman Kent, the intelligence estimating grand master, added that "Soviet inaction would be somewhat less embarrassing if Fidel were liquidated at the outset." Kent may have suspected or overheard whispered snippets in the executive dining room that such a plan was afoot.[24]

FOR DES, OCTOBER 1963 was to be the month of no return. The pace of coup promotion activities accelerated under a global effort code-named MHAPRON. Its purpose was to coordinate interlacing operations of many types, all concentrated on rupturing the Cuban military. SAS at Langley, JMWAVE, and the large Cuba branch at the Mexico City station were the legs of the ambitious, lavishly funded operational tripod.[25]

The newly inaugurated Voice of the Rebel Army covert radio station was broadcasting six nights a week from Swan Island. The programming, according to a CIA document, was "designed to inspire army units to unite and rise up in a coup." Military listeners were assured that if they rebelled, they would receive American support regardless of how closely they had been allied with the regime. It was time, they were urged, to restore the revolution to the democratic values the rebel army veterans had fought for before Castro betrayed them by turning to communism.[26]

Operation AMTRUNK geared up that fall. Ramón Guin, an army captain and former colleague of Cubela's in the struggles against Batista, was recruited on the island by an Agency penetration agent. He was designated AMTRUNK–10. The hope was that he would identify and recruit other disaffected military men to join with him and then link up with Cubela in a coordinated revolt. Although Guin's revolutionary and military credentials were flimsy—he never held a troop command or important government post, and had few contacts in the Castros' circles—he became the unlikely figurehead of this second cabal.

Cubela liked Guin and said he was willing to conspire with him. But he told Sanchez of concerns about his old friend's "nervous condition" and drinking problem. Thirty-year-old Guin was an even weaker reed in intrigue and coup instigation than Cubela. By November 9 there had been no progress. JMWAVE had provided Guin with an OWVL radio. He was asked if other prospective conspirators had yet been enlisted. They had not.[27]

From the start, neither Miami nor Langley had been enthusiastic about the AMTRUNK scheme. It had "a very high flap potential," Shackley warned headquarters. He was overruled; the plan had enthusiastic White House backing. The president was persuaded by a prominent journalist friend with contacts among Cubans on both sides of the Florida Straits that he could help split Castro's military. A critical 1977 Agency review of the operation stated that "pressure was exerted on CIA by Higher Authority." Another postmortem speculated that the journalist may have been double-dealing, reporting everything back to Castro.[28]

Shackley was alarmed that AMTRUNK was in fact a dangle-and-deception ploy run by Cuban intelligence. FitzGerald and Helms soon agreed, though they had no choice but to continue down the presidentially prescribed dead-end path. Ultimately, Shackley was vindicated: in 1977 an Agency report concluded that "the activity appears to have been insecure and doomed to failure from its inception." It was yet another of the many ingenious DGI double-agent operations run against the Agency, no doubt also masterminded by Fidel himself.[29]

In Miami, Shackley was doing his share to keep the coup cauldron simmering. He befriended Al Burt, the Latin America editor of the *Miami Herald,* providing him access to an important new Cuban defector. Rolando Santana was a captain in Cuban intelligence, a survivor of the 1956 landing when Fidel launched his guerrilla war, and a veteran of the insurgency that ensued. In mid-October 1963 Burt published a series of exclusive interviews. Santana, then sequestered in "a Miami hideaway," was quoted as saying what sounded like the text of a script written by Des FitzGerald: "There are men inside Cuba just waiting for a chance" to move against the regime. "They are in the rebel army and the government. When they find something solid to rally around, they will fight."[30]

Meanwhile, the JMWAVE navy was operating more aggressively in Cuban and surrounding waters. Sabotage and commando raids and infiltrations were stepped up. On-island casualties, civilian and militia, were rising. The Cuban economy was in shambles. Through October Castro grew progressively more incensed, fearing some unknown assassin might get close enough to him to succeed.

That was exactly what Nestor Sanchez hoped to achieve when he sat down with Cubela again, this time in Paris, on October 5. They met in the fashionable home of John Neville "Red" Stent, a senior Paris-based CIA officer. Stent lived in the affluent Saint-Cloud suburb, not far from Versailles. Cubela had been there before and may have been invited up into the attic to appreciate Stent's impressive collection of miniature lead soldiers. Cubela was generally more relaxed than he had been in Porto Alegre and was in what Sanchez described hopefully as a "confessional" mood. But, vacillating as usual, the Cuban was also on edge and recalcitrant.[31]

"Uninterested in unimportant tasks," as Sanchez put it in his cable to FitzGerald, Cubela still refused to use the secret writing skills he had been taught. Sanchez had planned to provide him with OWVL communications equipment instead, but concluded Cubela would refuse that as well. The critically important question of how this star agent would communicate securely with the Agency once back in Cuba organizing a coup was never resolved. It was probably a main reason why, in the contingency plans, FitzGerald included provisions for the "special teams" that would infiltrate Cuba and handle communications between coup leaders and the Agency.

Cubela had reached a crossroads. He had been prattling for over a year about wanting to fulfill a historic mission by killing Castro. Now he was pressed to commit to a specific plan. In response, he also upped the ante, insisting on assurances that he was being taken seriously in Washington, and by the topmost administration officials. Sanchez cabled Des that Cubela was "highly depressed," believing his value and ability to alter the course of Cuban history were not sufficiently appreciated. Sanchez reassured him; "his case was receiving consideration at the highest levels." He meant Bobby Kennedy, and by extension the president, and may actually have told Cubela exactly that.

When I met with Sanchez in the summer of 2008 to discuss Cubela, he told me that he had conferred privately in 1963 with the attorney general to discuss Cuban operations. Years after his retirement from CIA and a tour during the Reagan presidency as the Pentagon's top civilian Latin America official, Sanchez was reluctant to discuss matters he considered still classified. He admitted, though, that he had met with Bobby Kennedy at Hickory Hill, the Kennedy mansion near CIA headquarters. Sanchez said he went there "on a few occasions." He would not tell me how often or provide details of the discussions.[32]

They are not difficult to reconstruct, however. Cubela was Sanchez's principal, nearly exclusive, responsibility, and the attorney general was surely informed of progress in the operation during those visits. Their talks were not likely to have been confined to the Cubela case; FitzGerald probably instructed Sanchez to discuss progress in other areas of the far-flung Cuba program. Sanchez, the trusted intermediary in some of the most sensitive CIA operations ever undertaken, did volunteer during our meeting that "Des FitzGerald and Bobby really wanted to terminate the Castro regime."

A wrap-up cable to Des after the October 5 meeting in Paris came as close as anything Sanchez ever put on the record admitting that he was engaged in an assassination conspiracy. He wrote that as he and Cubela were leaving Stent's home, Cubela expressed again his wish to return to Cuba "to undertake the big job." Despite all the red flags and doubts about Cubela's reliability, he became the Kennedy administration's shining hope to decapitate the Castro regime. Caution and common sense were thrown to the Caribbean winds.[33]

Still in Paris, Sanchez met with Tepedino on October 10 and the morning of October 11. The jeweler conveyed Cubela's latest thinking—and new demands—that had coalesced in the days following the meeting at Stent's. The stunning new twist explained in Sanchez's cable to headquarters on the eleventh was that Cubela demanded a meeting with a senior administration official—and not just any official. He "prefers GPFOCUS." That was the tart Agency cryptonym for Robert Kennedy. The attorney general was so involved with SAS operations that there had to be a secure way to refer to him in communications.

Sanchez reported that Cubela wanted Bobby's personal assurances of American support "for any activity he undertakes" against Castro. The evidence is compelling that it was another euphemism for assassination.[34]

When researching his biography of Robert Kennedy, Evan Thomas found that the attorney general received a phone call from FitzGerald on October 11. Des and Bobby spoke frequently about Cuba operations, and it is difficult to imagine they did not discuss Cubela's demand for a meeting in that conversation. Helms was asked during one of his Senate testimonies if Des briefed Bobby about Cubela's demand. The guarded response was: "I would have thought he would have." Sanchez testified that he "assumed" Kennedy had been informed.[35]

It was an "untidy arrangement," Helms told the Church Committee, referring to the attorney general's involvement in the CIA's Cuban activities. He added that the president wanted Bobby "involved in these matters." A seasoned case officer was assigned to work exclusively for Bobby. Charlie Ford, using the alias Rocky Fiscalini, conducted dangerous meetings for the attorney general with international Mafia gangsters presumed to still have useful contacts in Cuba. Ford shared a cubicle office with Sanchez in SAS quarters, but neither ever discussed his work with the other.[36]

Bobby Kennedy maintained off-line relationships with a number of militant Cuban exiles, visiting Miami to encourage them and to hector JMWAVE personnel. "It was a gross violation of security," Helms wrote, "and played hob with operational discipline." But there was no skirting Bobby's interventions. His amateur freelancing in espionage took some strange turns. The penetration agent who had infiltrated Cuba and recruited Ramón Guin to join the AM-TRUNK operation said Bobby had authorized him—unilaterally, it appears—to "offer large sums of money" to any Cuban air force pilot willing to defect with a MiG fighter jet.[37]

When we met in Miami, I asked Cubela why he had demanded a meeting with the attorney general. He said it was because he knew Kennedy "could get me all the material I wanted and needed to overthrow Castro." Bobby's outsize role was no secret in Miami, Havana, or Langley, but Cubela's demand was an unusually provocative one. To consult with the attorney general would be to sit down with the president's alter ego, his most trusted confidant and advisor. It would be nearly the equivalent of a meeting with the chief executive himself. Dean Rusk, the secretary of state, said in an oral history interview that in foreign policy, Bobby "meticulously followed the president's instructions . . . he never freewheeled." Others who worked with the brothers said the same. Cubela was proposing to entangle both Kennedys in a conspiracy that, one way or the other, was intended to result in Fidel Castro's death.[38]

Sanchez lobbied hard for the meeting. From Paris, he cabled FitzGerald that the answer Cubela got "may be crucial point in our relationship." Any reasons given to discourage such a meeting "will certainly not satisfy AMLASH . . . We must be prepared to face the request." Sanchez was a calloused case officer, with a hard edge; he knew he was recommending something extremely unusual and dangerous. Agents, even the best and most trusted ones, are rarely indulged in the way Cubela was demanding.

And the Cuban remained an unknown quantity, as Helms himself admitted in his memoirs. Sanchez acknowledged the "implications, risks, and problems" associated with exposing the Kennedy brothers to what could easily be a Cuban double-agent operation. Still, he recommended that the "highest and profound consideration" be given to Cubela's demand.[39]

Implicitly, he was urging that it be approved that Des consult with Kennedy. Sanchez was convinced that they were at a watershed, that without a meeting between Cubela and the attorney general, the Cuban would bolt and abandon his relationship with the Agency. Sanchez thought, or desperately wanted to believe, that the potential benefits of a meeting outweighed the considerable risks. Like Helms and FitzGerald, he was feeling the weight of Bobby Kennedy's pressures to move the plot along.[40]

AS SANCHEZ CONSULTED with Cubela in Paris, millions of Cubans were suffering the consequences of the worst natural disaster in the island's modern history. Powerful Hurricane Flora first struck on Friday morning, October 4, and then lingered erratically over the eastern provinces for another four and a half days. Hurricane-force winds and unprecedented rains continued uninterrupted. The CIA, in a national intelligence estimate devoted exclusively to the storm, described it as "the worst that ever hit Cuba."[41]

Flora turned demonic loops, whirling stationary for fourteen hours over a single flattened and flooded region. Hurricane experts in Miami had never heard of anything like it. Fidel said that a "tidal wave came, not from the sea, but from the mountains." More than eleven hundred perished in Oriente Province alone, tens of thousands were homeless, and vast croplands were inundated. The entire town of Mayarí, near Fidel's birthplace, was swept away. It was said he nearly drowned trying to ford a surging river near there. Although the Cuban media trumpeted that he was pulled out by a local peasant, concerned about his finely honed image of invulnerability, Fidel never mentioned it.[42]

He directed recovery efforts, bivouacking in the countryside, marshaling scarce resources, and, in his own imperious fashion, consoling the families of victims. The Kennedy administration offered emergency relief through the Red Cross, but relations had been so inflamed that Castro rejected it as a gesture of obscene hypocrisy.

"We are honored by not accepting it," he thundered from a Havana television studio. He issued an angry communiqué: "The enemies of our homeland do not hide their joy . . . the pain of the humble gives joy to the people's malicious enemies."[43]

He was outraged because there had been no pause in what he considered a CIA reign of terror, even as the millions affected by Flora were still grieving over their dead and struggling to find food and shelter. American malice, he thought, had never been more tauntingly inhumane.

"They are cynics, brazen, shameless liars . . . they took advantage because of the hurricane."

He meant Kennedy and the CIA, and Cuban exile contract agents, and he was not exaggerating. In the tense weeks of the hurricane cleanup, there were coordinated incursions intended to raise tensions on the island and help set the stage for the coup.

The first bloody encounter occurred only a day after Flora had finally veered off to the north, away from the island. CIA commandos infiltrated by sea, killing two civilians when their sabotage mission went awry. In a national broadcast,

Fidel claimed that "of the seven individuals who took part, five have already been captured."[44]

"These have been the activities of the counterrevolutionaries and the CIA after the hurricane," Fidel shouted. Then, grimacing, he pounded the table in the television studio.

"They have been harboring illusions that this is the time. . . . Right away they thought of invading. . . . Go ahead and launch an invasion."[45]

It was another acknowledgment that he was alarmed, knowing he was looming large in American sights. His admirers have often said that throughout his long public career, Fidel was fearless, never blinking or wavering in the face of danger. It is a myth that falsely glorified him. In October and November 1963, he lived in dread of what the Americans were preparing to do.

As the AMLASH conspiracy was advancing, the CIA struck again late on the night of October 21, several hours after the moon had set. The sabotage mission off the far southwestern coast of the island was like so many other incursions, but it ended tragically. Cuban military forces awaited the intruders in ambush. Four exile frogmen were captured as they came ashore. Another six launched from the CIA mother ship onto a second speedboat were fired on by Cuban aircraft and patrol vessels but managed to escape, eventually reaching Panama.[46]

Amid the chaos, Cuban fighter jets shot up a Liberian-flagged freighter carrying bauxite ore from Jamaica that happened to be passing close to the CIA mother ship, which was disguised as a hydrographic research vessel. The incident was a nagging international news event for days. The Kennedy administration denied any knowledge, but Helms had to explain to other senior Washington officials what had gone wrong. Cuban intelligence, he had to admit, penetrated what he called "the reception committee" of Agency assets on the island. One or more had been doubled. The Cubans "laid a trap," he said, for the arriving commandos. The declassified record of that meeting identified the operation as Number 3105, high in the sequence of Kennedy-era commando raids.[47]

The damage done to Agency operations was substantial. Covers were blown, skilled agents were lost, equipment was captured, and sensitive CIA covert methods were laid bare. The two most dependable ships—the *Rex* and the *Leda*—were so compromised by all the press coverage that they had to be taken out of service. And worst of all, the Agency's ability to operate clandestinely on the island was severely compromised. Fidel was encouraged with the progress his special forces had made against the enemy.[48]

He was dealing simultaneously with the hurricane aftermath and the CIA. During those arduous weeks in October, he seemed to be everywhere. While orchestrating every step of the government's response to the storm, he personally commanded the intelligence and security forces that surprised the captured CIA infiltrators and the naval and air elements that attempted to seize or sink the CIA mother ship. He was an inexhaustible presence on Cuban radio and television. Frenetic action and discourse were always his best therapy when under stress. Characteristically, he was also retaliating in kind, lashing out in many directions. It was then that Cuba's first "Africa Corps" was dispatched to Algeria. Raúl spoke to the departing volunteers on October 9, telling them that "a sister country was under attack from reactionary imperialist forces."[49]

Fidel authorized Piñeiro to accelerate armed subversive actions against a number of countries. Operation Flora, a landing on the coast of the Dominican Republic just days after Hurricane Flora, inserted guerrillas fresh from Cuban commando training camps. An embryonic insurgency initiated operations in the rugged northwestern mountains of Argentina with Cuban participants. If it grew, Che Guevara planned to travel to his native country to join it; the Bolivia plan developed much later. The future defector Vladimir Rodríguez Lahera—AMMUG—had several meetings with Piñeiro at DGI headquarters to coordinate a shipment of explosives to Salvadoran communists. One of Che's tomes advocating guerrilla insurrection was recirculating prominently in the official media. "We should not fear violence," he argued; it is "the midwife of new societies."[50]

The most promising target was still Venezuela. A CIA analysis said it was the only country where Cuba was expecting "imminent revolutionary victory." The guerrilla front there received virtual diplomatic recognition when it opened an official liaison office in Havana. Cuban media devoted inordinate attention to the guerrillas, charging that Kennedy was planning to intervene with military force. Then, on November 1, a Cuban vessel seconded to the DGI delivered three tons of weapons and ammunition to a remote beach on the Venezuelan coast. Submachine guns, mortars, recoilless rifles, and demolition supplies were buried in a trench in the sand. A local fisherman discovered the cache in Falcón State on November 1, before the guerrillas could get to it. Now the Betancourt government, which Fidel had endeavored so aggressively to overthrow, had the upper hand.[51]

CIA took credit as well. In Senate testimony Helms suggested that the fisherman who discovered the arms cache was a handy foil. The success against the DGI was really the result of painstaking intelligence work, a joint effort by the Agency and Venezuelan security working with a penetration agent in the guerrilla movement. Two Cuban defectors told me that the same CIA agent—Francisco Carballo Pacheco, El Espia Pacheco—who worked in Cuban army mapmaking and later compromised the May 1967 guerrilla landing at Machurucuto had betrayed this incursion as well.

The next step was to prove that the arms originated in Cuba. Writing for the *Daily Summary*, CIA analysts told how Cuban intelligence had endeavored to grind off all serial numbers and identifying inscriptions from the weapons. Using special acids, Agency technicians were able, nonetheless, to "raise the numbers and shields" of three of them. The identifiers corresponded to weapons known to have been delivered to Cuba from Belgium in 1959 and 1960. The analysts concluded there was "definite proof" the weapons "came from Cuba."[52]

In his memoirs, Helms tells of taking one of the captured submachine guns to show Robert Kennedy. "Half an hour later we were in the White House, answering the President's questions." When they were done, Helms slipped the weapon into the canvas travel bag in which he had brought it in. He recalled that "as the president turned to shake hands, I said, 'I am sure glad the Secret Service didn't catch us bringing this gun in here.' The President's expression brightened. He grinned, shook his head and said, 'Yes, it gives me a feeling of confidence.'" Three days later Kennedy traveled in the fatal motorcade in the streets of Dallas.[53]

IT TOOK MANY YEARS, but the truth about Rolando Cubela's true loyalties gradually emerged. Evidence of his duplicity had been accumulating since the mid-1960s, and now, with what I have learned from a knowledgeable Cuban defector and a long-ignored CIA document, it can be stated unequivocally that he conspired with Fidel.

The first hint came from Castro himself. On May 2, 1966, he met with *New York Times* correspondent Herbert Matthews, whose archived notes of their conversation were not released for public use until a number of years later. Matthews quoted Fidel this way: "Cubela was a weak, neurotic type that they nursed along, but he was not getting the jobs he thought he deserved and he was in bad company."[54]

Matthews spoke to interior Minister Ramiro Valdés the next day. Cubela, the latter said, "had been reduced to supervisor of medical education in a big Havana hospital, and his friends realized his discontent and neurotic nature, so he was, in a sense being watched."[55]

Valdés spoke definitively about Cubela nineteen years later, on June 5, 1985, in a meeting with another visiting journalist. "Yes, we had information about his trip abroad, that he had contacts with the CIA, that he had a mission to assassinate Fidel. We knew this." The admission, stored at the University of Miami's Cuban Heritage Collection, seems to have gone unnoticed by earlier researchers.[56]

But *how* did Valdes know of the assassination plan, and when was it compromised? Was there an informant close to Cubela? Could the crafty jeweler Tepedino have been a double agent? Had Cubela himself been reporting to Cuban intelligence, perhaps from the first meeting with a CIA officer in Mexico City? Weatherby was asked to comment on that possibility by the Church committee. He said: "It is always possible they suspected him, or knew of it . . . but this does not make him a double agent." Perhaps then, Cubela just talked too much, spent too freely, vacationed too lavishly, made himself conspicuous, and came under DGI surveillance.

In May 1997, Ricardo Alarcón, the long-serving president of the rubber-stamp Cuban legislative body, the National Assembly, was the first authoritative source to suggest the answer. Alarcón was close to Cubela in 1960 when they served together in the top two positions in the University of Havana student federation. Author Richard Mahoney asked him about Cubela during a Havana interview. He said, "Cubela may have been a Castro plant."[57]

It was in the spring of 2011 when I was finally convinced that Alarcon had been right. It was then that I met Miguel Mir, another DGI defector living in the United States. He had joined the DGI in 1973 at the age of sixteen, later serving at different times on the personal security squads of Fidel, Raúl, and Valdés. He had worked his way up into those absolutely trusted positions, putting him in daily proximity to the top leadership. From 1986 until 1992, Mir was a principal bodyguard and security officer for Fidel.

It was during the first year of that assignment, as a DGI lieutenant, that Mir also served as chief curator for sensitive military and security archives. His title was Military Historian for Fidel Castro's Personal Security. Mir told me that in that position, he was custodian of the regime's records of historical memorabilia related exclusively to the commander in chief. They were kept in a secret vault at a military facility near Havana.

He told me, "I read documents there about Rolando Cubela, stating that he was a double agent." They dated from the 1961 to 1963 period. There were thousands of photos and records about Fidel. The archive, created by Castro's aide and one-time paramour Celia Sánchez, memorialized him. "It was a record of all the attempts against his life," Mir told me. "That's why these were kept and not destroyed."

I have no reason to doubt what Mir shared with me about this and other sensitive intelligence matters. What he saw in the archives indicates that Cubela was dangled in March 1961 in Mexico City and that he went on to report everything that took place in his meetings with CIA officers to Fidel and the DGI.

Even more recently I discovered yet more convincing evidence of Cubela's double game. Carlos Tepedino admitted during an aggressive CIA polygraph examination in August 1965 that Cubela "had strong connections with Cuban intelligence and was probably cooperating with them in various ways." He "had daily contacts with them . . . worked with them closely . . . knew what was going on in intelligence circles." Even worse, Tepedino said that Cubela had told "everyone" about his CIA relationships; "everyone knew." And, as Hal Swenson suspected, Tepedino admitted that Cubela had never tried to organize "a conspiracy to overthrow Castro and had no plan or followers who would work with him to achieve that." Tepedino said that "a group as such was nonexistent." AMLASH had been toying with his CIA handlers all along.[58]

Results of the interrogation were shared with the Church committee and some of its contents vaguely summarized in the committee's final report in April 1976. But Tepedino's startling admissions attracted no further attention. Until now they have not been cited as a smoking gun proving Cubela's duplicity and collaboration with Cuban intelligence, and thus with Fidel himself. The nine-page polygraph report was not declassified until 1998, and it was then filed away at the National Archives amid approximately a half million pages of CIA records relating to the Kennedy assassination. It was effectively lost until coming to my attention in October 2011.[59]

But why did the CIA officers familiar with the case insist until their deaths that Cubela had been a reliable secret agent even after the results of Tepedino's polygraph exam were written up in September 1965? A copy of that report is known to have been shared with headquarters Cuba operations officers. Yet Helms, Halpern, and Sanchez ignored it—or were never informed. They were not queried about it during testimonies before the Church committee, nor were Swenson, Shackley, Weatherby, and other CIA officers. The polygraph results were not mentioned in the 1967 inspector general's report on assassination plots.

An intentional cover-up? Quite possibly the information was too incriminating, too embarrassing for those involved. If it were known conclusively outside of CIA that Cubela had worked with the DGI all along, haunting concerns about possible Cuban government involvement in Kennedy's death inevitably would have been raised. In any event, it appears that Tepedino's reluctant confessions were filed away in 1965 with the hope that they would never have to be explained.

TEN

GREAT MINDS

DES FITZGERALD LONGED TO PLAY A DASHING ROLE IN THE CLOAK-and-dagger world he loved, but he was too senior an executive to go into the streets doing case officer work. It was Cubela who provided him just such an opportunity and the chance to perform as leading man in one of the most ill-advised capers in CIA history. Des decided to go to Paris and present himself to Cubela as Bobby Kennedy's personal emissary.

He wanted to take the Cuban's measure, confirm what he had been hearing from Sanchez. Smoldering curiosity compelled him, and in no small measure so did vanity and hubris. Bill Hood, coauthor of Helms's autobiography and a veteran of CIA and the OSS, told me that Des "was impetuous and so self-confident that he had to assess Cubela personally. He typically thought he knew best, and was willing to take risks to do so."

Ted Shackley, whom Des consulted, urged FitzGerald not to go; it was too hazardous for someone of his stature and visibility. Hal Swenson also was worried. He knew how good Cuban intelligence had become. "Probably I was better informed than anyone." Hal said, "my disapproval of it was very strong. Des FitzGerald knew it, and preferred not to discuss it with me." Des shut out the counterintelligence expert most qualified to warn him of the dangers.[1]

Potentially the most important vote—Bobby Kennedy's—may have tilted the balance. The precarious coup plan hinged on Cubela; he was indispensable and had to be encouraged. So, with an eye more on the political imperatives than the operational risks, Helms approved it. "I agreed that Des go to Paris and meet the Cuban under whatever high-level guise he might contrive."[2]

FitzGerald had a backup plan in the event Cubela refused to confer with anyone other than the attorney general. The CIA was prepared to fly Cubela from an American air base in France directly to one in the United States. No passport or paperwork would be required. "First class treatment and accommodations" would be provided, according to a declassified SAS document. Presumably then Cubela would have been taken somewhere impressive to rendezvous secretly with Bobby Kennedy. It seems improbable that such a contingency plan could have been put on paper without the attorney general's consent.[3]

Strangely enough, there was a precedent, of sorts. Oleg Penkovsky, one of the most valuable penetration agents in the history of western intelligence, provided information about Soviet missile programs and Kremlin political intrigue. He was a colonel in military intelligence but, unlike Cubela, was a fully vetted and trusted spy. He too pressed for a meeting with a top American official, hoping to be feted for his bravery and to have an opportunity to lobby for tougher American policies against the Soviets. Bobby Kennedy did agree to a clandestine meeting. Sadly, however, Penkovsky was arrested in Moscow in October 1962 and executed before one could be arranged.

For his own meeting, FitzGerald planned a show that could have come straight out of a vintage Hollywood movie. He wanted the rendezvous to be held at some splendid location where Cubela and Sanchez would be awaiting his grand entrance. The Paris station was instructed to be sure Cubela observed his arrival so he would be aware of FitzGerald's importance as an august American dignitary. Des wanted to be slowly driven up to the meeting place in a Cadillac limousine, chauffeured by a liveried Agency officer. He ordered that a countersurveillance team be deployed in the neighborhood. And in case he had not considered enough embellishments to sufficiently impress Cubela, he instructed Paris "to make it as impressive as possible."[4]

The station must have offered some useful suggestions, because Sanchez cabled it on October 21 that "great minds think alike . . . present plan is for Dainold (FitzGerald's pseudonym) to meet with AMLASH 29 October" between five and eight in the evening. Des traveled without disguise, using the alias James Clark, and, as Helms remembered, "did not trouble to affect any more high-level credentials than his appearance and manifest self-confidence suggested."[5]

He arrived in Paris that morning. The meeting with Cubela came off as planned, though with improvisations. David Laux, the CIA case officer who chauffeured, was not in uniform and not behind the wheel of a limousine. He drove Des in what he described to me as his "beat-up old Peugeot." Laux said, "I don't recall that we took any special evasive actions or worried about surveillance." Running a little late, they were in a hurry. Des congratulated Laux for maneuvering through the chaotic evening rush-hour traffic as aggressively as he himself would have. "If you ever decide to give up Agency work, you can always get another job as a Paris taxi driver." Laux told me FitzGerald, "as always, was relaxed and bursting with self-confidence."[6]

The meeting was at Red Stent's home. Cubela told me he had no recollection of observing Des's arrival but remembered he was genuinely impressed and satisfied that he had indeed met with a ranking American official close to the attorney general. Many years later he still believed FitzGerald was a blood relative of the Kennedys. Des conveyed Bobby's commitment to the operation convincingly, with élan and in high style. Cubela told me he could not recall if he saw a personal message from Kennedy. Considering the attorney general's reckless interest in the case, Des may well have showed the Cuban a signed letter of encouragement.[7]

The unlikely pair—Fidel's premier double agent and Bobby Kennedy's understudy—sat side by side. Sanchez translated and, back at headquarters two weeks later, prepared a memorandum for the record. It is the only surviving contemporaneous account of what is purported to have occurred. Des told Cubela that the Kennedy administration would support a coup to remove the Castro dictatorship. Ironclad assurances were given: "The United States is prepared to render all necessary assistance to any anti-communist group" that succeeds in "neutralizing the present Cuban leadership." The implication was that a coup would be bloody and Fidel would be killed. In Senate testimony a dozen years later, Sanchez reluctantly conceded that Cubela talked that day about "getting at the leadership first."[8]

The only record from FitzGerald himself comes from interviews in 1967 with the CIA inspector general. Des revealed that Cubela "spoke repeatedly of the need for an assassination weapon." He wanted a high-powered rifle with a telescopic sight or another weapon to kill Castro from a distance. Sanchez added that he also asked for grenades and a smaller, handheld weapon, such as a pellet or poison dart gun. Des insisted, however, that he told Cubela he wanted no part of a murder plan.[9]

Manny Gunn, the obedient doctor instructed to fabricate the assassination weapon, remembered it differently, saying that FitzGerald knew what it was for—"but didn't want to know." In a sworn affidavit, Sam Halpern agreed; the weapon was fabricated "in response to urgings by AMLASH for a means to start the coup by killing Castro."[10]

FitzGerald never had to speak about the operation on the record. Nor did he have a chance to reconcile the contradictions between what he told the inspector general and all that the declassified record has subsequently revealed. The inspector general's report was completed late in May 1967. Des's death two months later during a vigorous game of tennis in blistering heat at his Virginia estate spared him the indignity of having to be grilled under oath about Cubela and whatever understandings he had with the Kennedys. Little of substance from FitzGerald's SAS personal files is known to have survived, and the notes of his and all the other interviews with the inspector general were destroyed on Helms's orders. It was thought at the time that everything about the AMLASH adventure would be buried deep in CIA archives, stored in brown envelopes sealed with black tape to ward off nosy file clerks, never again to see the light of day.[11]

Until his death, Des remained confident that if John Kennedy had not been murdered, together they would have taken Castro down. In March 1964, then in a new position as western hemisphere division chief, FitzGerald traveled to Buenos Aires on a grand tour of the many CIA outposts in his expanded realm. Joseph Burkholder Smith, a young case officer in the Argentine capital, wrote about the visit years later. During a pep talk and briefing session in the station, Des talked about Cuba and JMWAVE.

"If Jack Kennedy had lived," he told them, "I can assure you we would have gotten rid of Castro by last Christmas." Smith pressed him. "What do you mean by 'gotten rid of?' "Just say I mean he wouldn't still be doing business in Havana" was the response. Author Evan Thomas tells a similar story. Des made a friendly wager with a White House official on November 13, two weeks after the Paris meeting with Cubela. He bet $50, against two-to-one odds, that Castro would be gone before the 1964 presidential election. He had that much confidence in his supposedly star penetration agent.[12]

Cubela had done his double job convincingly. In Havana, the case must have been handled with the same care as it was in Langley. Most likely it was Fidel who trapped and turned Cubela in the first place and then managed the operation, as he did so many other doubles cases. It would have been characteristic of him to have Cubela demand a meeting with Bobby Kennedy, probably expecting the request would be denied, as it should have been. When Des substituted at Red Stent's home in Saint-Cloud, Fidel had ultimate proof of how expertly CIA and the attorney general could be manipulated. By then Castro was sure that he had full control of the two-sided operation.

A few other Cuban double agents had been run against CIA before Cubela, but in some ways he was the role model for the many subsequent ones. His vacillations and quirks were partly innate, genuinely reflective of his peculiarities, but they were also dramatic contrivances used to gain operational advantage. In this sense, he was the forebear of the double agent "Robert," previously described, who presented himself as rebellious and eccentric when working with the Agency in the 1980s and of another double who acted out the role of naïf. When Aspillaga's defection exposed them, both were heralded by the Cuban media for their ingenuity. Odd behavior would always be counterintuitive for a true spy or mole, but for the Cubans it has often been key to the genius of their tradecraft.

Aspillaga tells a joke to explain the sporting gamesmanship of their methods. There was an old, cantankerous, and rich Cuban who died. Before his death he met with his executor and described in the minutest detail how he wanted his funeral to be staged. One kind of flower but not another. The music and procession had to be exactly what he prescribed. He designated the attendants and pallbearers, and what they should wear. He provided the eulogy and obsequies. The old man left nothing to chance or to the whims of his heirs. But finally, his executor said to him in exasperation. "But why? Why should you care about all that? You'll be dead." The old man laughed and said simply, *"Para joder."* It translates roughly as "Just to screw around with them."

Cubela was run against the unsuspecting CIA for another two and a half years, luring others into acts of treason and betraying them. Meeting periodically with Sanchez, he continued to lobby unsuccessfully for American help in killing

Cuban leaders, probably because Fidel wanted to know if Lyndon Johnson also wanted him dead. Still known as AMLASH, Cubela worked with Manuel Artime, leader of one of Bobby Kennedy's "autonomous" exile organizations, pretending again to plot Fidel's murder.

In June 1965, two months before the incriminating polygraph interrogation of Tepedino, CIA finally shut down the operation. Then it was Fidel's turn to ratchet up his charade. Cubela and Ramón Guin—AMTRUNK–10—were arrested in Cuba in March 1966 and put on trial. They were condemned to death, but within days Fidel commuted the sentences to prison time. In Cubela's case, it was characterized as an act of magnanimity for a hero of the revolution gone astray. He was never added to Fidel's demonology of "big traitors." Castro tried to explain his leniency in a convoluted speech at the University of Havana, but his words rang false.[13]

Fidel mentioned nothing about Sanchez and Porto Alegre, the meeting with FitzGerald in Saint-Cloud, or any of the Kennedy-era assassination plotting. For another nine years the regime said nothing about those conspiracies. Cubela spent more than a dozen years in Cuban prisons, but always as a trusty. It was reported that he acted as an informant and enjoyed free run of one prison. He served as an inmate doctor, with privileges. His family visited regularly, and he lived well.[14]

The incarceration of an outstanding double agent may seem inexplicable at first. It was necessary, however, to perpetuate the fiction. Releasing him after a conviction for treason would be untenable, seeming to confirm what is now known about his treachery. Castro may have worried that their secret would not be safe if Cubela were freed; he could be tripled by the CIA, as sometimes happens, or talk too loosely. Perhaps the jeweler Tepedino would lure his friend into real opposition. It turned out there was no need for concern, however. Now living abroad, the former AMLASH has never wavered in upholding all the lies of his double life.[15]

FIDEL KNEW THE DETAILS of the Saint-Cloud summit within hours. His carefully laid trap had snapped shut. Now he had a bird in the hand, definitive evidence from the highest level of the government in Washington that the Kennedys and CIA were plotting his death. He knew the initial volley of shots was to be aimed at him.

Restless and energized, he again moved to the offensive. He was righteously enraged and wanted the world and everyone important in the Cuban leadership to know the war with the Americans had reached a dangerous new stage. In a marathon tirade televised on October 30—a day after Des's meeting with Cubela—he excoriated CIA. All of his top security and intelligence advisors, and a phalanx of prominent regime officials, were present in the studio in a show of force and solidarity. He revealed that he was aware of the full range of American perfidies. CIA, he said, carries out "subversion, espionage, coups, and similar villainies" against Cuba.[16]

Seated before TV cameras and a cluster of microphones, Castro alternated between feigned fury and smug satisfaction. He condemned saboteurs, spies, and commandos but all the while was surely thinking mainly of assassins. A tableful of evidence was arrayed in front of him, proving a fresh CIA plot to smuggle arms and explosives into Cuba for use by dissidents. Detonators, ammunition, and hand grenades had been concealed in gallon-size cans of fruit and vegetables and flown into Havana by two Canadians whom Castro claimed were CIA agents.[17]

Cuban media coverage of the show highlighted a colorful can of fruit, *fruta bomba* conserve. Literally that means "bomb fruit," but it is also a standard Cuban euphemism for papaya, which in the argot of the streets has an obscene meaning. The "bomb fruit" was supposedly canned by a delectables firm called Siboney in Miami. But the cans were too heavy with explosives and attracted the attention of Havana airport security. SAS, where all this was concocted, had displayed a delicious sense of humor that even its DGI opposite numbers must have grudgingly admired.[18]

Three days later, on November 2, another media spectacular featured three of the CIA commandos captured in the failed October 21 landing. Fidel did not appear this time, turning the proceedings over to an army *comandante* and three young security officers who conducted a live inquisition of the captives. Faced with the choice of confessing all or standing before an execution squad, they were cooperative, volunteering excruciating details about how the CIA mother ships and infiltrators operated.[19]

One of the elite interrogators, Lieutenant Juan Antonio Rodríguez Menier, later rose through ranks to become DGI Center chief in Budapest, then ultimately had a change of heart. As already revealed, he fled in 1987—Cuba's devastating year of the defectors—and won asylum in the United States, where he remains, living under an assumed identity.[20]

The target audiences for these shows were domestic. Fidel wanted to mobilize and motivate Cuban defenses. The Ministry of Interior battened down security hatches and upgraded its vigilance against all imaginable threats to the leadership. JMWAVE was receiving reports from the island of a severe security crackdown, according to one source, the worst since just before the Bay of Pigs. Leaders were preoccupied by increasing acts of spontaneous sabotage by dissidents and the rising tempo of coastal raids. The armed forces began using newly acquired Soviet helicopters to defend against them. In a late 1963 assessment, CIA analysts wrote, the armed forces had achieved a "higher level of combat capability" than ever.[21]

Military preparations reached unprecedented levels. Less than two weeks after Fidel spoke, Raúl announced the revolution's first military draft. Boys as young as sixteen and men as old as forty-five were subject to three years of compulsory service. In the CIA *Cuba Daily Summary,* analysts detailed an unconfirmed agent report that Fidel had made an emergency trip to the Soviet Union sometime in the middle of November to confer secretly with Khrushchev. At a minimum, the rumor reflected the increased tension and uncertainty on the island.[22]

The military buildup was in response to the American threat. Inductees were needed to strengthen the armed forces and to man the Soviet military equipment that had been flooding in. Deliveries—nine full shiploads of military materiel in 1963—included as many as 700 tanks, 20,000 military vehicles, 700 antiaircraft guns, and more than 100 MiG jet fighters, 41 of them the most advanced model. A capable and modernized military was emerging and the numbers of troops would soon swell to become the second largest force, after Brazil, in Latin America. CIA analysts judged the military leadership to be loyal to the regime. Purges, they wrote, had eliminated "anti-Castro elements." There was little chance of "widespread disaffection" because precautions had been taken "to assure political reliability of the officer corps, even at the expense of military proficiency."[23]

The analysts were right. Had they been consulted about the viability of a military coup led by Rolando Cubela, they would have expressed profound skepticism. But they knew nothing of the agent code-named AMLASH or of FitzGerald's high hopes for him. They could have told Des that Cubela was not one of the three or four top officials in the regime, as was believed in SAS. They knew he held no troop command and was not esteemed by most of his colleagues. The analysts would have thought of him as an unlikely leader of a successor government.[24]

And true enough, Cubela was not pretending to make any progress. More than two weeks after the meeting with FitzGerald in Paris, SAS was still trying to determine if Cubela had enlisted anyone else in a plot. No one had, but he was complaining again. The promised CIA support had not been provided. From New York, Tepedino reported that Cubela was irate because he had not received the equipment that "promised a final solution." He was acting petulantly but also telling CIA exactly what it wanted to hear about the assassination plan. Tepedino said that if Cubela "does not get what he wants, he'll get fed up."[25]

They did not have to worry or wait much longer. Whatever Cubela demanded would be provided. On November 19, JMWAVE was instructed to conceal an arms cache on the Cuban coast, including rifles with telescopic sights, grenades, and pistols. As mentioned, Cubela also wanted a small, light assassination weapon—something he could use against Fidel in close quarters and that would allow him a reasonable chance of making a safe getaway. Manny Gunn went about designing what was surely the most bizarre, and laughable, assassination weapon in the history of modern espionage.[26]

But time was short. Sanchez planned to fly to Paris in days to supply the equipment to the impatient Cubela, who was known to be returning soon to Cuba. The idea was that he could carry the weapon in a pocket and it would arouse no suspicions. Prototypes were still being tested only a day or so before Sanchez's scheduled departure, so whatever was fabricated could not be sent securely to Paris, as Sanchez would have preferred. Gunn struggled through most of a day and night, discarding a number of unworkable models, before finally perfecting one he thought would work.[27]

The weapon was an ordinary-looking Paper Mate pen, but instead of a ballpoint cartridge, it was fitted with a retractable syringe. Cubela would need to purchase a bottle of Black Leaf 40, a common nicotine alkaloid household poison, when he returned to Cuba, and fill the chamber of the pen. The poison could be bought over the counter; it usually was festooned with a black-and-white skull and crossbones warning on the label.[28]

Once the device was loaded, the rest would supposedly be simple. Sanchez said, "You push the button and the needle comes out." Cubela would only have to scratch Castro's skin lightly for a small amount of the poison to be lethal, or so it was thought at CIA. The metal tip was so fine that Fidel might not even feel it. It would be no more noticeable than a scratch on a man's neck from an overly starched collar. Halpern said Cubela "just barely might get away with it."[29]

Sanchez carried the murder weapon from Washington in the breast pocket of his suit. Late in the afternoon of November 22, he and Cubela convened alone in a Paris safe house. By then they had spent many hours together, but they had still developed no real rapport, as usually occurs in case officer–agent relationships. In my meetings with each man decades later, I could not coax either into saying anything pleasant about the other. When I interviewed Sanchez and heard his gruff insistence that Cubela had been a true and reliable asset, I wondered whether he could really have believed it.[30]

Sanchez told Cubela where to find the cache of weapons and grilled him again about who might join him in the conspiracy. Nothing in the available records suggests that either Sanchez or FitzGerald harbored doubts as the plot, they believed, was coming to closure. In his postmortem cable, carefully worded to exclude any mention of the poison pen or its purpose, Sanchez tried to be upbeat. He was encouraged because Cubela's "operational thinking appeared much less foggy than before." Yet no dependable means of secure communications had been established. Most critically, headquarters was told, Cubela was "fully determined to pursue his plans to initiate a coup."[31]

Before Sanchez got around to exhibiting the pen, he told Cubela how FitzGerald had contributed to a speech President Kennedy delivered four days earlier. It was Kennedy's last important foreign policy address and, appropriately, it concerned Latin America. He spoke on November 18 in Miami Beach to a dinner audience that included Latin American media executives, journalists, and a large contingent of Cuban exiles. The *Miami Herald* reported that the president was interrupted three times by applause during the twenty-five-minute speech, each time when he spoke of the ultimate downfall of Fidel Castro.[32]

Kennedy included in his remarks a faintly disguised message intended for Cubela and his putative allies. The language Des claimed to have drafted was meant to assure the plotters of American support. That unusual presidential demarche apparently had been approved after the November 12 policy meeting Kennedy chaired in the Cabinet Room of the White House. Two senior SAS staffers noted for the record that afternoon that "the president will emphasize the importance of increasing internal resistance . . . leading to a coup." And afterward,

SAS was pleased with the results. The speech, Langley believed, had significantly bolstered the coup plotters "to whom the remarks were addressed."[33]

The Miami Beach audience heard blunt talk about Cuba. Castro had "betrayed the original goals of his revolution." He had "led a small band of conspirators who had stripped the Cuban people of their freedom." He "handed over the independence and sovereignty of the Cuban nation to forces beyond the hemisphere." Cuba had become "a victim of foreign imperialism, a weapon to . . . subvert the other American republics." It was the most strident and comprehensive denunciation of Castro and his policies Kennedy ever uttered while in office.

Most provocatively, he promised that when sovereignty was restored, "we will extend the hand of friendship and assistance to a Cuba whose political and economic institutions have been shaped by the will of the people." Referring to Castro's dictatorship, he said that "no Cuban should feel trapped." When we met in Miami, Cubela told me he could not remember anything about the speech. But Sanchez informed headquarters that Cubela had been pleased "to read a copy" and "even more pleased to hear that Mr. Clark"—FitzGerald's alias—had helped to prepare it.[34]

White House sources churned the speech into a major news event. Reporters were told that Kennedy's words were meant as a call for the Cuban people to evict Fidel. The next day, the *Miami Herald* wrote that "Kennedy offered hope to Cuban exiles in Florida . . . that the time is not far distant when their native land will be free again and they can go home." Al Burt, the *Herald* reporter close to Ted Shackley, wrote that Kennedy's words "seemed an appeal to elements in Cuba . . . almost an invitation to the Cuban people to throw out the Castro brothers." The *Dallas Times Herald* reported that Kennedy "all but invited the Cuban people to overthrow Castro and promised them support if they do."

In the same editions on November 19, the Dallas press for the first time carried block-by-block details of the route the president's motorcade would follow three days later. It was then that Lee Harvey Oswald first became aware that Kennedy would pass beneath the windows of the Texas Book Depository where he worked. Oswald probably also read what Kennedy had said in Miami Beach and the Dallas paper's interpretation of it.

It was after dark in Paris when Sanchez finally removed the Paper Mate pen from his jacket pocket. The last of Cubela's many demands was being met. The weapon, however, was not one of Manny Gunn's finer achievements. Sanchez re-

membered disdainfully: "It wasn't that good." Cubela agreed as soon as Sanchez
began to explain how to use it. "He showed it to me; I didn't accept it." Neither
man remembers exactly what became of the pen. Cubela told me he was sure he
did not keep it and thus contradicted Cuban government accounts that, after the
meeting, he tossed it into the Seine.[35]

Cubela remembered that the rendezvous "ended abruptly with a phone call."
FitzGerald was on the line. His voice was different, emotion stifling his standard
bullish grandiosity. He told Sanchez that the president had just been shot in
Dallas.[36]

Des had heard the breaking news while hosting a luncheon for a foreign diplomat at the City Tavern, a historic club in the Georgetown neighborhood of
Washington. He was always a gregarious host, and Cuba was his obsession, so it
is difficult to imagine that Castro was not a staple of the table talk that afternoon.
The gathering dissolved immediately, the Agency men rushing back across the
Potomac to headquarters, about fifteen minutes away. They would need to get
cables out to field stations, though they had no idea yet what they would write.

The Paris meeting also broke up immediately. Sanchez said Cubela was vis-
ibly moved by the news from Dallas. As they were going out into the Parisian
night, the Cuban asked him, "Why do such things happen to good people?" It may
have been a sincere reaction, but knowing now of the man's duplicity and schem-
ing, it is difficult to believe he did not share Castro's loathing of Kennedy. Most
likely the remark was another example of his finely honed performance skills.[37]

Another reaction was hauntingly prescient. Not long after, when reports of
Oswald's arrest first were aired by the news media and nothing was known about
him, Sam Halpern commented to an SAS colleague, "I sure hope the guy was not
involved in Cuba in some way."

Fidel was at his Varadero beach house when he heard that Kennedy had been
shot. He too was hosting a lunch for a distinguished foreign visitor. Jean Daniel,
the lead correspondent of the progressive Parisian weekly *L'Express* and one of the
most distinguished members of the French press corps, had been visiting the island since late October. He and Castro had already spent about two days together.

Daniel remembered there were about a dozen people—he and his wife,
Michelle, Fidel, and nine or ten other Cubans—all sitting around a casual table
when the phone rang. Cuba's figurehead president was calling from Havana with
the news. It was still preliminary, arriving very soon after the first bulletins about

the gunfire in Texas filled American airwaves. The others heard Fidel say, "*¿Como? ¿Un atentado?*" "What? An assassination attempt?"[38]

Daniel and his wife remembered Castro seeming to be genuinely shocked. She recalled that he almost immediately wanted to know who the American vice president was, as if he were already convinced that Kennedy would not survive. Soon it was learned that the president was dead, and Fidel expressed alarm. "They will have to find the assassin quickly, otherwise you watch and see, they will try to blame us."[39]

Why he said that cannot easily be explained. The news media had not yet publicized Oswald's Marxist beliefs, Cuba infatuations, and trip to Mexico City. Castro may have thought he was vulnerable because of all his angry rhetoric directed at Kennedy, in particular the threatening interview with Daniel Harker eleven weeks earlier. Oswald's threat to kill Kennedy as he was departing the Cuban consulate in Mexico must also have been on Fidel's mind. But, assuming what Aspillaga told me about Fidel's foreknowledge of the assassination is correct, much more was known in Havana than has ever been admitted.

INTELLIGENCE AND LAW ENFORCEMENT officers everywhere know to be skeptical of coincidences. Most of them, of course, are actual happenstance, odd convergences. Yet a coming together that appears innocent enough may have been devised with ulterior motives. Fidel arranged the Varadero luncheon with care and with the expectation that Jean Daniel would write one or more widely circulated articles.

Two soon appeared in the *New Republic,* an important New York weekly. The first, an eyewitness account, was entitled "When Castro Heard the News." Because it was written by a European intellectual of unimpeachable reputation, Fidel would never be asked to explain where he was when Kennedy was killed. There would be no speculation that he might have been at DGI headquarters with Redbeard Piñeiro or in a war room at Raúl's defense ministry. Whether he contrived it or not, the Varadero luncheon provided Fidel with an airtight alibi. "It was one of those incredible historical coincidences," he told an interviewer in 1984.[40]

Daniel's visit proved even more fortuitous for Fidel because of another coincidence. On the day Kennedy was killed, the Frenchman was acting as the president's unofficial emissary to explore with Castro possibilities for improving relations.

Kennedy had never entrusted anyone else with such a mission. Nothing would have come of it because the chasms dividing the two countries were unbridgeable. All the same, the talks, which ranged over two days as Daniel conferred with Castro, first in Havana and then Varadero, provided Fidel with another seemingly perfect alibi that is still widely believed today. Soon after Kennedy's death, Fidel, the Cuban media, and the DGI's intelligence machine began to promote the legend that, with Daniel's help, progress had been made toward a historic American-Cuban reconciliation.

Daniel had met with Kennedy in the Oval Office on October 24. The president was loquacious and charming, introducing his visitor to the First Lady and then chatting amiably about French politics. He got to the point quickly: "I'd like to talk to you about Cuba."

He knew Daniel would be traveling there intending to interview Castro, and there were things he wanted Fidel to know. Kennedy made clear that he hoped he and Daniel could consult again in Washington to hear Castro's responses. "Our conversation will be much more interesting when you return." This type of back-channel communication was a typical problem-solving technique for Kennedy. His brother may have told him that FitzGerald would be meeting with Cubela a few days later; perhaps he wanted to explore a diplomatic option before it was too late.[41]

He hoped the clever and observant Frenchman would provide him insights and explanations, clues to the character, motives, and psychology of the leader he considered more intriguing than any other on the world stage. Daniel told me when we met forty-seven years later that he thought Kennedy had two principal reasons for enlisting him as a messenger. He believed the president had come to doubt the aggressive policies he had pursued toward Cuba and "was seeking a way out." Further, Kennedy was puzzled by Castro. The curiosity was mutual. Daniel said, "Castro and Kennedy had a hunger about knowing the other. They were fascinated with each other."[42]

The démarche for Fidel's ears only was kept secret in Washington. Kennedy knew that if word of it leaked, his Republican opponents would use it against him to great advantage. They would charge that he was going soft on his nemesis Castro. Kennedy's friend James Reston of the *New York Times* had written that, with respect to Castro, "the natural instincts of the nation are against the president. Cuba is too close." Sensitive to the political risks, Kennedy kept even his closest advisors in the dark. Neither the White House press secretary nor national security advisor knew of the meeting until after the president's death.[43]

Kennedy had authorized other tentative and unofficial contacts with Castro. Only one bore fruit. During a dozen meetings with Fidel, James Donovan, a garrulous New York lawyer, arranged in December 1962 for the release of the Cuban exile prisoners captured at the Bay of Pigs. At around the same time he also negotiated the repatriation of three CIA officers imprisoned after being caught red-handed installing listening devises in Havana in 1960. With these negotiations complete, Donovan reported that Fidel wanted to engage in a dialogue to reduce tensions; he was anxious to win relief from the intensifying American campaigns against him.[44]

Through most of 1963 Castro signaled that supposed interest in a variety of ways. The wife of a former Dutch ambassador in Havana contacted CIA. She claimed that Fidel was "desperate for a rapprochement because of the economic chaos in Cuba." Richard Helms compiled a list of a half dozen agent reports all suggesting Cuban interest in a dialogue. One said that Castro was indicating that he wanted better relations because of pressure from Soviet leader Khrushchev. But he was only adopting a conciliatory pose, the source said, "for the time being." Other approaches were made through Lisa Howard, an American journalist whom Donovan introduced to Castro, and William Attwood, accredited as an American ambassador to the United Nations. None of these straws in the wind brought either negotiations or the pause in aggression that Fidel desired.[45]

Daniel's first meeting with Castro had been on the night of November 20 in Havana. "I had practically given up hope," he wrote, "when on the evening of what I thought was to be my departure date, Fidel came to my hotel." The usually nocturnal Castro arrived at the Havana Libre—previously the Havana Hilton—at the busy corner of L and 23 Streets in the old Vedado neighborhood two hours before midnight. Knowing of assassination plotting, his personal security was elaborate. Eight to twelve armed and ready men traveled with him wherever he went. Among his guards was one who prepared all his meals and always served him, even in restaurants.[46]

Castro and Daniel talked in the Frenchman's cramped room for six hours. They faced each other across a small table and later sitting together on the bed. At times Fidel perched on the arm of a chair, his hands in constant motion. Knowing that Cubela was on his way to the rendezvous with Sanchez in Paris where he likely would receive a murder weapon, he must have wondered if Daniel was bringing a belligerent ultimatum from the White House. What hypocrisy would Kennedy be peddling now?

At first, the message was conciliatory. Daniel said Kennedy wanted Fidel to know that he had sympathized with his original revolutionary objectives and deplored the Batista dictatorship. The corrupt, Mafia-connected ruler had embodied all the worst historical sins the United States had committed in its dealings with Latin America. Kennedy asked Daniel to convey his belief that no other country had suffered as much humiliation and exploitation as pre-Castro Cuba. It was an adroit introduction that played well to Castro's ego and his interpretation of history.[47]

As Daniel remembered when we met in New York, Kennedy had asked him to convey two important points. He wanted to assure Castro that "I don't care about communism. I have good relations with Tito in Yugoslavia and with Sékou Touré in Guinea. . . . I have only one enemy. It is communism in the Soviet Union and their allies." Daniel remembered Kennedy adding that "I am indifferent to Castro being a communist." The president could deal with Castro if he was independent of Moscow and stopped intervening in Latin America. He had made the same points in his Miami Beach speech. Those were the only problems, he said. "As long as this is true, nothing is possible. Without it, everything is possible."[48]

Kennedy mainly had Tito in mind. The Yugoslav leader had broken with the Soviet Union in 1948, declaring himself an independent Marxist. Later he was a founder of the nonaligned bloc of nations and maintained cordial relations with both Washington and Moscow. Kennedy reminded Daniel during their Oval Office meeting that he had greeted Tito just three days earlier, "right here," on the South Lawn of the White House. "And our discussions were most positive."

Could Castro somehow be induced into becoming the Caribbean Tito? The possibility had been on Kennedy's mind for more than a year. In July 1962 he had mused with Herbert Matthews about how Castro might "turn Tito." The journalist recalled that Kennedy was attracted to the idea and wanted to know what "we could use as bait." The nonaligned Marxist Touré, the president of Guinea, a small country on the west coast of Africa, was another example of what Kennedy had in mind.[49]

No one who really understood Fidel believed, however, that he could ever "turn Tito." Kennedy's top Latin America advisor, Assistant Secretary of State

Edwin Martin, a shrewd policy bureaucrat with a deep understanding of Castro, had warned a few months earlier that there was no chance Fidel would ever change his stripes. He is "a true revolutionary," Martin told a high-level policy group; there is "no possibility" that he would ever defect from the Soviet fold. And even if he were to move closer to the United States, it would be for tactical and fleeting reasons. "He would not stay bought." The implication was that Castro could not be trusted. He would renege on any deal in which he benefited from American concessions. Furthermore, according to Martin, how could the United States replace the Soviet Union as Cuba's economic benefactor? The annual tab amounted to about $5 billion.[50]

The intelligence community was of a similar mind. A June 1963 national intelligence estimate acknowledged "fragmentary indications of an interest" by Fidel in better relations, but only as one of numerous alternatives he was considering. He was motivated, the analysts wrote, by the hope of reducing the danger of US intervention and to gain time to consolidate the regime. Those responsible for the estimate had scant knowledge of the CIA covert war but were correct in attributing Castro's interest in dialogue to his fear of the quickening pace of American aggression.[51]

As the late-night hours at the Havana Libre melted away, it became clear that Edwin Martin and the analysts were right. Kennedy's overture through Daniel had fallen on deaf ears. Fidel would not become another Tito or Touré. He would not stop supporting and encouraging Latin American guerrillas and revolutionaries. Just a few weeks earlier he had told Matthews, the *New York Times* reporter, "[O]f course we do subversion, the training of guerrillas, propaganda! Why not? This is exactly what you are doing to us."[52]

Castro would never forswear Marxist beliefs or the alliance with Moscow. He snapped at Daniel, "I don't want to discuss our ties with the Soviet Union. I find this indecent." The revolution and its ideology were irreversible. Fidel's hatred of the United States was implacable. He told Daniel that he and Cuba must be "accepted as we are." That was his bottom line, and it never changed during all his years in power.[53]

By that dictum, any Cuban concessions to improve relations would be tactical, on the margins. Havana would never feel bound to constrain its revolutionary foreign policies or venomous anti-American propaganda. The revolution was irreversible. It would continue to support like-minded revolutionaries in Latin

America and anywhere else. Not a penny would be paid in compensation for the confiscated American properties in Cuba. The large Soviet military force still on the island would stay. Even if relations improved, Cuban intelligence would continue to target Washington policy makers and Miami exiles and to run aggressive active measures campaigns against American interests.

Fidel's intransigence about his core beliefs had been manifest many times before. In an anniversary speech on July 26 he shouted to a massive crowd in Revolutionary Plaza, "What do they want? For us to make some ideological concessions? We will not . . . they will have to negotiate with the Cuban Marxist-Leninist government." British novelist Graham Greene, author of *Our Man in Havana,* a black comedy about the foibles of intelligence operatives, was there that day. He was amazed with Fidel's ability simultaneously to entertain and to indoctrinate the masses. When Castro mentioned the Bay of Pigs, Greene wrote, a young man "went down on fours in front of me to make pig noises."[54]

Anti-imperialist rancor crowned the strategic position Fidel hewed to for the rest of his life. Twenty-three years later, Kennedy's Boswell, historian and White House aide Arthur Schlesinger, visited Cuba and spoke with Carlos Rafael Rodríguez, then the third most influential figure in the regime. Rodríguez told him, "[W]e want normal relations with the United States, but normal doesn't necessarily mean friendly . . . we would like coexistence on the basis of mutual respect." It was another rendition of Fidel's "accept us as we are."[55]

Over the years, Castro rejected earnest petitions from at least four subsequent American presidents. It was always for the same reasons. Anti-Yankee animosities dominated Fidel's worldview. He had always sought grandeur on the world stage, fame, power, and glory as a leader of Latin American and third-world revolutionary causes. His vision reflected a warrior's hubris, the desire to emulate the conquerors and heroes he had revered since childhood: Alexander the Great, Julius Caesar, and Napoleon. As Fidel had said in a speech in January 1963, "Mr. Kennedy, there is much blood between us."[56]

Perpetual confrontation with the United States was the legitimizing prerequisite for his titanic ambitions. Castro knew he could never be a transcendental figure on the world stage if he was perceived as shackled to the United States. Protracted David-and-Goliath conflict with the American superpower would be inevitable until some future president might just accept him on his own terms.

FIDEL WOULD HAVE TALKED all through the night at the Havana Libre, but Jean Daniel was exhausted. When they adjourned it was with the understanding that Fidel would be back after dawn to take the Daniels to Varadero. The next morning, at the wheel of a jeep, Castro drove eastward about seventy-five miles along Cuba's north coast to the beach house. Security was heavy. The defector Rodríguez Menier says that in those days, Castro was always accompanied on road trips by a truck bristling with communications gear and another carrying a 35 mm cannon to protect against possible air attack.[57]

The conversations about Kennedy continued through the rest of that day and the next. With Fidel's rejection of Kennedy's Tito proposal, the Frenchman's mission was essentially complete. In the last few days of his life, Kennedy remained at the same impasse with Castro as before. There was to be no exit from their lethal conflict. And there probably would not have been any meeting of the minds if Kennedy had been elected to a second term in 1964. Neither man had the slightest intention of compromising on issues of fundamental importance.

Yet a myth about Castro's and Kennedy's maneuverings with each other in the fall of 1963 has persisted. Respected historians and analysts have argued that before the assassination in Dallas, the two leaders were close to reconciling. Some even seem to have concluded that rapprochement would have been nearly inevitable in a second term. Robert Dallek, a prestigious Kennedy biographer—who makes no claim to being a Cuba or Fidel Castro expert—asks: "Who can doubt that a Cuban-American accommodation might have been an achievement of Kennedy's second four years?"[58]

Similarly, Ted Sorensen, an intimate Kennedy advisor and speechwriter, wrote in 2008 that Kennedy gradually acquired a "grudging respect for Castro" and believed that one day they would have "enjoyed a personal dialogue in which private mutual admiration might well have played a part." He raised the Tito possibility. Sorensen knew Kennedy well, but not Castro, and failed to explain how Fidel could have been persuaded to abandon everything he believed in. Sadly, Sorensen was taken in by decades of Cuban disinformation and wishful thinking. Sam Halpern described the possibility of a Kennedy-Castro rapprochement in 1963 as "sheer, utter nonsense."[59]

The belief in a Kennedy-Castro reconciliation has thrived because Cuban media and intelligence have been masterful and unrelenting. After November 22, 1963, Fidel almost never spoke or wrote about Kennedy without asserting that they were on the verge of a rapprochement. Despite all the evidence to the contrary, he claims that he admired and respected the president. These positions have been pushed by Cuban illegals, influence and penetration agents, and by DGI active measures aimed mainly at American audiences.

In an autobiographical interview a few years ago, Fidel lavished praise on Kennedy, saying his death "touched me and grieved me." Shameless, he told John F. Kennedy Jr. in Havana of his admiration for the president, "how brave he had been" and how relations might have been repaired if he had lived. These themes have cascaded in Castro's rhetoric and through Cuban media and intelligence programs for nearly fifty years. Their objective has been to exonerate Fidel and his intelligence chieftains of any responsibility for Kennedy's death.[60]

But during his conversations with Daniel, CIA assassination plots against him were much on Fidel's mind. For no apparent reason during the late-night session at the Havana Libre, he told the French reporter that he was not the least fearful for his life. Danger was "his natural milieu." If he was murdered, that would only enhance his revolutionary causes and strengthen his allies in Latin America, he said. At another point in their discussions, when he was speaking of Kennedy, Fidel said, "Personally, I consider him responsible for everything."[61]

He volunteered even more cogent language demonstrating his knowledge of the plots against him. He told Daniel, "They have tried everything against us, everything, absolutely everything, but we are still standing." When I met with Daniel in April 2010, I asked him what he thought Fidel had meant by this last comment. "It is very clear," he responded without hesitation. "Fidel wanted me to know that the Americans had tried to assassinate him. Yes, the journalist I was, I knew what he meant."[62]

Daniel was ninety years of age when we talked, although he looked and acted fifteen years younger. He had traveled to New York from Paris to be the keynote speaker at a tribute to his old friend Albert Camus. His memories of his long-ago meetings with Fidel were still vivid.

ELEVEN

CONSPIRACY
OF SILENCE

CIA OFFICERS REMEMBER FEELING AS IF THEY HAD BEEN "KICKED in the belly by a donkey." It was a few hours into the first meeting with Aspillaga in a Virginia safe house in the summer of 1987. One by one, he had exposed the more than four dozen double agents Cuban intelligence had been running for years against an unsuspecting CIA.

Cubela had paved the way for that new generation of doubles and dangles. His successors in the ruses had been paid handsome sums, were showered with awards and gifts, congratulated, and in some cases befriended by their American handlers, all the while doing Fidel's bidding. Clever disinformation was offered up to confuse and distract Agency efforts. Pursuing false leads, CIA officers were sprung into wild goose chases and operational dead ends. Espionage tradecraft and undercover personnel were compromised. The DGI acquired advanced American communications and other sensitive technology, which it shared with the KGB. CIA programs and recruitments that might have paid real dividends were shelved because so many officers and resources were already committed to managing the agents believed to be good. No lives were lost, but CIA pride was badly scarred.

It was reassuring to learn that there had not been a single instance of skimming of operational funds by case officers or any malfeasance. The Cubans would have ballyhooed any such lapses, but all those involved in the operations had performed honorably and professionally. It is a curious commentary on the ethics of intelligence jousting that Fidel and the DGI did not resort to fabricating tales of financial wrongdoings. They respected nearly all of the men and women pitted against them. The Americans had been careless, overconfident, deceived in ways they had thought unimaginable, but none had been dishonest or disloyal.

Until Aspillaga's defection, a ranking CIA officer ruefully remembered, "[W]e lost the espionage war to the Cubans." It was a humbling admission of how poorly the Agency fared against the world-class adversaries whom it had so dangerously underestimated. A period of regrouping and licking of wounds followed as the Americans studied Cuba's often ingenious tradecraft and unexpected audacity. Only then did Fidel's orchestrating role as his country's preeminent spymaster begin to be appreciated.

As he spilled Cuban secrets, Aspillaga's extraordinary value as a newfound ally was validated. The CIA cryptonym assigned to him is a measure of that value. Although it remains classified, the cryptonym was not chosen at random, pulled out of a database by what used to be known in the Agency as cryptic reference officers. What can be revealed is that the code name assigned to him constituted a private, inside-Langley boast of just how highly CIA had scored against Cuban intelligence. A multitude of reports of general interest were issued as the debriefings continued over an extended period. Hundreds of operational leads were developed.

It was learned that the DGI was a formidable and creative foe but not a juggernaut. Tiny told of lapses in tradecraft and fallibilities in its operating culture. When working in Havana, he had learned of deep-cover sources that should have been securely fenced off. Compartmentalization at headquarters had been sloppy. By the best practices, no single officer should have been entrusted with all the doubles cases he monitored and went on to compromise. Security was often lax. Before he had been dispatched to Bratislava, he ought to have come under scrutiny, if not suspicion, for his occasional jokes about defecting. Such comments are like open musings about suicide by a depressed person; they need to be taken seriously.

To this day Aspillaga remains the most valuable Cuban intelligence officer ever to have changed sides. A death sentence may still hang over him, meant to be executed by former colleagues who are among the best judges of the damage he did. As far as I know, no one at Langley ever suspected him of fabricating, exaggerating, or withholding information. His record is unblemished; nearly everything he reported could be confirmed in one fashion or another. Some of it I have been able specifically to verify in interviews with another DGI defector. One of the CIA officers who engaged with Tiny from the start told me, "I never doubted his bona fides." No one else familiar with his reporting did either.

Not surprisingly, though, his two most astonishing revelations—Fidel's Armageddon letter and the orders Aspillaga received on the morning of November 22, 1963—seem to have been greeted skeptically. Tiny told me that his American debriefers thought his father's rooftop story about Fidel's apocalyptic, late-night missive to Khrushchev too bizarre to be believed. It was hearsay; it could not be verified or corroborated. There was no way to evaluate the senior Aspillaga's credibility or to confirm his access to Castro. It seemed preposterous that a leader known for his cool strategic calculations could have advocated nuclear holocaust. In 1987 the account was easy to disregard. A few years later, though, the two Aspillagas were vindicated when Castro himself confirmed that bizarre episode.

Tiny's story about Fidel having advance knowledge that Oswald would shoot at Kennedy in Dallas on its surface appears just as implausible. Yet it must be evaluated with the defector's impeccable reporting record in mind. First, however, it is worth reviewing what he remembered.

He was at work in Jaimanitas early on the morning of President Kennedy's death. As usual, his intercept equipment was directed toward detecting CIA agents and infiltration teams. He had never had any other assignment, and until that morning did not deviate from the standing priority. Around 9:00 or 9:30 A.M. Eastern Time, he received a coded message by radio to walk to the second small structure where he also worked, a hundred yards or so away and use the secure phone there to call his headquarters.

Headquarters ordered him to cease all his tracking of the CIA. Tiny told me, "The *jefatura* wanted me to stop all my CIA work, all of it" and to redirect the antennas "from Langley and Miami toward Texas." Listen to ham radio and other transmissions, he was ordered, and "if anything important occurs," inform us immediately. About four hours later the shots rang out in Dallas. His conclusion in that first telling—and every other time we discussed it—was the same: "They knew Kennedy would be killed . . . Fidel knew."

Tiny never discussed this experience with anyone until after his defection. "I did not even tell my father." He was sure the information would have been too dangerous to share with other Cubans. He feared his knowledge would get back to Fidel, and he would be marked for execution. I have often wondered if a desire to get the Jaimanitas story safely on the public record after so many years was a contributing reason for Tiny's decision to defect. He never told me that, saying rather that he fled after losing faith in Castro and communism and because of his admiration for Alpinista, the CIA officer he had worked against in Havana. But perhaps, like the rooftop stories that reflect so adversely on Castro's character, Tiny also wanted the world to know what he learned the morning Kennedy was shot.

He told me that he is certain he shared his memory during his initial rounds of debriefings, with CIA officers exactly as he did with me. One officer remembers that to be true. But it is not known from unclassified sources what happened next. Two other CIA officers he dealt with told me they have no recollection of such a ground-shaking revelation. Perhaps it was thought to be so incendiary—and suspect—that it was quietly cocooned, not put on paper, recorded, or repeated to anyone outside a small circle at CIA headquarters. Under the circumstances, temporizing may have seemed the best option, the most prudent way to deal with a matter of such historic significance. After all, if it leaked that an otherwise unimpeachable, high-level Cuban intelligence defector had arrived with new information about the Kennedy assassination, a public outcry might have been unavoidable.

Ronald Reagan was in the White House. Cuba was a pariah state for him and many in his administration, the target of muscular policies not seen since the Kennedy years. American and Cuban military personnel had fought each other—for the first and only time—in October 1983 in the small Caribbean country of Grenada. Nineteen American soldiers were killed, as were twenty-four Cubans. Castro was supporting the Marxist guerrillas in El Salvador and the sibling Sandinista regime in Nicaragua. In Washington, there were few more urgent national security priorities in 1987 than these Cuban-inspired revolutionary threats to American interests. Even tentative evidence of a Cuban hand in Kennedy's death could have sparked a clamoring for punitive action. Apparently Tiny's remarkable story was squirreled away. This is the first time it has entered the public record.

WHEN I TOOK THE INITIATIVE through government channels in the summer of 2007 to meet with Tiny, bureaucratic sensitivities—perhaps even all institutional memory of the Jaimanitas story—must have long since faded. My intention, I made clear, was to write about Cuban intelligence and for Aspillaga to be a primary source. There was a precedent; I knew that another author, not connected to CIA, had interviewed him in the 1980s.

No constraints were imposed on me other than the contractual obligation I have—like all former CIA employees—to clear what I write about intelligence matters with the Agency. Except for about a dozen words that I agreed to delete, my treatment here of everything he told me is uncensored. No one in CIA, or anywhere else, has tried in any way to influence or alter this long-overdue accounting of Aspillaga's most sensational revelation.

I had no knowledge of what he would reveal until we sat down together for our first interview. So, I was surprised . . . and skeptical. In all of our meetings I asked him to retell the story, and he did so in good humor, again and again, with no inconsistencies or deviations. I remained dubious, nonetheless, peppering him with variations of these three questions: Was he sure he remembered the incident accurately, especially the time when he received those orders from his headquarters? Why did he assume Fidel himself knew that Kennedy would be shot at? And weren't there alternative explanations for what he remembered?

It is in the marrow of intelligence officers to look for flaws in evidence, to seek corroboration or countervailing information, and to play devil's advocate. My first instinct was to discount the story. I knew how young Tiny was the day Kennedy was killed, and how new he was to intelligence work. Adolescent exuberance or the fog of the more than forty-three years that had passed between November 1963 and August 2007 could have distorted his memory of that morning. His recollection might have evolved, possibly under the influence of other Cuban exiles eager to implicate Castro in the most notorious crime of the twentieth century. Perhaps he had stitched the story together long after his defection. There were so many reasons to be cautious, despite my knowledge of his consistently accurate reporting record.

Obviously, there could be other, more innocent explanations for what he remembered. The orders from his headquarters might have been a perfectly routine requirement. Redbeard Piñeiro could have been reporting to Castro on everything Kennedy was saying about Cuba during his campaign swing through Texas. Fidel knew the provocative speech in Miami Beach a few days earlier had been intended in part to bolster the imaginary coup plotters. Perhaps there would be other veiled messages to Rolando Cubela worth monitoring. Castro was meeting with Jean Daniel and would have been keenly interested in any other demarches Kennedy might be trying to convey.

Tiny and I went over his memory of that long-ago morning time and time again. I hoped he could provide details that might substantiate his story—perhaps the names of others with similar memories or who shared his suspicions. Alternatively, I thought the story might somehow unravel under scrutiny. I listened for errors, contradictions, anything that might prove it wrong. But I heard nothing that enhanced or detracted from his account. At the same time, I was impressed that he did not embellish even as I urged him to provide more details. He was rarely willing to describe anything he did not know firsthand or from trusted colleagues. "I don't like to speculate," he told me. I asked him, for example, if he believed "Fidel had ordered that Kennedy be killed." His response was quick, and I found it reassuring: "I cannot tell you that, but at the very least Castro knew they were going to kill him."

I was curious about Fabian Escalante, a suave and prominent Cuban counterintelligence general who is rumored to have traveled secretly to Dallas on November 22. The authors of one of the few Kennedy assassination conspiracy books that indict Castro and Cuban intelligence quote a source that makes that claim. Others I know have raised the same possibility, even linking Escalante directly to Oswald. I asked Aspillaga if there could have been such connections. "I can't tell you that," he said. "I think you have to be careful with that information. Castro could have sent people to spread disinformation." For emphasis he repeated it: "You have to be careful." The implication was clear. Cuban intelligence is masterful at fomenting rumors that lead to dead ends, as this one did, all meant to embarrass anyone who points to Cuban complicity in Kennedy's death.[1]

Tiny is sure his interpretation of the orders from his headquarters is valid. He did not consider it speculation at all. He based that conclusion on his subsequent experience working in increasingly more responsible positions in intelligence and counterintelligence. He was acquainted with Interior Minister Ramiro Valdés and understood his operating style. He knew that Fidel was involved in every important intelligence issue and therefore, looking back, was confident that the orders he received that fateful morning had originated with Valdés and Castro. He told me, "My principal work, the most important, went directly to Fidel."

Even during that first month of his duty in Jaimanitas, Aspillaga could tell what was routine and what was unprecedented. "The most important thing for Castro was to confront the CIA," he told me repeatedly, and yet, that morning, "they told me to drop all my work on the CIA and point my antennas to Texas. The CIA could enter Cuba and nothing would happen." Never again during his tenure at the intercept station did he receive similar instructions. The requirement to track the CIA was removed for only that one day. Tiny refused to retreat from his judgment: "Castro knew one hundred percent that they were going to shoot at Kennedy." "You don't have any doubt?" I persisted. "No, no, no," he replied.

Gradually, despite considerable reluctance to be drawn into the miasma of assassination conspiracy theories, I decided that Aspillaga's memory of November 22 had to be taken seriously. His ability to recall details and names had proved almost photographic. It did not make sense to discount this one recollection when, as far as I could tell, everything else he reported about Castro and Cuban intelligence had proved to be accurate. His retellings of the Jaimanitas story betrayed no fabrication or exaggeration. He had nothing to gain from convincing me. He has no interest in this book and asked me for nothing in return for sharing his story.

After our first meeting adjourned, I began searching through the few hundred pages of the memoir he had given me earlier in the day. It is an English-language translation of the original he composed in Spanish in 1990. Would the Jaimanitas story also be in those pages? I considered it a critical test, likely a reliable way to rule out the possibility that he had concocted the story sometime long after his arrival in the United States. I scoured the manuscript. It contained essentially the same brief, unadorned account, written sixteen years earlier. In ended this way: "I am absolutely convinced, and have always been, that I was instructed to monitor [ham radio and other transmissions in Texas] before the assassination attempt occurred."

Eventually I was able to locate a copy of the original Spanish-language version of the manuscript from a retired government official. The English translation was accurate. At least I could be confident Aspillaga had not invented it for my benefit.

As I continued to assess the Jaimanitas story, I was impressed that Tiny was always cautious, refusing to accuse Castro of actual involvement in the assassination. He never wavered from the critical distinction between Fidel simply knowing in advance and somehow being involved in what transpired. He did not claim that Fidel wanted Kennedy dead or that he plotted against his nemesis. It was, he said, that "Fidel wanted to know what was going to happen . . . if he [Kennedy] was really going to be killed or not." Tiny did not try to persuade me that Oswald was a DGI asset or even that he remained in contact with Cuban intelligence after leaving Mexico City and settling in Dallas. He always discussed these matters calmly, not in rushed, fevered tones like the denunciations of Castro sometimes heard from militant Cuban exiles.

By the time we sat down together for the third time, a year after our first meetings, and he again recounted the events of November 22, 1963, I had come to believe he was telling the unvarnished truth. I thought—as with his report about the Armageddon letter—that he should be vindicated. For better or worse, his Jaimanitas memory needs finally to be put on the public record.

As I later discovered, other solid evidence seemed to bolster his account. Jack Childs's Operation SOLO report to the FBI, and a second by the British journalist, about Oswald's shouted threat to kill Kennedy seemed to dovetail with Tiny's recollection. I knew his account was not a false corroboration of those earlier ones. He had no knowledge of either of those sources and was not familiar with the book by John Barron that described Childs's conversation in Havana with Fidel. If Aspillaga is right that Castro knew Kennedy would be targeted by a gunman in Dallas on November 22, it seems reasonable to assume that he—Castro—knew it would not be just *any* gunman but Lee Harvey Oswald who would pull the trigger. It would be the same man who had threatened to do just that at the Cuban consulate in Mexico City.

Piñeiro and Valdés would have informed Fidel about Oswald after receiving reports from DGI officers at the consulate. Castro later said there were concerns that Oswald could have been a provocateur, that if he had been granted a visa to go to Cuba, "he would have compromised us." That suspicion alone would have required DGI officers to file a report to Havana, and such a report would have

been of sufficient gravity to reach Fidel. A headquarters file on Oswald had probably already been opened, started when he made contact with Cuban officials in
Los Angeles in 1959 during his service in the Marine Corps. It would have grown
in 1963 with copies of the evidence of his militance he had brought to Mexico and
because of his conspicuous pro-Castro activities in New Orleans.

Yet, speaking on different occasions about the Warren Commission and the
investigations of the House assassinations committee, Fidel said, "We gave them
all the information we had." In fact, his government provided very little information, and nothing of value. The Cubans gave photos and three documents, all
irrelevant to the investigation, to the House committee when members visited
Havana in April 1978. One was a tendentious anonymous essay entitled "Imperialism's Political, Economic, and Military Organizations and Agencies of Crime
such as the CIA." The Cubans provided nothing about Oswald's conversations
with Cuban officials in Mexico City or his earlier activities in three US states that
surely would have been of interest to the DGI.[2]

Meeting with committee staff and three congressmen in his office, Fidel
denied knowing anything about Oswald's threat in Mexico. He claimed that, if
he had, "it would have been our moral duty to inform the United States." Remarkably too, considering his violent and conspiratorial history, his capacity for
cynicism and guile, he told the congressmen, "I was one of the naive people who
thought these things could not happen." It was the performance of a lifetime.
Christopher Dodd of Connecticut, one of the congressmen present, was taken
with the melodrama. He told Castro, "I have been deeply impressed by your statements. I find your logic compelling." His became the majority view; in its final
report, the committee concluded that Castro's government "was not involved" in
the assassination." Committee members did not consider the possibility that Fidel
had foreknowledge and could have warned the White House.[3]

Others were skeptical of the Cuban claims. Robert Blakey, the committee's
staff director who doubled as its chief counsel, along with Richard Billings, another senior investigator, ultimately demurred from some of their colleagues' key
findings. They did not believe Castro. Instead, in a joint memoir published in 1981,
they concluded that Jack Childs's report about Oswald's threat was more credible than Fidel's denial. "We were inclined to believe that Oswald had uttered the
threat." They wrote that "unlike the committee, [they thought that] the Cuban

government withheld important information. . . . We also believed [Castro's regime] kept a careful eye fixed on its own best interests . . . [that] warranted not telling us the truth."[4]

The Cubans had cooperated with the committee's investigation to a point while simultaneously obstructing it. Blakey requested meetings with Piñeiro, Foreign Minister Raúl Roa, and the Mexico City mystery woman Luisa Calderon. They were unavailable: She was supposedly ill; Roa was too busy; and Piñeiro was "out of the country." Rogelio Rodríguez López, identified by Laddie Rodríguez Lahera as the deputy DGI chief in Mexico City who had likely seen or dealt with Oswald, was posted in East Germany. He could not be interviewed either, although a Cuban intelligence official told the committee that Rodríguez claimed to have had no contact with Oswald.[5]

When he met with House investigators, Eusebio Azcue, the consul in Mexico, labored to promote a once-popular but preposterous conspiracy theory: that it was an Oswald imposter he confronted at the consulate. None of the others who dealt with the assassin in Mexico City agreed with him, but Azcue stood his ground. "It is my truth," he claimed. And Fidel vouched for him: "[H]e is a person you can trust." It seemed suspicious too that after the committee staff said they did not need to meet with Cubela, their Cuban Ministry of Interior handlers insisted that they do so. A predictably rehearsed Cubela came out of prison to testify. During those committee sessions, and ever since, the Cubans have peddled disinformation: The CIA sowed lies to cover its own role in the Kennedy assassination; powerful reactionary forces in the United States have conspired to protect "the real assassins."[6]

A member of the Church Committee believed for the rest of his life that it was Castro who perpetrated a cover-up. Robert B. Morgan, a North Carolina Democrat, was one of three members of the committee's assassinations subcommittee that focused on Kennedy's death. He spoke to me during the summer of 2009 from his home in Lillington, in the sandy eastern lowlands of his state. The former senator told me, "I believe John Kennedy's death resulted from his administration's efforts to kill Castro. . . . How could Castro have said what he did at the Brazilian embassy and meant anything innocent? That could not have been a coincidence."

Morgan was eighty-three when we talked. I called him without any introduction or warning and was impressed when he immediately responded to my questions with absolute recall. More than four decades after his subcommittee completed its investigation, he was still unnerved by its findings. He volunteered that "Cubela, and all that, has been an obsession for me ever since those days." Convinced that Cubela was a double agent, Morgan had pushed that view forcefully when Nestor Sanchez testified in 1975, but to no avail. He told me, "I am as strong in my opinion that Castro and Cubela were working together as I am about anything I've ever done."

Before his election to the Senate, Morgan had been a country lawyer, state senator, and attorney general. He prosecuted numerous cases, he told me, including "capital crimes, murders, even before the Supreme Court." Because of that experience, he believed that he would have convicted Fidel of complicity in Kennedy's death—if he could have participated in some imaginary trial. "If I ever had tried it in court, it would have been as strong a circumstantial case as I've ever known." The senator's views were not incorporated into the final report of the Church Committee. He was hospitalized as the subcommittee's findings were being drafted. "I left approval of the document to my staff. But I disagreed with it."

Many other prominent political figures—beginning with President Lyndon Johnson—believed there was a Cuban hand in Kennedy's murder. Former secretary of state Alexander Haig wrote that Johnson "believed until the day he died that Fidel Castro was behind the assassination." Haig, who had worked at the Pentagon as a lieutenant colonel in the office that supported Des FitzGerald's paramilitary operations, observed that Johnson's concerns "were amply justified." There *had* been a cover-up. The full Warren Commission was not told about the American murder plots against Fidel. The reputation of the dead president had to be protected, Haig concluded, against the "terrible suggestion that Castro had acted in self-defense."[7]

Warren Commission scholar Max Holland quotes Johnson. Days before he retired from the Oval Office, the president told a respected newsman, "I'll tell you something [about the assassination] that will rock you. Kennedy was trying to get to Castro, but Castro got to him first." Later, the then-former president, in a conversation with two magazine editors, reiterated his belief that there had been a conspiracy. "I never believed Oswald acted alone, although I can accept that he pulled the trigger." Holland also points out that in the first hours after Robert Kennedy's assassination in Los Angeles in June 1968, Johnson's first instinct was to wonder if Castro was behind that too, inflicting double-barreled revenge against the brothers he knew had plotted against him.[8]

Richard Russell, a senior senator from Georgia who served on the Warren Commission, refused to sign off on its final report if it ruled out a conspiracy involving Cuba. The compromise language that was agreed to stated that, based on "the evidence before it," Oswald had not been involved in a conspiracy. Richard Helms also intermittently betrayed doubts. Testifying before the Warren Commission, he said, "I would assume the case will never be closed." In 1978 he was more expansive when speaking to the House assassinations committee: "[U]ntil Cuban intelligence in Havana is prepared to turn over their files . . . it is going to be extraordinarily difficult to tidy up this case, finally and conclusively."[9]

THE ENTIRE TRUTH ABOUT CUBAN COMPLICITY in Kennedy's death is not likely ever to be known. Ornate tapestries of deception and disinformation woven over decades in Havana have obscured most of the underlying truths. Fidel's obfuscations and fabrications are believed almost everywhere, perhaps nowhere more than in Cuba. The regime's domestic propaganda has been so pervasive that virtually the entire population is convinced that Kennedy was the victim of a right-wing conspiracy.

Whatever relevant records may once have been preserved in Cuba were probably destroyed long ago. Miguel Mir, the DGI defector who served as one of Fidel's elite bodyguards, informed me of a directive requiring the destruction of sensitive documents that could someday compromise the leadership. He said it was most rigorously enforced in the ministries of interior and defense. Files are checked monthly for incriminating material. Mir said there are special burn ovens in each of the two ministries' major departments. Aspillaga agrees that records about Oswald have disappeared but holds out the hope that some remain, forgotten in dusty corners of different government archives.

It is not likely that more than a few Cubans survive who have firsthand knowledge of the murder in Dallas. Piñeiro and José Abrahantes, in late 1963 both in positions to have seen or heard something, are dead. Other than the Castro brothers, former interior minister Ramiro Valdés probably knows more than anyone on the island. As of this writing he is seventy-nine years old, a member of the Communist Party politburo and a vice president of the councils of state and ministers. He is one of the few surviving *historicos,* leaders who trace their revolutionary lineage to July 26, 1953. But he is unlikely ever to betray the sensitive secrets he shares with Fidel, even if his influence wanes in the regime of old rival Raúl Castro.

Today, if Luisa Calderon is still alive, she would be in her late sixties (she was born in March 1943). She probably lives obscurely, in retirement somewhere on the island. As of August 1978, fifteen years after returning home from Mexico City, she was working in Havana for a government radio station as an English language editor. According to the norms of Cuban tradecraft, it is highly unlikely she has been allowed to stray far from home. The defector Rodríguez Menier wrote that when agents are compromised, "they are given work that provides a higher standard of living [but] under no circumstances are they ever allowed to travel abroad." Calderon has not spoken on the record about her experiences in Mexico when Oswald visited or the day of the assassination. Her case remains one of the most tantalizing of all those associated with Oswald.[10]

Vladimir Rodríguez Lahera—AMMUG—heard suspicions expressed at DGI headquarters that Calderon had been recruited by CIA, although he also knew that Piñeiro flatly rejected that possibility. It turned out Redbeard was right; reliable declassified CIA documents from the late 1970s show she was never an Agency asset. She was, however, a loyal deep-cover DGI officer. Did she have dealings with Oswald during his five-day stay in the Mexican capital? Could she have overheard his threat to kill Kennedy? Might they have been in touch after he went to Dallas? Did she have prior knowledge of the assassination, as she seemed to suggest in the recorded phone conversation? These are some of the questions that have never been put to her because the Cuban government has kept her incommunicado for decades.[11]

If a post-Castro government is ever willing to pursue these leads, open any surviving records, and make witnesses available, I believe that Cuban government foreknowledge of John Kennedy's death might be proven beyond a reasonable doubt. Until such a breakthrough, however, the additional evidence that Aspillaga and Laddie Rodríguez Lahera provided, combined with Jack Childs's report, form the basis for reasoned speculation. A case can be built on the answers to two critical questions: What happened in the Cuban consulate to have caused Oswald to threaten Kennedy's life? And how did Fidel and the DGI know that Oswald would take aim at Kennedy when his motorcade passed the Texas Book Depository in Dallas?

I put the first question to a former CIA officer, one of the best, who worked against Cuban intelligence for many years. He was willing to speculate but prefers to remain anonymous. Here, verbatim, is what he told me:

> The Cubans at the embassy must have first thought Oswald was a CIA provocateur. Thus, they would need to do considerable checking: with headquarters, the KGB, fraternal organizations and intelligence services, even radical groups influenced by them but perhaps not under their control. But they would also have given him a good dose of their *"trabajo politico,"* that is, plenty of propaganda and indoctrination in Cuban revolutionary policies and concerns. That would have undoubtedly included denunciations of the CIA and the attempts to kill Castro. They would have encouraged him to go back to Texas and get busy in their behalf, by supporting their positions. But they would *not* have enlisted him in an assassination plot. They however, would have planted the seed in him. The *"trabajo politico"* would have agitated him, given him new, even violent impulses. This I think is where Oswald got the idea for the assassination.

The disturbed young Castro acolyte was an ideal target for such a psychological shakedown. In a 1967 press statement, Oswald's brother Robert said, "since Lee had always been so easily influenced, someone had to put him up to the crime."[12]

It is known that he had tried to impress the Cubans with his devotion to the revolution, activism on behalf of their causes, and eagerness to take up arms for Fidel. He might have boasted of his near miss in the attempt the previous April to murder retired General Walker. Castro's threat against Kennedy in the Daniel Harker interview had been published in the New Orleans *Times Picayune* less than three weeks before Oswald's arrival in Mexico. He had probably read it, understood why Castro had threatened Kennedy, and identified with Fidel's self-portrayal as the innocent victim of savage American imperialism.

Under the circumstances, it would have been logical for Manuel Vega, Rogelio Rodríguez, and Alfredo Mirabal—the three senior DGI agents in Mexico City—one, or all three together, to have stoked Oswald's loathing. The devious, America-hating Azcue may also have participated. Such propaganda and motivational gambits were standard practice for Cuban operatives abroad, whether they were persuading young Latin Americans to take up arms in their countries as guerrillas or coaxing young North Americans into cooperative covert relationships. They were good at what they did, and Oswald would not have needed much encouragement.

So, when he left the consulate and shouted his intent to kill Kennedy, it must have been as the war cry of a fully primed soldier for Fidel. If he could not get a visa to travel to Cuba, Oswald would have to be satisfied doing the revolution's work in Texas, as soon as he had good opportunities, and to do more than merely again hand out "Viva Fidel" leaflets. There is another term—like trabajo politico—that is commonly used by Cuban intelligence. It sums up a favorite practice in their tradecraft, often used in false-flag and deception operations: *dandole cuerda*, or "winding him up."

Arriving in Dallas from Mexico City on the afternoon of October 3, Oswald rented a furnished room in the Oak Cliff section of the city, then moved a week later to another nearby room on North Beckley Street. Marina and their daughter, June—a second daughter, Rachel, was born later that month—were living in a suburb with a friend. Oswald visited them almost every weekend except the one before the assassination; otherwise he kept to himself, living like a monk. At the rooming house, he kept a shortwave radio purchased in the Soviet Union and apparently listened in the evenings to English-language Radio Havana propaganda broadcasts. Vincent Bugliosi, author of an exhaustive 1,500-page study of the assassination, writes that "more likely than not Lee Oswald was hearing Havana's every complaint."[13]

As already shown, they reached a fever pitch in the weeks preceding Kennedy's death. Hurricane Flora began pounding the island a day after Oswald arrived in Texas. On October 11 Cuban press and radio reiterated Fidel's denunciation of American humanitarian relief as "hypocritical." Castro's heated televised appearances later in October and early November, when he excoriated CIA commando and sabotage attacks, received blanket coverage in official Cuban media. Bugliosi quotes a radio broadcast on Thursday, October 24; there is a good chance Oswald heard it in his eight-dollar-a-week rented room.[14]

The CIA acts under the direct orders of the president . . . when they launch a pirate attack against the Cuban coast, and murder a militiaman or a teacher, when they commit acts of sabotage . . . they are acting under the direct orders of the U.S. president.

Listening to these broadcasts and reading *The Worker* and *The Militant*—Marxist publications that idolized Castro and railed against American imperialism—Oswald was steeped in the latest Cuban propaganda. The Warren Commission noted that he told an acquaintance in Dallas, "apparently in all seriousness, that you can tell what they wanted you to do . . . by reading between the lines." *The Militant*, a weekly Trotskyite publication out of New York, published translations of the full texts of Castro's more important speeches. The October 7 issue quoted a speech Fidel delivered on September 28, saying "[W]e cannot consider ourselves at peace with an imperialism that is increasing its efforts to strangle us."[15]

On October 16, Oswald began work at the Texas Book Depository. On November 11, *The Militant* ran a lengthy exposé of the CIA's October commando raids and delivery of the fruta bomba and other canned explosives. As a faithful subscriber, Oswald no doubt read "[e]very decent American should be outraged at the fact that the U.S. government has responded to the hurricane disaster . . . by stepping up sabotage raids." His outrage, always close to the surface, was intensifying.

On November 8, the *Dallas Morning News* had informed its readers that Kennedy would visit the city on November 22. The first hint that the president might speak at the Dallas Trade Mart, and thus possibly pass near the Book Depository, was published on November 15. But it was not until Tuesday, November 19, that, as noted, the local papers printed the exact motorcade route. Covering that story, the *Dallas Times Herald* also reported on Kennedy's speech in Miami Beach the day before. It headlined on its front page: "Kennedy Virtually Invites Cuban Coup." It is safe to assume that by then Oswald had become aware of some of the deadliest American covert programs as well as Kennedy's call for a military uprising to topple Fidel.[16]

Only during the three days before the assassination could Oswald have begun pondering the opportunity that had materialized. The president would pass directly below the windows of the building in which he worked. That Tuesday night, Radio Havana broadcast details of another of the CIA's continuing commando raids on Cuban shores. If Oswald had not truly hated Kennedy before—as Marina later reported—during the last weeks of his life he obviously came to despise the president.[17]

His Mannlicher-Carcano rifle was wrapped in a blanket in the garage of the family home where Marina was staying. He spent the night before the assassination with her, and in the morning carried the rifle to the Book Depository wrapped in paper, describing the package as containing curtain rods.

None of the investigations into Kennedy's death turned up evidence that Oswald remained in contact with Cuban intelligence after he left Mexico City. But assuming that Aspillaga's story is reliable, there is no other reasonable explanation for how the DGI could have known in advance of the assassin's intentions.

A clandestine relationship would not have been difficult in Dallas. Scores of Cubans, most of them newly arrived refugees, were being resettled there. By November 1963, at least 125 had formed a tight-knit émigré community. A Cuban-American woman, prominent and active there, told me she was sure Oswald was involved with some of them and claims to have met him. Another émigré, now in his late eighties, also spoke to me about the Dallas exiles. In 1963 he was a fearless warrior with Comandos L, one of the most aggressive of the anti-Castro exile organizations based in Miami. "We had a group in Dallas," he told me, "there were seven of us; 'Roberto' was the chief." Such firebrands would have been prime targets for DGI penetration operations. Dallas, therefore, would have been similar to Miami and New Orleans, where the much larger Cuban communities seethed with pro- and anti-Castro intrigue.

Oswald could easily have been in touch with someone reporting to the DGI, whether an illegal, a cut-out, or a trusted Cuban agent. But there was an easier way for him to communicate his intentions. He had kept the phone number of Silvia Duran, the Mexican receptionist at the Cuban consulate in Mexico City; her number was inscribed clearly in his address book that was seized among his other belongings after he was apprehended. He may simply have called that number and talked to Duran, who had befriended and probably dated him during his visit the previous September. A call from a Dallas pay booth could have been all that was necessary for the DGI to learn of his plan to fire on the president. "On Friday, I am going to do what I told you I would" is all he would have needed to say.[18]

But it might have been Luisa Calderon who received his call. She is known to have answered Duran's phone when the latter was not at her desk. A cable from the Mexico City station to Langley shows that on December 2, 1963, a male American caller "asked for Silvia Duran who was not there." Calderon spoke to the man instead. Her English was fluent after having lived in Miami with her parents from 1951 until 1960. If in fact she spoke to Oswald shortly before the assassination, it could explain why she told an unidentified caller soon after Kennedy's death that: "I learned of it almost before Kennedy."[19]

However contact was established, Oswald might have gone further. He could have made clear that his vantage point on the motorcade route would likely give him an easy, clean shot. He might have boasted of his Marine Corps credentials as a marksman. Aspillaga's Jaimanitas story suggests that Cuban intelligence took him seriously.

Redbeard Piñeiro, Ramiro Valdés, and Fidel would have been informed promptly of Oswald's intentions. And then, on the morning of November 22, not knowing precisely what Kennedy's timetable in Dallas would be, headquarters would have issued orders to Tiny a few hours before Kennedy's arrival in Dallas from Fort Worth where he had spent the night. The few Cuban officials who knew of Oswald's plan must have wondered whether the strange young American would carry out his threat. It was probably considered unlikely at best but worth monitoring. Aspillaga's assignment was to listen and report back to his superiors the first indications that shots had been fired.

Fidel was with Jean Daniel at the Varadero beach house. Daniel told me that "the night before we spent hours and hours with Fidel," but even though Kennedy's messages for Fidel had been delivered and rejected, the visit was extended for another full day. When I told Aspillaga where Fidel was when he received news of the assassination, his reaction was immediate. He raised his voice: "It was a *medida activa*," an active measure or covert action, elaborate *fidelista* theater. Castro "was in a public place with someone not even Cuban," Tiny said. "It's an indicator." He meant the beach house luncheon had been planned as a cover story, an alibi, because Fidel wanted to be in the presence of distinguished foreign witnesses when he heard the news bulletins from Dallas.

VINCENT BUGLIOSI CORRECTLY POINTS OUT that "the overwhelming majority of Americans, as well as most conspiracy theorists, have discarded the theory that Cuba was behind the assassination." The Warren Commission found "no evidence" of Cuban involvement. In 1976 the Church Committee found "no evidence that Fidel Castro or others in the Cuban government plotted Kennedy's assassination." As noted, three years later, the House assassinations committee reached a similar conclusion. In the 1990s, five million pages of CIA and other US government documents were declassified and no smoking gun pointing to a Cuban assassination plot emerged. The few authors who suspect a Cuban hand have not made convincing arguments for a conspiracy and have offered no hard evidence. Thus, for nearly everyone with an interest in the assassination, the case has been closed.[20]

It is therefore with trepidation but with confidence in Aspillaga's good faith and memory that I am proposing a more nuanced but hardly less heinous possibility that has never been broached before. I believe that Castro and a small number of Cuban intelligence officers were complicit in Kennedy's death but that their involvement fell short of an organized assassination plot.

Cuban intelligence officers in Mexico, carrying out standard operational procedures, exhorted Oswald. They encouraged his feral militance. Later they believed he would shoot at Kennedy. But it was his plan and his rifle, not theirs. The hot-headed consulate walk-in proved to be a viable candidate to avenge the Kennedy brothers' simultaneous plotting against Fidel. As much as Castro feared and loathed the president, and surely wanted to "be rid of him," organizing an absolutely deniable assassination plot against him was probably beyond Cuban capabilities in 1963.

Whatever contacts Oswald must have had with Cuban intelligence after he left Mexico were deniable. They would not be traceable to the DGI or Fidel. Had he lived to be interrogated at length and tried for murder, no Cuban partnership with him could have been proven. There is no reason to believe that there was a Cuban illegal or penetration agent—or anyone for that matter—armed and ready to shoot at Kennedy from the grassy knoll near the Book Depository. No one can prove that Oswald planned his attack with anyone else, least of all a Cuban. If he had plans to flee to Cuba after killing Kennedy, no such evidence has ever surfaced. He was a troubled loner all his life; likely he thought of himself as a martyr for Fidel and a hero for global revolutionary causes. He wanted a place of his own in history.

Relying mainly on reporting by Vladimir Rodríguez Lahera, Jack Childs, and Florentino Aspillaga, a plausible case can be made that the Cuban role was passive and opportunistic. But despite his sanctimonious claims about "moral obligations," Castro was not tempted to warn American authorities of Oswald's plan. He and his regime have lied endlessly about the assassination, spawning deceptions and disinformation ever since. Fidel made his decision to lie within about twenty-four hours of the president's death. In broadcast speeches on November 23 and 27, he lied about his and the DGI's prior knowledge of the assassin that appears to have dated to 1959. His initial cover-up suggests that he knew there was much more that had to be concealed.

Fidel compounded the Cuban cover-up in 1978 when he met with the House delegation. As mentioned, the congressmen could not confront him with the

Operation SOLO report of his conversation with Jack Childs because it was still highly classified. It was vastly easier for him to repudiate the parallel report by the English journalist about Oswald's shouted threat to kill Kennedy. As a result, Castro's robust denial has stood the test of time. He lied to the committee about his threats during the interview with Daniel Harker. He pretended that he and Kennedy were en route to a rapprochement and that he admired the president and grieved his death. To cynically advance these deceptions, over the years he courted Kennedy family members and aides, in the process gaining measures of reflected immunity.

The truth is that Fidel hated and feared Kennedy and was delighted when he was gunned down. The enemy he would later describe as "the greatest and most dangerous adversary of the Revolution" had been eliminated. Through his premier double agent Rolando Cubela, Fidel knew every detail of the imaginary conspiracy to kill him as the first step in a coup to extinguish the revolution. He had wanted to be certain that Robert Kennedy was pushing all the buttons in Des FitzGerald's SAS and that he was sponsoring the murder plot, presumably with the silent support of his brother in the Oval Office. By having Cubela demand a meeting with the attorney general, Fidel got the answer he expected: The Kennedys were indeed conspiring against him. On November 22, 1963, Fidel's motive and Oswald's were the same.

Castro told the House delegation it would have been insane for him to have become involved in a conspiracy against Kennedy. "Nobody would have thought of that." But nobody thought either that he was capable of drafting the Armageddon letter. Since his first days in power, Fidel was the world's most idiosyncratic and unpredictable major leader. Underestimating him proved to be one of the worst mistakes CIA ever made.

Fidel's largely passive but knowing role in the Kennedy assassination should be considered in the context of his history of remarkably audacious behavior. Eventually, for example, he admitted his role in the destruction of an American U-2 and its pilot during the missile crisis. Yet the first reports about that incident, including one from a reliable CIA spy, were discounted because the story sounded so far-fetched.[21]

Cuban military and paramilitary interventions in third-world conflicts, beginning with Algeria in 1963—later in Angola, Ethiopia, and Nicaragua— surprised Washington officials like bolts from the blue. In 1996 Fidel ordered

Cuban fighter jet pilots to shoot down civilian aircraft flown by American citizens, members of a militant Cuban exile group, even though they were in international air space. Four men were killed.

Castro impelled massive seaborne migrations of disaffected Cubans to south Florida on three occasions. Each time, he correctly calculated that he could act with impunity. He is now known to have run an ultra-secret four-man assassination squad and to have targeted many enemies—prominent and humble—for execution. Cuba profited from the international narcotics trade and from counterfeiting of American dollars, according to the defector Jorge Masetti, who had firsthand knowledge of both practices. For Fidel, nothing was off limits in his half-century war with American imperialism. He and Cuban intelligence proved nimble masters in the art of plausible denial, rarely being caught red-handed in their deceptions. In Washington, the beguilingly false assumption in case after case was that Fidel could not possibly act so precipitously.[22]

There is a revealing, perhaps unguarded passage in the speech Fidel delivered the night after Kennedy was shot. It is one of the clearest expositions he has ever offered about his elastic theory of justifiable homicide. His dictum covered the dictators Rafael Trujillo, Fulgencio Batista, Anastasio Somoza, and Augusto Pinochet—all of whom he conspired to assassinate. Including John F. Kennedy among them takes no stretch of the imagination. Fidel said:

> [S]ometimes, cases in the midst of a civil war, in the midst of a fierce repression during which the revolutionaries see themselves forced to defend themselves, they find themselves forced to kill to defend themselves.

In Kennedy's case, Fidel chose to defend himself through a conspiracy of silence. Since the Bay of Pigs invasion, he had been at war with Kennedy. The aggressive American campaigns to unseat and kill him had gained intensity and momentum in the fall of 1963 and were coming to a crescendo. He was more worried than he had ever been. By his own twisted reckoning, he was acting in self-defense on November 22, 1963, by taking no action to deter Oswald or warn American authorities.

AFTERWORD

DURING THE KENNEDY YEARS, LITTLE WAS OFF LIMITS IN THE
intelligence wars waged across the Florida Straits. CIA had the authority to plot
Castro's assassination, so covert actions designed to compromise Cuban officials
would hardly have been considered morally objectionable—even if innocent targets might be executed for treason. That possibility loomed through the more
than three years the Agency ran an especially sensitive and ethically questionable
operation apparently code-named AMROD. It continued in force until March
1966, covertly implicating prominent Cuban officials in capital crimes.[1]

According to a declassified CIA summary of the case, it was designed to stir
dissension in the Cuban leadership and sow discord between Havana and its
Soviet patrons. Originally approved by an interagency coordinating committee
in 1962 when Bill Harvey was running Task Force W, it reached full velocity a
year later, coinciding with Des FitzGerald's efforts to divide the Castros' armed
forces. It was a supercharged effort, one too sensitive to be mentioned even in
large group meetings with the president in attendance. I have found no record
that he or the attorney general was briefed on AMROD, but given its scope and
success, and their interest, there can be no doubt that it was brought to their attention privately.[2]

Two prominent Cubans—a deputy defense minister and a diplomat at the
Mexico City embassy—were tarred and were lucky to escape with their lives.
Sixty-two-year-old Joaquín Ordoqui was the principal target. One of four dep-
uties in Raúl's ministry, he also served as armed forces quartermaster. An "old
communist"—that is, a founding member of the pre-revolution Communist

Party—he remained especially close to the Kremlin. Tensions flared early in 1962 when Castro and his "new communist" followers, nearly all veterans of his guerrilla movement, condemned the older generation of Marxists for engaging in pro-Soviet subversion. Fidel launched a purge of those "sectarians" who were allegedly more devoted to Moscow than to him. Dozens were disgraced and exiled. In reality, the show Castro staged was mostly smoke and mirrors meant to demonstrate his absolute authority and to weed out a few rivals. But the affair was closely tracked in Langley and provided appealing operational opportunities.[3]

The objective was to jolt fault lines in the leadership, with the added hope that Moscow would side with Cuba's "old communists" against Fidel. Generous Agency resources at headquarters and in Mexico City were devoted to carrying it off. The large Mexico station—with about forty CIA personnel in late 1963—was up to the task. It surreptitiously photographed most people entering or leaving the Cuban diplomatic compound and tapped at least six phone lines there, including the ambassador's. By late 1963, CIA had recruited about fifty agents in the Mexican capital to work against the Cuban target, including two inside the embassy. Declassified records show that, wittingly or not, the Cuban chargé, code-named AMRIFT, played a critical role in the AMROD operation.[4]

It was one of the more remarkable covert operations ever run against Cuba's leaders. In April 1963, counterfeit documents falsely attributed to a disaffected CIA agent in Mexico were passed to a Cuban embassy official, probably AMRIFT. The documents made it appear that Ordoqui was a CIA agent and that he had handed over sensitive military information in the run-up to the missile crisis. According to a CIA record of the operation, "the Cubans accepted the spurious papers and paid for them per our demand." Additional deliveries of falsified documents were made through the summer, and the eager DGI paid several thousand dollars more. At first, nothing seemed to happen to Ordoqui, although there can be no doubt he was put under round-the-clock audio and visual surveillance.[5]

In November, as the Cubela conspiracy was ripening and there were still no signs of new political turmoil in Havana, fifty-year-old Maria Teresa Proenza was also targeted. The respected Cuban cultural attaché in Mexico was an "old communist" friend of Ordoqui's. A celebrity and socialite, Proenza was a former personal secretary of the acclaimed Mexican muralist and painter Diego Rivera. Her enormous influence in Mexican artistic and intellectual circles, hardcore communist beliefs, and virulent anti-American attitudes caused her to become the Agency's newest victim. Another document sale falsely fingered her to the DGI as a CIA agent. Within weeks she was recalled to Havana and put under house arrest.[6]

The first Cuban reactions to the deceptions were not evident until the following March. A young communist protégé of Ordoqui's was arrested and tried for capital crimes to which he confessed. In reality, however, when the death sentence was carried out, he was a surrogate for Ordoqui. "It was really a trial of the latter," according to the CIA summary of the operation.

The deadly charade was typical of Fidel's operating style, and there were few among the island's political elite who misunderstood. Ordoqui was too closely connected to the Kremlin to be put up against the execution wall, especially as relations had warmed following Fidel's long sojourn in the Soviet Union the previous spring and as economic and military subsidies increased. In 1964, he had no taste for another sweeping purge of Cubans beholden to Moscow.[7]

But Ordoqui was not given a free pass; he was arrested that November as the sale of counterfeited documents continued apace in Mexico City. His wife, a cabinet minister, was detained too. AMROD stayed on track for another sixteen months, CIA document counterfeiters artfully producing new ones, all so seemingly authentic that they were totally believable to Cuban intelligence. Finally, according to an official record of the operation, and for unknown reasons, "the Cubans ceased taking an interest in it."

Only a few relevant documents have been declassified, so it is not possible to tell how many other Cuban officials may have been affected. Two years after the last ersatz papers were sold, however, Fidel unleashed a second purge of "old communists." In the aftermath of that so-called microfaction affair, only a handful of the old-guard Marxists remained in important positions. Operation AMROD may very well have been decisive in their collective downfall.

The three defendants survived and eventually were paroled. Ordoqui died of natural causes in Cuba in 1973. His wife was allowed to live out her years in Spain. Proenza remained in Havana, where she was interviewed in 1978 by the House assassinations committee. She was a close friend of her Havana neighbor Luisa Calderon; "I see her often now," she said. Unverified but credible reports had also linked Proenza to Oswald during his visit to Mexico. She denied any knowledge of him, saying she knew nothing either about his threat, reported by Jack Childs, to kill Kennedy. Proenza gave no indication of knowing that she had been framed by the enemy CIA.[8]

To my knowledge, this story has never been aired publicly before. Published references by two CIA officers, however, do seem to point at AMROD. In their memoirs, David Phillips and Ted Shackley appear to mention it in fleeting, shielded terms. Phillips, who was in charge of covert operations against Cuba at the Mexico City station beginning in mid-1963, wrote that the targeted cultural affairs officer was "energetic and bright, despised Americans, and had hatched . . . dirty tricks aimed at CIA." Although he disguised the nature of the operation and depicted Proenza as a man, Phillips's description neatly fit her. Not surprisingly, he says nothing about how dangerously she was compromised or that she might easily have been executed as a CIA spy.[9]

Shackley was more critical in his brief reference to an operation that closely resembles AMROD. But his complaint was not on moral grounds. He wrote that "[i]n a limited sense this was indeed a success because it caused some disruptions and discord in the enemy's bureaucracy." On balance, he thought the case was largely a lark that did little more than give CIA "the satisfaction of poking Fidel in the eye." Perhaps he was not aware of the show trial and execution of Ordoqui's young disciple, the sacrificial lamb in the affair. And perhaps the cold-blooded Shackley considered the operation just as fair and routine as the commando and sabotage campaigns he ran that resulted in considerable loss of life on both sides of the clandestine war with Cuba.[10]

It is not known when Fidel and his intelligence chiefs realized how grandly they had been deceived. No Cuban official or any state media has commented on the case. It is not their practice to admit to any such embarrassing calamities, especially since they paid dearly for the flow of forged documents. But by the mid- to late 1970s, they apparently had learned of the deceptions, perhaps from CIA turncoat Philip Agee, who had some knowledge of the case. I have concluded that since that time, the Cubans have toiled to exact revenge. They chose a single target.[11]

If, as seems likely, Dave Phillips was the Mexico City principal in charge of AMROD, a long-running disinformation campaign against him—continuing today, long after his death—is probably a maliciously calculated case of Cuban retribution. According to some Kennedy assassination conspiracy theorists who have been taken in by the disinformation, Phillips used the alias Morris or Maurice Bishop when supposedly meeting with Oswald as his CIA case officer.

Cuban intelligence may not have been the first to promote the canard, but counterintelligence general Fabian Escalante soon became one of its most prolific propagators. Cuban government commentators and others have repeated it ad nauseum. The CIA has denied any knowledge of Bishop and that it had dealings with Oswald, and Phillips successfully sued publications in the United States and Britain that alleged he used that alias to meet with Oswald. Of course he could not sue Cuban government media, and, undeterred, they have continued to proclaim the infamous lie that he was a CIA conspirator in Kennedy's assassination. Even some otherwise sensible American scholars have been taken in.[12]

NO OTHER ADVERSARY INTELLIGENCE SERVICE has enjoyed gloating rights comparable to Cuba's since the 1930s and 1940s, when more than five hundred Americans assisted Soviet intelligence. Those fellow travelers were seduced by the myths of a Marxist paradise or traveled there and naively came away enamored and eager to help. Others were born in Russia before emigrating or identified with the Kremlin because of shared ideology. Americans have conspired for Fidel for the same reasons and also because, like Lee Harvey Oswald, they idolized him and were persuaded that he and revolutionary Cuba were the innocent victims of brutal Yankee imperialism. For nearly all the converts, working for Castro has been an unremunerated labor of love.[13]

In most years since the early 1960s, the number of Americans assisting Cuban intelligence—moles and spies, doubles, access and influence agents, spotters, sycophants, and support assets—probably add up to between three and five hundred. Some of them—say, when meeting with Cuban operatives posing as diplomats or cultural affairs officials and accepting tasks or guidance from them—may not be aware they are actually aiding Cuban undercover programs. But most Americans in such situations who sympathize with Cuban government objectives cannot have any illusions about whom they are serving.

As early as September 1963, the *Miami Herald* reported that Castro's intelligence agents had penetrated "every facet of the Cuban exile movement." DGI operative Gerardo Peraza, who defected in 1971, knew that more than three hundred recruited Cuban agents were then working for Fidel in Miami alone. Today, the numbers throughout the United States are probably comparable, and the underground infrastructure that supports them is probably better than ever. That is partly due to the loss of other intelligence priorities. Since the disintegration of the Soviet bloc, Cuban support for foreign revolutionaries has withered. Similarly, from the 1960s through the 1980s, illicit acquisition of American technology and manufactured goods was a costly Cuban intelligence priority. That has also faded in recent years as legalized trade and contacts across the Florida Straits have multiplied. The result is that nearly all Cuban intelligence resources have been directed to focus on Washington and Miami.[14]

Espionage and counterintelligence have been the beneficiaries. Infiltrating sleeper agents and illegals is astonishingly easy for Cuban intelligence. At least thirty thousand émigrés arrive every year in the United States from the island and meld into American society. Twenty thousand of them come under the terms of an immigration agreement concluded with Havana during the Clinton administration. The remainder travel by way of third countries, or on small craft to Florida, but usually are not repatriated as long as they reach American soil.

All qualify a year later to begin the process of acquiring citizenship under the terms of the Cuban Adjustment Act, legislated in 1966 at the height of the cold war. These antiquated immigration laws and rules—which apply only to Cubans among all émigré nationalities—work to the continuing great advantage of Cuban intelligence. For this reason, and because they are discriminatory and outdated, they are no longer justified.

The Cuban intelligence threat is compounded by liaison and sharing agreements it maintains with other regimes and groups hostile to American interests. Sensitive information acquired through espionage is provided in exchange for reciprocal favors, profit, or as a show of ideological solidarity. Civilian and military technology and American spyware have been compromised this way. Ana Montes, the Cuban mole in the Defense Intelligence Agency, was arrested just a day before she would have gained access to secret targeting data for the October 2001 military operations against al Qaeda and the Taliban in Afghanistan. The Pentagon feared that she would pass sensitive military plans to her Cuban handlers in time for them to warn the enemy. She is reported to have given the Cubans copious details of secret American electronic eavesdropping systems that may have been shared with other countries. And Montes was suspected of having provided information about US military and intelligence operations in Central America during her long service for Cuban intelligence.[15]

But American counterintelligence capabilities have improved dramatically in recent years. Only four Cuban spies were arrested in the United States between 1959 and 1995. Then, beginning in September 1998 and through 2011, about four dozen Cuban agents have been prosecuted or neutralized. More than thirty were members of the sprawling Avispa, or Wasp, network wrapped up that year.[16]

Since their arrests, six other American citizens working for Cuba have been prosecuted successfully. Carlos Alvarez, a Florida International University professor, and his wife, Elsa Prieto, a university counselor, pled guilty in Miami to conspiracy. Mariano Faget, a naturalized American born in Cuba, was convicted in 2000 of spying while he served as an upper-level official of the Immigration and Naturalization Service. The prosecutions of Ana Montes, Walter Kendall Myers, and his wife, Gwendolyn, have been discussed already. Still others, some prominent in academic circles, who wittingly assisted Cuban intelligence have been neutralized as viable secret assets without being criminally prosecuted.

The Montes case remains the most troubling. She spied for sixteen years, rising into steadily more sensitive and responsible positions in the intelligence community. She first came under suspicion early in 1996 and was interrogated that November by a Defense Intelligence Agency security officer after consultations with the FBI. Although he believed that she lied to him and found her evasive and manipulative, remarkably, she was allowed to resume her sensitive work as a political and military analyst on Cuba. The wiser course would have been to reassign her to some other specialty or country desk while investigating her further. At least then her utility to Cuban intelligence would have been minimized.[17]

I have learned that the FBI also missed opportunities that could have led to Montes much sooner. Miguel Mir, the Cuban intelligence and security officer who served for six years on Fidel's personal security squad, defected from his post at the Cuban diplomatic mission at the United Nations in May 1996. He told me of information indiscreetly shared with him by two of the most senior officers at the large Cuban intelligence Center in New York. In retrospect, he believes that both colleagues were making indirect references to Montes.[18]

The first incident occurred in early 1995. Mir drove to Washington from New York as a security escort for intelligence lieutenant colonel Luis Carrera, who was allegedly Montes's principal contact in the United States at the time. During the boring drive south, Carrera boasted, "I have contact with a very important person who works at the highest levels of the American government." He provided no details, but Mir believes the purpose of the trip was for Carrera to meet secretly with Montes or, more likely, to execute a brush pass with her somewhere in the Washington subway system in order to clandestinely provide or receive sensitive materials. Mir recalls Carrera later said it took two or three tries to effect the exchange.

The second fragment of information came from a conversation the defector had in New York. In February 1996, the outspoken Mir had a confrontation there with the visiting Cuban foreign minister. The next day, Center chief José Odriozola summoned Mir to be privately admonished in the secure *cabina,* a plastic enclosure within a larger room where sensitive conversations could he conducted without fear of audio interception. Mir told me how Odriozola reprimanded him, saying: "It is really ironic; you were given the twentieth-anniversary-year Ministry of Interior medal and many other honors, how could you have been so lacking in respect for the foreign minister?"

Odriozola was a senior and experienced intelligence officer who had previously served as Paris Center chief. Other defectors have also described him to me, and his name is included in the list of DGI officers I received from Aspillaga. But in rebuking Mir, this veteran operative committed fundamental errors of tradecraft, violating basic rules of compartmentalization when he revealed this information: "We have penetrated the Congress of the United States," he bragged, "the Senate, and the Pentagon, and we have a very powerful operating network . . . and you have been so disrespectful of us!! We should send you back to Cuba, but because of your accomplishments, we will let you remain here."

Mir later concluded that his boss was referring to the Wasp network in Miami and to Montes. A few months later—a day before he was scheduled to return to Cuba, his tour of duty in New York completed—Mir defected.

He told me he provided these leads to the FBI in May 1996. It is possible that they helped investigators in the search that five years later led to Montes. But there is no reason to believe they were factored in when she was interrogated at DIA a few months later. The published account by the security officer who grilled her makes no mention of information provided by a defector. Were the tips Mir passed on from the two senior Cuban intelligence officers disregarded or considered too vague and ambiguous to pursue?[19]

American authorities have never revealed how Montes finally came under sufficient suspicion to be put under surveillance and then caught red-handed in espionage. The Defense Intelligence Agency security officer who wrote about her case stated only that "a tidbit of information that might help identify a Cuban spy surfaced within the counterintelligence community."

He did not elaborate, and no details of the evidence trail surfaced during Montes's prosecution. The mysterious tidbit could have come from another defector or an intercept of Cuban communications. Montes or her handlers may have made an incriminating error in the way they arranged contacts. A colleague or family member could have become suspicious and reported her to the FBI. Most embedded spies are ferreted out in one or another of these fashions.

But I suspect that in her case, the critical tidbit came from an egregious error committed by Fidel Castro himself. He was surely Montes's ultimate case officer and followed her with intense interest. He probably met with her in Havana. But his health—and mental acuity—were deteriorating by 2000, after earlier life-threatening surgeries. In June 2001 he was filmed for the first time faltering during a speech. He appeared disoriented and dizzy, nearly collapsing before being carried off by aides. Nothing like that had ever happened before, and the international press reported that he had briefly lost consciousness. In two subsequent appearances that summer, audiences squirmed in embarrassment as he became strangely incoherent for short spells. Something, both physical and cognitive, clearly was wrong.

I cannot support my surmise about Fidel's responsibility for Montes's arrest with hard evidence. It is based mainly on my understanding of how he and Cuban intelligence have operated. I suspect that Fidel, in a disoriented state, boasted when he was among other Cuban officials of an extraordinary, high-level spy working for him in Washington. Odriozola and Carrera had both bragged in a similar unguarded way to Mir, who had no need to know.

When he was younger and fitter, Fidel would never have made such a fundamental error. But as he aged and began declining mentally, he was driven more powerfully than before by narcissistic excess. He sought gratification and congratulations. He wanted others to know of his accomplishments. If, as I suspect, he boasted of his super-mole Montes, he may have provided some identifying information; for example, that it was a woman or an American of Puerto Rican descent. One of the Cubans who heard him, duly impressed and perhaps later a defector, may have provided that information to American authorities. It would have been considerably more than the tidbit the Defense Intelligence Agency investigator cited, and it would have set in motion the counterintelligence dragnet that snared Montes.

If this is correct, ironically it was Fidel Castro, the infirm supreme spymaster, the modern world's most venerable and intuitive intelligence boss, who compromised one of the most valuable secret agents he ever handled. There is a strange justice in supposing that Cuba's seemingly infallible, prescient, and Machiavellian leader for so many decades could have in the end failed so abjectly. But I believe this is exactly what happened.

TOO ILL TO CONTINUE AS PRESIDENT, Fidel stepped aside provisionally in July 2006 and definitively in February 2008. Today, eighty-five years old and rarely seen in public, his continued decline is irreversible. Meanwhile, his legacy is being cautiously dismantled, his enormous failures on the home front implicitly acknowledged by his successors. Under the presidency of his brother Raúl, the emphasis has been on bread rather than revolutionary circuses, on problem solving at home rather than global grandstanding. Raúl has assembled a new leadership team nearly entirely of his own choosing.

Fidel no longer serves as supreme spymaster. Intelligence operations are now in the hands of distinctly lesser men, bureaucrats and military officers for whom the long covert war with the Americans cannot possibly have the same exhilarating meaning as it did for Fidel. War with the Yankee imperialists was always his personal crusade, the unyielding raison d'être of his revolution. As long as he lives and his brother rules Cuba, the conflict he wanted and needed will be honored in Cuban propaganda, but it will never again determine nearly everything else in national policy.

Raúl has little firsthand experience in the intelligence operations and conspiracies Fidel thrived on. He is more cautious and pragmatic, and he has always delegated responsibilities. Not ruled by lifelong vendettas, he is less inclined to order the executions of enemies or traitors. When he speaks in public, he does so softly, with none of the pageantry or vitriol that accompanied Fidel's performances. Raúl pays lip service to his brother's hatred of the United States and the need for continued vigilance—as if recent administrations in Washington were still plotting coups and assassinations—but he clearly has higher priorities than baiting and condemning the Americans. When Fidel is gone, the anti-Yankee obsession will likely expire with him.

Eighty years old as I write these words, Raúl is unchallenged in power and likely will rule until he too falters physically or mentally. His health, like Fidel's, is a state secret, but the odds are high that he also suffers from serious ailments and debilities, some no doubt related to his decades of heavy drinking. The greatest burden on his leadership, however, is the fact that Fidel is still alive, still issuing "reflections" that are circulated by the Cuban media. Probably they are composed now by others in Fidel's entourage, which suggests that a hard-line, *fidelista* sect still is powerful in the leadership. These commentaries rarely critique Raúl's decisions, but it is also clear that the younger brother self-censors in order to avoid that. As much as he might like to, it is extremely unlikely that Raúl will flatly repudiate any of Fidel's sacrosanct policies of the past while his brother lives.

Boxed in this way, Raúl has focused on remedying Cuba's dire economic crises. More than five years in power in his own right, however, he has little to show for the effort. He has publicly promised some radical changes—such as laying off as many as a million public sector workers—only to retreat, no doubt fearing public unrest. He has talked incessantly about implementing agrarian reform, but here too his measures have been halfhearted and cautious.

He is tough—though not as ruthless as Fidel always was—in dealing with Cuba's small but valiant internal opposition. Pro-democracy groups, independent journalists and librarians, and a world-famous blogger, among many other scattered voices of dissent, continue to pressure the regime, especially by bringing international scrutiny to its appalling human rights record.

Raúl will continue to cast about for ways to force efficiencies and reduce expenditures. He knows how perilously close to economic calamity Cuba balances. If the enormous subsidies provided by gravely ill Venezuelan president Chávez should end, the lights in Havana would literally dim and a severe recession, like the one that occurred after the collapse of Soviet subsidies, would be inevitable. In this climate of uncertainty and cost-cutting, the virtually unlimited resources Fidel devoted to intelligence functions have probably diminished. I am not aware of accurate estimates of the number of active Ministry of Interior or intelligence personnel today, but it is likely that foreign intelligence, at least, has endured cutbacks through early retirements and reassignments.

Capabilities have all but certainly diminished. Raúl's cronies, the elderly military officers who now run intelligence, are pale, plodding successors to the swashbuckling Redbeard and his founding generation of inspired, audacious operatives. The new leadership is more on the defensive because it faces more determined American counterintelligence efforts than ever before. Many Cuban operatives must doubt the urgency of their missions as they confront the American enemy that cannot possibly seem as threatening as it did before. Faltering morale would be one of the worst consequences of all the new challenges and constraints Cuban intelligence faces. That explains why the regime maintains a deafening drumbeat of propaganda in support of the Wasp spies in American prisons.

Some of the defectors who have been quoted in these pages believe that until the 1989 Ministry of Interior purges, intelligence professionals were the most sophisticated, enlightened, and progressive elite in Cuba's governing apparatus. Many in the DGI were attracted to the reform movement that fractured the communist bloc between 1989 and 1991, and some officers may actually have plotted against the Castros. I have asked some of my defector sources if the service, now known as the Intelligence Directorate (the DI), could someday be the wellspring of reformist dissent and lead the way to a pluralist, entrepreneurial, even democratic Cuba. Alternatively, might some wily and barnacled intelligence veteran employ his guile, and that of colleagues, to rise to the top of the political heap? It happened in Russia.

The answers vary, but generally my sources conclude that the innovative, iconoclastic spirit they remember when civilians ran intelligence has been muffled during the last twenty years of military dominance. On balance, then, the defectors I consulted are inclined to speculate that a hard-line, authoritarian leader is more likely to emerge from the Cuban military or intelligence services than a democratic reformer. I imagine they are right.

Some of the more extreme DGI practices that Fidel demanded in his day—pumping sleeping gas under closed doors, running a personal squad of assassins, hunting down prominent foreigners—may well have been abandoned by new, more cautious Ministry of Interior chieftains. Only time, and tough American counterintelligence efforts, will tell, however, just how aggressive and creative Cuban espionage remains. Until there is a comprehensive normalization of relations with Havana, however, it would be folly for American officials again to underestimate Cuba's remarkable foreign intelligence abilities.

Somewhere along that inevitable path toward reconciliation—which now cannot be too far in the future—I hope that a Cuban comes forward with evidence to corroborate what Tiny Aspillaga told me about his memory of the morning of November 22, 1963. Confirming that Fidel knew of Oswald's intentions to shoot President Kennedy—and did nothing to deter the act—would not stifle the warring among rival assassination conspiracy theories or dissuade those who insist that Oswald did not act alone that day. But additional evidence from somewhere in Cuban archives, from Luisa Calderon, or from another Cuban witness would confirm what I now believe was Fidel Castro's most despicable decision during his nearly five decades in power: to stand aside, build an elaborate alibi, lie and dissemble, launch decades of disinformation pointing at others, all the while maintaining a conspiracy of silence about the murder of John F. Kennedy.

NOTES

AUTHOR INTERVIEWEES

Dariel "Benigno" Alarcón Ramirez (by phone)
Florentino "Tiny" Aspillaga
Lazaro Betancourt
Francisco Compostela
Jaime Costa
Rolando Cubela (AMLASH)
Jean Daniel
Samuel Halpern
Roberto Hernández del Llano
William Hood (by phone)
David Laux
José Maragon
Rolando Martínez
Keith Melton
Miguel Mir
Robert Morgan (by phone and correspondence)
Félix Rodríguez
Nestor Sanchez
Juan Sanchez Crespo
I. C. Smith
Sally Swenson Cascio (by phone and correspondence)
Carlos Tepedino (AMWHIP)
Gustavo Villoldo (by phone)
Joaquín Villalobos
and many others who prefer to remain anonymous

SOURCE ABBREVIATIONS

CC   Church Committee (Select Committee to Study Governmental Operations with
Respect to Intelligence Activities, United States Senate; chaired by Senator Frank
Church, Idaho)
CHC   Cuban Heritage Collection, University of Miami
FBIS   Foreign Broadcast Information Service
HA   Hoover Institution Archives, Stanford University

HSCA   Select Committee on Assassinations, United States House of Representatives
IGR   Report on Plots to Assassinate Fidel Castro, CIA Inspector General, May 23, 1967
JFKOH   John F. Kennedy Library Oral History
NARA   National Archives and Records Administration

CHAPTER 1: BETTER THAN US

1. CIA, "Clandestine Services Cuban Collection Program," NARA, 104-10310-10005.
2. James J. Angleton, CC testimony, June 19, 1975.
3. Juan Antonio Rodríguez Menier, *Cuba Por Dentro* (Miami: Ediciones Universal, 1994), p. 61.
4. Gerardo Peraza, Subcommittee on Security and Terrorism, Judiciary Committee testimony, February 26, 1982.
5. Oleg Kalugin, *The First Chief Directorate* (New York: St. Martin's Press, 1994), p. 192.
6. *The CIA War Against Cuba,* televised by the Cuban government, July-August 1987; author interviews with Florentino Aspillaga; I. C. Smith, *Inside: A Top G-Man Exposes Spies, Lies, and Bureaucratic Bungling Inside the FBI* (Nashville, TN: Nelson Current, 2004), p. 96.
7. David R. McLean, "Western Hemisphere Division, 1946-1965," Vol. 1, p. 234. NARA, 104-10310-10001.
8. "Seven Men: One Fist and One Heart," *Granma Weekly Review,* August 2, 1987.
9. "Espionage and Counterespionage in Havana," *Granma Weekly Review,* July 19, 1987.
10. "Our Man in the CIA" and "Angel Mateo," *Granma Weekly Review,* July 19, 1987.
11. J. C. Masterman, *The Double-Cross System in the War of 1939 to 1945* (New Haven, CT: Yale University Press, 1972), p. 15.
12. Zayda Gutierrez Perez, "The Improvement of Political-Operational Work Against the Intelligence Services of the USA Through the Intelligence Activity of Penetration Agents," Ministry of State Security, German Democratic Republic, 1987. I am grateful to Chuck Lane who provided me a copy he translated from the German.
13. Richard Helms, CC testimony, June 13, 1975.
14. Author interview with Miguel Mir.
15. Smith, *Inside,* pp. 95-96.
16. Ibid.
17. *The CIA War Against Cuba.*
18. "Espionage and Counterespionage in Havana."
19. McLean, "Western Hemisphere Division, 1946-1965," p. 234.
20. Ibid., pp. 234-235.
21. Alan H. Flanigan interview, Foreign Affairs Oral History Collection of the Association for Diplomatic Studies and Training, National Foreign Affairs Training Center (NFATC), June 16, 1997.

CHAPTER 2: ON FIDEL'S ORDERS

1. Florentino Aspillaga, unpublished manuscript.
2. Author interview with Florentino Aspillaga; *The CIA War Against Cuba,* televised by the Cuban government, July-August 1987.
3. David Leppard, "The Men from Havana," *Sunday Times* (London), September 18, 1988; *Time,* September 26, 1988.
4. Ibid.
5. Author interview with José Maragon.

6. Aspillaga manuscript.
7. Author interview with Lazaro Betancourt.
8. "Castro Speaks on Dominguez, del Pino Cases," FBIS, July 2, 1987.
9. Brian Latell, *After Fidel: The Inside Story of Castro's Regime and Cuba's Next Leader* (New York: Palgrave Macmillan, 2005).
10. Ibid.; "Castro Speaks on Dominguez, del Pino Cases."
11. Juan Antonio Rodríguez Menier, *Inside the Cuban Interior Ministry* (Washington, DC, Jamestown Foundation, 1994), p. 5.
12. *Granma* editorial, September 2, 1989.
13. Rodríguez Menier, *Inside the Cuban Interior Ministry,* p. 64; José Ramón Ponce Solozabal, *Al Final del Arco Iris: Un Psicologo en el Contraespionaje Cubano* (Miami: Grupo de Apoyo a la Democracia, 2005), p. 211.
14. Rodríguez Menier, *Inside the Cuban Interior Ministry;* Jorge Masetti, *In the Pirate's Den* (San Francisco: Encounter Books, 1993), pp. 122, 136; Aspillaga manuscript.
15. Author interview with Roberto Hernández del Llano.
16. Aspillaga manuscript.
17. Author interview with Hernández del Llano; Gerardo Peraza, Subcommittee on Security and Terrorism, Judiciary Committee testimony, February 26, 1982.

CHAPTER 3: ROOFTOP STORIES

1. Rolando Bonachea and Nelson Valdes, *Revolutionary Struggle, 1947-1958, Selected Works of Fidel Castro* (Cambridge, MA: MIT Press, 1972), p. 23.
2. Ibid., p. 24; Robert E. Quirk, *Fidel Castro* (New York: Norton, 1993), p. 25; Georgie Anne Geyer, *Guerrilla Prince* (Boston: Little, Brown, 1991), p. 64.
3. Leycester Coltman, *The Real Fidel Castro* (New Haven, CT: Yale University Press, 2003), p. 38.
4. Tad Szulc, interview with Max Lesnick, CHC, August 10, 1984.
5. Memorandum for the Record, NARA 104-10308-10197.
6. Szulc, Lesnick interview.
7. Brian Latell, *After Fidel: The Inside Story of Castro's Regime and Cuba's Next Leader* (New York: Palgrave Macmillan, 2005), p. 87.
8. James Blight, Bruce J. Allyn, and David A. Welch, *Cuba on the Brink: Castro, the Missile Crisis and the Soviet Collapse* (New York: Pantheon Books, 1993), p. 109.
9. Ibid., p. 110.
10. The text can be found in Fidel Castro and Ignacio Ramonet, *Fidel Castro: My Life* (New York: Simon & Schuster, 2006), pp. 278-279.
11. Tad Szulc response to Peter Kornbluh, *Washington Post Book World,* November 15, 1992.
12. Laurence Chang and Peter Kornbluh, eds., *The Cuban Missile Crisis, 1962: A National Security Archive Reader* (New York: New Press, 1992), pp. 195-196.
13. William Taubman, *Khrushchev: The Man and His Era* (New York: Norton, 2003), pp. 150, 169.
14. Nikita Khrushchev, *Khrushchev Remembers: The Glasnost Tapes* (Boston: Little, Brown, 1990), p. 177.
15. FBIS, October 1, 1990.
16. Khrushchev, *Glasnost Tapes,* p. 183.
17. Oleg Troyanovsky, "The Caribbean Crisis: A View from the Kremlin," *International Affairs* (April-May 1992): 153.
18. Blight et al., *Cuba on the Brink* p. 107.
19. Fidel Castro interview with Robert McNeil, February 20, 1985.

20. Blight et al., *Cuba on the Brink,* pp, 106-134; Khrushchev, *Glasnost Tapes,* p. 178.
21. "Memo for the Record, STEEL-1," NARA 104-10308-10197.
22. Jorge Domínguez, "Foreword," in Blight et al., *Cuba on the Brink,* p. xiii.
23. Henry Kissinger, *Years of Renewal* (New York: Simon & Schuster, 1999), p. 816.
24. Fidel used that number in a fundraising speech at the Flagler Theater in Miami, November 20, 1955, in Bonachea and Valdes, *Revolutionary Struggle,* p. 286. In Antonio Rafael de la Cova's authoritative volume, *The Moncada Attack* (Columbia: University of South Carolina Press, 2007), p. 266, he says that sixty-one of Castro's men were killed.
25. FBIS, April 22, 1963.
26. Fidel Castro interview with Julio Scherer, *Proceso,* September 21, 1981.
27. Brian Latell, National Intelligence Council Memorandum, "Castro Agonistes: The Mounting Dilemmas and Frustrations of Cuba's Caudillo," November 1981, author's archive.
28. Ibid.
29. Author interview with Moncada survivor Jaime Costa.
30. Anatoly Dobrynin, *In Confidence: Moscow's Ambassador to America's Six Cold War Presidents* (New York: Times Books, 1995), p. 85.
31. Brian Latell, "The Dilemmas and Anxieties of Cuba's Aging Leader," in *Cuban Foreign Policy: The New Internationalism,* ed. Jaime Suchlicki and Damian Fernandez (Miami: University of Miami Press, 1985), pp. 30-55.
32. Fidel Castro, "Nuclear Winter," *Granma,* August 23, 2010.
33. Castro speech on inauguration as president, FBIS, March 6, 2003.

CHAPTER 4: COME TO CUBA

1. Orlando Castro Hidalgo, *Spy for Fidel* (Miami: E. E. Seaman, 1971), p. 37.
2. David A. Phillips, *The Night Watch* (New York: Athenaeum, 1977), p. 77; author interview with a former CIA officer.
3. David A. Phillips, "Castro's Spies Are No Longer Teenagers," *Retired Officer,* January 13, 1982; David A. Phillips, *Secret Wars Diary* (Bethesda, MD: Stone Trail Press, 1989).
4. "Biography of Rogelio Rodríguez, Diplomat and Member of Cuba's Foreign Member Intelligence Service," NARA 104-10072-10222.
5. Jorge Castañeda, *Utopia Unarmed* (New York: Knopf, 1993), p. 54.
6. Richard Helms, CC testimony, June 13, 1975.
7. "The Organization of the General Directorate of Intelligence," CIA report CS-311/00115-64, NARA 104-10185-10149.
8. CIA defector report, January 15, 1965, NARA 104-10239-10409. The source added that when an agent returns to his country after training, he is expected to find a job and support himself. In extreme cases, the DGI subsidized agents but not indefinitely.
9. John McCone, Statement to the House of Representatives Committee on Foreign Affairs, February 19, 1963.
10. Castro Hidalgo, *Spy for Fidel,* p. 39.
11. Ibid., p. 40.
12. Christopher Andrew and Vasily Mitrokhin, *The World Was Going Our Way* (New York: Basic Books, 2005), p. 49.
13. *New York Times,* June 29, 2010.
14. Andrew and Mitrokhin, *World Was Going Our Way,* p. 49; Gerardo Peraza, Subcommittee on Security and Terrorism testimony, Judiciary Committee, U.S. Senate, February 26, 1982.

15. "Debriefing Report of Defector from Cuban Intelligence Service," NARA 104-10247-10389.
16. McCone, Statement.
17. AMMUG report, August 20, 1964, NARA 104-10239-10442.
18. AMMUG reports, NARA, 104-10239-10427 and NARA 104-10185-10111.
19. McCone, Statement.
20. Statement of President Betancourt to Organization of American States Investigating Committee, December 9, 1963, in OAS Council series, February 18, 1964, p. 10.
21. Fidel Castro, "The Bolivarian Revolution and the Antilles," Granma, February 7, 2010.
22. McCone, Statement.
23. Luis Baez, Secretos de Generales (Barcelona: Editorial Lozada, 1996), p. 122.
24. Author interviews with Lazaro Betancourt, Juan Sanchez Crespo, and Norberto Fuentes.
25. Baez, Secretos de Generales, p. 122.
26. Ibid.; Castro Hidalgo, Spy for Fidel, p. 49.
27. David Phillips, CC testimony, July 31, 1975.
28. Baez, Secretos de Generales, pp. 27-28.
29. Jorge Castañeda, Companero: The Life and Death of Che Guevara (New York: Knopf, 1997), p. 342.
30. Castro Hidalgo, Spy for Fidel, p. 49.
31. Jon Lee Anderson, Che: A Revolutionary Life (New York: Grove Press, 1997), p. 701.
32. Ibid., pp. 698-699.
33. Castañeda, Companero, p. 379.
34. Markus Wolf, Man Without a Face (New York: Random House, 1997), p. 310.

CHAPTER 5: AT DAGGERS DRAWN

1. "Excerpts: Draft History: John A. McCone," NARA 104-10301-10000; thanks to Keith Melton for technical advice.
2. Ted Shackley, Spymaster: My Life in the CIA (Dulles, VA: Potomac Books, 2005), p. 65.
3. Ibid.; Robert Wallace and H. Keith Melton, Spycraft: The Secret History of the CIA's Spytechs from Communism to Al-Qaeda (New York: Dutton, 2008), p. 438; author interview with Keith Melton.
4. Shackley, Spymaster, p. 52.
5. José Maragon, author interview.
6. Author interviews with captains of the covert navy.
7. Ted Shackley, CC testimony, August 19, 1975; Shackley quoted in Don Bohning, The Castro Obsession (Dulles, VA: Potomac Books, 2005), p. 130.
8. Tom Karamessines, CC testimony, April 14, 1976; Sam Halpern, interview by Ralph Weber, NARA 104-10324-10002.
9. Richard Helms, Rockefeller Commission testimony, 1975, NARA 157-10005-10376; Helms, CC testimonies, April 23 and June 13, 1975.
10. Helms, Rockefeller Commission and CC testimony, April 23, 1975.
11. Regarding the Puerto Rico station: Bill Sturbitts, Rockefeller Commission testimony, April 16, 1975, NARA 157-10011-10083.
12. Brian Latell and Michael Warner, interview with Sam Halpern, April 7, 1998, NARA 104-10324-10000; regarding Houston and Robert Kennedy: Walt Elder, CC testimony, August 13, 1975; regarding JMWAVE opening: Sturbitts, Rockefeller Commission testimony.
13. James Angleton, CC testimony, September 17, 1976.

14. James Angleton, CC testimony, September 19, 1976.

15. Sam Halpern, CC testimony, April 22, 1976.

16. David R. McLean, Excerpts History of WH Division, 1946-1965, NARA, 104-10301-10001; "Minutes of Special Group (Augmented) Meeting," July 12, 1962, NARA 157-10014-10082.

17. "Clandestine Services Cuban Collection Program," NARA 104-10310-10005.

18. McLean, Excerpts History of WH Division.

19. Helms, CC testimony, September 11, 1975; Evan Thomas, *Robert Kennedy: His Life* (New York: Simon & Schuster, 2000), pp. 119-120.

20. Bohning, *Castro Obsession*, pp. 84 and 130; Sturbitts, Rockefeller Commission testimony.

21. David Corn, *The Blond Ghost* (New York: Simon & Schuster, 1994), p. 16.

22. Shackley, *Spymaster*, p. 69.

23. Shackley, CC testimony.

24. "Participacion Directa de la CIA en Ataques a Cuba," *Bohemia*, November 8, 1963; Corn, *Blond Ghost*, p. 105.

25. FRUS, *Cuban Missile Crisis and Aftermath, 1961-63*, Vol. 11, p. 886.

26. Helms, CC testimony, September 11 and July 17, 1975.

27. Helms, CC testimony, July 18, 1975; interview with Samuel Halpern by Dr. Mary S. McAuliffe, January 15, 1988, p. 16, NARA 104-10324-10003.

28. Marshall Carter, CC testimony, September 19, 1975; Bohning, *Castro Obsession*, p. 153; Helms, Rockefeller Commission testimony.

29. Garry Wills, *The Kennedy Imprisonment: A Meditation on Power* (Boston, Little, Brown, 1981), pp. 211, 234.

30. Church Committee, June 13, 1975.

31. Ibid.

32. Jack Bell, JFKOH, April 19, 1966.

33. Helms, CC testimony, June 13 and July 17, 1975.

34. "Report on the Plots to Assassinate Fidel Castro," May 23, 1967, NARA 104-10213-10101.

35. Max Holland, *The Kennedy Assassination Tapes* (New York: Knopf, 2004), p. 419.

36. Tom Parrott, CC testimony, July 10, 1975.

37. McAuliffe interview with Sam Halpern.

38. Regarding Soviet troops: see *The President's Intelligence Checklist*, November 29, 1963, NARA 104-10302-10028.

39. Charles Bartlett, JFKOH, February 20, 1965. Regarding the poll: see *Washington Post*, November 28, 1963.

40. Laura Bergquist, JFKOH, December 8, 1965.

41. Thomas C. Mann, *Be There Yesterday: The Adventures of a Career Foreign Officer, 1942-1966*, unpublished memoir. I am grateful to Peter C. Maffitt for sharing his copy with me. Thomas C. Mann, JFKOH, March 13, 1968; Allan Stewart, JFKOH, October 23, 1967.

42. Helms, CC testimony, June 13, 1975; Special National Intelligence Estimate, "The Effects of Hurricane Flora on Cuba," November 15, 1963, FRUS Supplement 719.

43. The unredacted and most complete account of the meeting can be found in "Minutes of the Meeting to Review the Cuban Program," signed by Bruce Cheever, November 12, 1963, NARA 104-10306-10014. A shorter version is at FRUS, *Cuban Missile Crisis and Aftermath, 1961-63*, Vol. 11, p. 886.

44. Ibid.

45. Ibid.

46. Ibid.

47. 303 Committee Meetings (January-December 1963), NARA 104-10306-10024; "Minutes of the Meeting."
48. Shackley, *Spymaster*, pp. 74-75. Bohning, *Castro Obsession*, pp. 162-165.
49. Ibid.
50. CC testimony, Marshall Carter, September 19, 1975.
51. Ibid.
52. Sturbitts, Rockefeller Commission testimony.
53. Ibid.
54. Bohning, *Castro Obsession*, p. 192.
55. "Minutes of Meeting"; Shackley, *Spymaster*, p. 72; Castro speech, March 13, 1966, FBIS.
56. "Minutes of Meeting."
57. Shackley, *Spymaster*, p. 69; Clandestine Services Cuban Collection Program, NARA 104-10310-10005.
58. Wills, *Kennedy Imprisonment*, p. 255.

CHAPTER 6: TYRANNICIDE

1. Regarding passport: NARA 104-10186-10328.
2. CIA report, May 26 1965, NARA 104-10186-10046.
3. CIA debriefing report, May 26-27, 1965, NARA 104-10186-10046; 104-10183-10343.
4. "Biographic Data," NARA 104-10247-10399.
5. "Forwarding of Tapes," May 1, 1964, NARA 104-10183-10284.
6. Raymond G. Rocca, "Memorandum for Deputy Director for Plans," May 11, 1964, NARA 104-10400-10105.
7. Author phone interview and correspondence with Sally Swenson Cascio.
8. Cable to Headquarters, April 24, 1964, NARA 104-10183-10280.
9. Dispatch from Ottawa to Chief, Special Affairs Staff, May 1, 1964, NARA 104-10185-10319.
10. Hundreds of pages of Rodríguez Lahera's reporting are available at NARA 104-10185-10398 and 1994:04.26.09.06:29:280005. "Debriefing Report of Defector from Cuban Intelligence Service," undated, NARA 104-10247-10389 is a detailed account of his case.
11. Harold Swenson, CC testimony, May 10, 1976; "The Organization of the General Directorate of Intelligence," CIA, July 8, 1964, NARA 104-10185-10149.
12. "Report on Cuban Documentation and Procedures of the General Directorate of Intelligence," CIA, July 22, 1964, NARA 104-10185-10135; "Selection and Training of Cuban Intelligence Agents Abroad," CIA, October 12, 1964, NARA 104-10186-10109.
13. "Memorandum for Director of Security," June 22, 1964, NARA 104-10185-10297.
14. "Request for Cover for AMMUG 1," May 11, 1964, NARA 104-10183-10280.
15. Ibid.; regarding other cryptonyms: see NARA 104-10185-10290; 104-10054-10014.
16. NARA 104-10234-10322.
17. Memorandum for the Record, March 6, 1964, NARA 104-10102-10117.
18. Memorandum for the Record, October 18, 1976, NARA 104-10506-10022.
19. Ops cable from Santiago, June 18, 1964, NARA 104-10234-10322.
20. Contact report, June 5, 1964, NARA 104-10216-10175.
21. "AMMUG Operational Target Analysis and Non-Surfaceable Leads," June 19, 1964, NARA 104-10183-10276.
22. Ibid.
23. "Forwarding of Tapes," NARA 104-10183-10284.

24. AMMUG Operational Target Analysis.
25. NARA 104-10187-10354; 104-10187-10373; 104-10187-10365; and 104-10187-10113.
26. Ops cables from San Salvador, September 24, 1964, NARA 104-10187-10144 and September 26, 1964, NARA 104-10187-10365; memorandum, November 4, 1964, NARA 104-10187-10354.
27. Roque Dalton, *Poemas Clandestinas* (Willimantic, CT: Curbstone Press, 1984), p. 141.
28. Jorge Castañeda, *Utopia Unarmed* (New York: Knopf, 1993), p. 64.
29. Ibid., p. 352.
30. Ibid.
31. Juan Antonio Rodríguez Menier, *Inside the Cuban Interior Ministry* (Washington, DC: Jamestown Foundation, 1994), p. 52.
32. Castañeda, *Utopia Unarmed*, p. 356.
33. Javier Rojas, *Conversaciones con el Comandante Miguel Castellanos* (Santiago, Chile: Editorial Adelante, 1986), p. 29.
34. Robert Kagan, *A Twilight Struggle: American Power in Nicaragua, 1977-1990* (New York: Free Press, 1996), p. 160.
35. John Lee Anderson, *Che: A Revolutionary Life* (New York: Grove Press, 1997), p. 749.
36. Ibid.
37. Author interviews with Gustavo Villoldo and Félix Rodríguez; Gustavo Villoldo, *Che Guevara: The End of a Myth* (Miami: Rodes Printing, 1999), p. 84; Félix Rodríguez, *Shadow Warrior* (New York: Pocket Books, 1989), p. 70.
38. William Harvey, CC testimony, June 25, 1975. Harvey appears to have been right, but may have been unaware of assassination plots undertaken by Stalin against Yugoslav president Tito. They are described in Robert Service, *Stalin: A Biography* (Cambridge, MA: Belknap Press, 2005), p. 592.
39. Author interview with Rolando Martínez.
40. Rolando Bonachea and Nelson Valdes, *Revolutionary Struggle, 1947-1958, Selected Works of Fidel Castro* (Cambridge, MA: MIT Press, 1972), p. 283.
41. NARA 124-90135-10285 and 104-10073-10117.
42. Author's phone interview with Dariel Alarcón Ramírez.
43. Jorge Masetti, *In the Pirate's Den* (San Francisco: Encounter Books, 1993), pp. 66-67.
44. Ibid.
45. José Maragon, author interview.

CHAPTER 7: MOUTH OF THE LION

1. "Selection and Training of Cuban Intelligence Agents Abroad," October 12, 1964, NARA 104-10186-10109.
2. "Debriefing of AMMUG: The Oswald Case," May 8, 1964, NARA 104-10088-10174; "Debriefing of Cuban Source," May 5, 1964, NARA 104-10054-10418.
3. Thomas Karamessines, CC testimony, April 14, 1976; Memo for the Record, October 18, 1976, NARA 104-10506-10022.
4. "Review of Selected Items in the Lee Harvey Oswald File Regarding Allegations of the Castro Cuban Involvement in the John F. Kennedy Assassination," May 23, 1975, NARA 104-10103-10271.
5. "Debriefing of AMMUG: The Oswald Case," May 7, 1964, NARA 104-10054-10439.
6. Silvia Duran, HSCA testimony, June 6, 1978.
7. Alfredo Mirabal, HSCA testimony, September 18, 1978; Eusebio Azcue, HSCA testimony, September 18, 1978. Both can be found at http://jfkassassination.net/russ/wit.htm#a.

8. J. Edgar Hoover, Warren Commission testimony, May 14, 1964.
9. NARA 180-10117-10101.
10. Vincent Bugliosi, *Reclaiming History: The Assassination of President John F. Kennedy* (New York: Norton, 2007), p. 562; Nelson Delgado, Warren Commission testimony, April 14, 1964.
11. Jean Davison, *Oswald's Game* (New York: Norton, 1983), p. 96; Gus Russo and Stephen Molton, *Brothers in Arms: The Kennedys, the Castros, and the Politics of Murder* (New York: Bloomsbury, 2008), pp. 68-69.
12. Bugliosi, *Reclaiming History*, p. 938.
13. Ibid., p. 940.
14. Marina Oswald Porter, HSCA testimony, September 13-14, 1978.
15. Albert H. Newman, *The Assassination of John F. Kennedy: The Reasons Why* (New York: Clarkson Porter, 1970), p. 23.
16. Cited by Bugliosi, *Reclaiming History*, p. 937.
17. Patricia Johnson McMillan, *Marina and Lee* (New York: Harper & Row, 1977), p. 340; Warren Commission Document 82.
18. Marina Oswald Porter, HSCA testimony; *The Warren Commission Report, issued September 24, 1964* (New York: St. Martin's Press, n.d.), p. 301.
19. Raymond G. Rocca memorandum to Deputy Director for Plans, "AMMUG Information on Lee Harvey Oswald," May 11, 1964, NARA 104-10400-10105; Rocca, HSCA testimony, July 17, 1978).
20. Howard Willens, HSCA testimony, July 28, 1978).
21. "Proposed Questions on Oswald Case," May 1, 1964, NARA 104-10052-10065.
22. "Debriefing of AMMUG: The Oswald Case," May 8, 1964, NARA 104-10088-10174.
23. Ibid; "Debriefing of Cuban Source," May 5, 1964, NARA 104-10054-10418.
24. CIA Office of Current Intelligence, November 29, 1963, NARA 104-10302-10029.
25. *Daily Summary*, November 29, 1963, NARA 104-10302-10022.
26. Ibid. Memo for the Record, STEEL-1, NARA 104-10308-10197.
27. *Daily Summary*, November 25, 1963, NARA 104-10302-10021; *Central Intelligence Bulletin*, November 25, 1963, NARA 014-10302-10006. "Castro on Death of President Kennedy," FBIS, November 26, 1963.
28. "Havana's Response to the Death of President Kennedy and Comment on the New Administration," FBIS Radio Propaganda Report No 12, December 31, 1963; *Current Intelligence Weekly Summary*, November 29, 1963, NARA 104-10302-10005.
29. CIA Bulletin, November 25, 1963, NARA 014-10302-10006; George Lardner Jr., "Castro 'Frightened' After JFK Killing," *Washington Post*, August 20, 1997.
30. "Havana's Response to the Death of President Kennedy."
31. WAVE to DIR, November 27, 1963, NARA 104-10079-10310. "Cuban Government Activities in Mexico," November 1976, NARA 104-10308-10025.
32. Fidel Castro, "An Impressive Gesture," *Granma*, April 24, 2009.
33. "Castro on Death of President Kennedy," FBIS, November 26, 1963.
34. *Daily Summary*, November 29, 1963, NARA 104-10302-10022.
35. "Castro Talks to University Students," FBIS, November 29, 1963.
36. Ibid.
37. "Debriefing of Cuban Source," May 5, 1964, NARA 104-10054-10418.
38. NARA 1993.07.19.15:59:57:590280. HSCA Box 18, #506.
39. "Debriefing of AMMUG: The Oswald Case," May 8, 1964, NARA 104-10088-10174; Ray Rocca, HSCA testimony, July 17, 1978.
40. Mirabal, HSCA testimony.
41. NARA 104-10054-10021.
42. NARA 104-10183-10284.

43. John Barron, *Operation SOLO: The FBI's Man in the Kremlin* (Washington, DC: Regnery, 1996), p. 113.
44. Ibid., pp. 43-44.
45. Letter from Jack Childs to Gus Hall, John Barron Collection, Box 1, Folder 17, HA; regarding CIA and Roa: "Interim Working Draft," February 10, 1977, NARA 104-10103-10072.
46. Letter from Jack Childs to Gus Hall; Memo from Jack Childs, John Barron Collection, Box 2, Folder 18, HA.
47. John Barron Collection, Box 1, Folder 17 and Folder 1, HA
48. Ibid.
49. Letter from Childs to Hall.
50. Hoover letter to Rankin, June 17, 1964, John Barron Collection, Box 2, Folder 5, HA; Gerald Posner, *Case Closed* (New York: Doubleday, 1993), p. 103.
51. Letter from Childs to Hall.
52. "SAC New York to Director, FBI," June 12, 1964, NARA 124-10274-10338.
53. Ibid.
54. Davison, *Oswald's Game*, p. 211; re McCone- John Goshko, "Oswald Reportedly Told Cubans of Plan to Kill JFK," *Washington Post*, November 13, 1976.
55. Davison, pp. 213-14.
56. Castro interview, HSCA, April 3, 1978.
57. CIA report, "Cuban Activities in Mexico," NARA 104-10163-10332; re Mirabal, NARA 104-10187-10330.
58. "Cuban Government Activities in Mexico," November 1976, NARA 104-10308-10025.
59. Respuesta al Cuestionario del Comite Selecto sobre Asesinato de la Camara del Congreso de los Estados Unidos a Luisa Calderon, NARA 180-10105-10341.
60. Cuban Government Activities in Mexico.

CHAPTER 8: WHIPLASH

1. "Report on Plots to Assassinate Fidel Castro," (*CIA Inspector General Report*, May 23, 1967, NARA 104-10213-10101); "Rolando Cubela Secades, New Cuban Military Attache to Spain," April 29, 1959, NARA 104-10400-10200.
2. "Biographic Data: Cubela Secades, Lazaro Rolando," November 1963, NARA 104-10215-10216; "Handwriting Analysis-AMLASH-1," April 7, 1965, NARA 104-10216-10441; Nestor Sanchez, CC testimony, July 29, 1975; "Mr. Weatherby," CC testimony, August 11, 1975.
3. Hugh Thomas, *Cuba: The Pursuit of Freedom* (New York: Harper & Row, 1971), p. 890.
4. IGR.
5. Edward Gunn, Rockefeller Commission testimony, May 17, 1975; IGR.
6. Tad Szulc interview with Ramiro Valdes, CHC, July 5, 1985.
7. William Harvey, interview, CC staff, April 10, 1975.
8. Lawrence Houston, CC testimony, June 2, 1975; Félix Rodríguez, *Shadow Warrior* (New York: Pocket Books, 1989), pp. 69-72; Scott Breckinridge, CC testimony, June 2, 1975.
9. William Harvey, CC testimony, June 25, 1975; IGR.
10. Mary McAuliffe, interview with Sam Halpern, January 15, 1988, NARA 104-10324-10003.
11. William Harvey, CC testimony, July 11, 1975; Richard Helms, *A Look Over My Shoulder* (New York: Random House, 2003), p. 152.

12. Regarding Harvey alias: NARA 104-10319-10013; also Bayard Stockton, *Flawed Patriot: The Rise and Fall of CIA Legend Bill Harvey* (Washington, DC: Potomac Books, 2006).
13. "TO Director; FROM Paris," October 12, 1963, NARA 104-10215-10381.
14. IGR; Memo for the Record, March 27, 1961, NARA 104-10215-10122.
15. "Anti-Communist Leaders Driven into Hiding at University of Habana," American Embassy, Havana, May 24, 1960, NARA 104-10308-10155; CIA cable to JMWAVE, June 8, 1961, NARA 104-10216-10022.
16. "Mr. Weatherby," CC testimony, August 1, 1975.
17. IGR.
18. IGR; "Mr. Weatherby," CC testimony, August 1, 1975; "Summary of Contacts with AMWHIP-1 and AMLASH-1," September 1962, NARA 1994.04.26.11.24:25:530007.
19. "Mr. Weatherby," CC testimony; CIA cable, August 3, 1962, NARA 104-10215-10073.
20. NARA 104-10295-10001.
21. "Mr. Weatherby," CC testimony; NARA 104-10216-10034.
22. "Summary of S/W Training & Issuance of Materials," August 29, 1962, NARA 104-10295-10001; NARA 104-10215-10210.
23. "Mr. Weatherby," CC testimony; Helms, *Look Over My Shoulder*, p. 229; "Castro Interview on Return from Soviet Trip," FBIS, June 6, 1963.
24. CIA Dispatch, December 7, 1962, NARA 104-10309-10006.
25. "Mr. Weatherby," CC testimony.
26. Ibid.
27. Halpern, CC testimony, June 18, 1975.
28. Helms, CC testimony, April 23, 1975; Donovan Papers, Box 39, HA.
29. "Prospects for and Limitations of a Maximum Covert Action Program Against the Castro Communist Regime," April 17, 1963, FRUS, Cuba, vol. 11, Supplement 655.
30. "Situation and Prospects in Cuba," NIE, 85-63, June 14, 1963, FRUS, Cuba, vol. 11, p. 834.
31. "Interview with Sam Halpern by Brian Latell and Michael Warner," April 7, 1998, NARA 104-10324-1000; Harold Swenson, CC testimony, May 10, 1976.
32. Juanita Castro, *Fidel y Raul Mis Hermanos: La historia secreta* (Miami: Aguilar, 2009), pp. 275-276; regarding Ramón: HA; Georgie Anne Geyer Collection, Box 13, Folder 17, and suggestive reference in Juanita Castro.
33. "Dispatch: Operational/TYPIC/MHAPRON/AMCROAK: Views of Bernardo Milanes López," NARA 104-10309-10007. Regarding recruitment: NARA 104-10308-10020.
34. Ibid.
35. "Operations to Split the Castro Regime," February 10, 1977, NARA 104-10103-10072.
36. The three were conducted by Ralph Weber, October 1987, NARA 104-10324-10002; Brian Latell and Michael Warner, April 7, 1998, NARA 104-10324-10000; and Mary McAuliffe, January 15, 1998, NARA 104-10324-10003.
37. Memo for the Record, November 12, 1963, NARA 104-10306-10014. "Briefing of the Joint Chiefs of Staff," July 31, 1963, NARA 104-10307-10010.
38. "Fidel Castro's Growing Military Power," December 13, 1963, FRUS, Cuba, vol. 11, Supplement 728; Piero Gleijeses, *Conflicting Missions: Havana, Washington and Africa, 1959-1976* (University of North Carolina Press, 2002), pp. 41-44.
39. Gleijeses, *Conflicting Missions*, p. 44.
40. ONE Draft Memo, May 7, 1963, NARA 104-10307-10023.
41. "Memo for the Director, New Covert Policy and Program toward Cuba," April 19, 1963, FRUS, Cuba, vol. 11, Supplement 656.
42. Ibid.

43. Memo for the Director, "Cuba a Year Hence," April 22, 1963, FRUS, Cuba, vol. 11, Supplement 665.
44. Memorandum to the DCI from Desmond FitzGerald, March 19, 1963, FRUS, vol. 11, Supplement 634.
45. Ibid.; "Contingency Plan for Cuba," October 31, 1963, NARA 104-10307-10007.
46. "Advertencia a Los Mandos Militares," *Bohemia,* April 5, 1963.
47. Mary McAuliffe, interview with Sam Halpern.
48. Memorandum from the Secretary of the Army's Special Assistant, April 9, 1963, FRUS, Cuba, Vol. 11, p. 754.
49. Author interview with Nestor Sanchez.
50. Ops cable from Porto Alegre to Director, September 7, 1963, NARA 104-10309-10006.
51. Ibid.; regarding photo: Un Panel de Comandantes, *Bohemia,* May 10, 1963.
52. Ops cable from Porto Alegre.
53. Sanchez, Rockefeller Commission testimony, May 19, 1975, NARA 178-10002-10335.
54. Interview with Halpern by Brian Latell and Michael Warner.
55. Helms, *A Look Over My Shoulder,* p. 229.
56. Helms, CC testimony, June 13, 1975.

CHAPTER 9: THE BIG JOB

1. Author interview with Nestor Sanchez; Rolando Cubela, HSCA testimony; author interview with Cubela.
2. "Extracts: AMLASH Comments on 13 Cubans," NARA 104-10215-10328.
3. Ibid.
4. Fidel Castro interview, HSCA, April 3, 1978.
5. Charles Porter, "An Interview with Fidel Castro," *Northwest Review* (Fall 1963).
6. "Castro Assails Kennedy Tactics," *New York Times,* September 9, 1963.
7. The most complete rendition of the original wire service story I have been able to find appeared in the *Spokesman-Review,* Spokane, Washington.
8. "Review of Selected Items in the Lee Harvey Oswald File," May 12, 1975, NARA 104-10322-10001.
9. Sam Halpern, CC testimony, April 22, 1976.
10. CC testimonies; IGR.
11. Fidel Castro interview, HSCA, April 3, 1978.
12. "AMTURVY Operation," NARA 104-10506-10031.
13. Arkady N. Shevchenko, *Breaking with Moscow* (New York: Knopf, 1985), p. 124; *Granma,* April 11, 2009.
14. Jack Bell, JFKOH.
15. Brian Latell and Michael Warner, interview with Sam Halpern, NARA 104-10324-10000; Evan Thomas, *The Very Best Men* (New York: Simon & Schuster, 1995), p. 200.
16. "Briefing of the Joint Chiefs of Staff," July 31, 1963, NARA 104-10307-10010; "Briefing by Mr. Desmond FitzGerald on CIA Cuban Operations and Planning," September 25, 1963, NARA 202-10001-10028.
17. Ted Shackley, CC testimony, August 19, 1975.
18. Briefing by Desmond FitzGerald, September 25, 1963; FRUS, Cuba, vol. 11, p. 871; Shackley, CC testimony; Thomas, *Very Best Men,* pp. 324-325.
19. "The Situation and Prospects in Cuba," NIE 85-2-62, August 1, 1962, FRUS, Cuba, vol. 11 Supplement 288.
20. Briefing by FitzGerald.

21. Nestor Sanchez, CC testimony, July 29, 1975; Richard Helms, *A Look Over My Shoulder* (New York: Random House, 2003), p. 230.

22. Mary McAuliffe interview with Sam Halpern; Halpern, CC testimony, June 18, 1975; IGR

23. "A Contingency Plan for a Coup in Cuba," October 31, 1963, NARA 104-10307-10007.

24. "Possible Soviet Reactions to an Anti-Castro Coup," October 28, 1963, NARA 104-10307-10020.

25. "Status of AMTRUNK MHAPRON Recruiting Efforts," April 17, 1964, NARA 104-10216-10110.

26. "Chronology of Significant Documents in AMTRUNK File," NARA 104-10213-10262.

27. IGR; "AMTRUNK Operation," February 14, 1977, NARA 1993.08.13.13:59:45:430028.

28. "AMTRUNK Operation," April 25, 1977, NARA 104-10308-10186.

29. David Corn, *The Blond Ghost* (New York: Simon & Schuster, 1994), pp. 102-103; "Operations to Split the Regime," February 10, 1977, NARA 104-10103-10072.

30. Al Burt, "Defector Reveals Anti-Castro Conspiracy," *Miami Herald,* October 20, 1963; Corn, *Blond Ghost,* pp. 113-114.

31. IGR; author interview with Dave Laux.

32. Author interview with Sanchez.

33. CIA ops cable Paris to DIR, October 7, 1963, NARA 104-10215-10372.

34. Ops cable from Paris, NARA 104-10215-10381.

35. Evan Thomas, *Robert Kennedy: His Life* (New York: Simon & Schuster, 2000), p. 271; Helms, CC testimony, September 11, 1975; Sanchez, CC testimony.

36. Interview with Sam Halpern by Brian Latell and Michael Warner, April 7, 1998, NARA 104-10324-10000; Helms, CC testimony, June 13, 1975; "Senate Select Committee Request (Charles Ford)," September 4, 1975, NARA 104-10309-10014.

37. Helms, *Look Over My Shoulder,* p. 230; "Chronology of Significant Documents"; IGR.

38. Author interview with Cubela; Dean Rusk, JFKOH, March 30, 1970.

39. Ops cable from Paris, October 11, 1963, NARA 104-10215-10381.

40. Ibid.

41. Special National Intelligence Estimate, "The Effects of Hurricane Flora on Cuba," November 15, 1963, FRUS, Cuba, vol. 11, Supplement 719.

42. FBIS, October 9 and October 21, 1963. In a speech on January 21, 1964, at a Kremlin reception, Fidel said: "Over a thousand workers and peasants perished."

43. Castro speech, October 20, FBIS, October 23, 1963; Castro communiqué, October 12, 1963, FBIS October 14, 1963.

44. Castro speech.

45. Ibid.

46. "Participacion Directa de la CIA en Ataques a Cuba," *Bohemia,* November 8, 1963.

47. "Minutes of the Special Meeting of the Special Group," November 5, 1963, NARA 104-10306-10024.

48. Ibid.

49. Piero Gleijeses, *Conflicting Missions: Havana, Washington and Africa, 1959-1976* (Chapel Hill: University of North Carolina Press, 2002), p. 43.

50. Regarding El Salvador and the Dominican Republic: NARA 104-10247-10389; regarding Che: *Cuba Socialista* (September 1963), and *Bohemia,* September 20, 1963; regarding Argentina: Jon Lee Anderson, *Che Guevara: A Revolutionary Life* (New York: Grove Press, 1997), pp. 576-579.

51. "Report on Cuban Propaganda," No. 11, FBIS, November 21, 1963.

52. Helms, CC testimony, September 11, 1975; Helms, *Look Over My Shoulder,* p. 226; *Daily Summary,* December 9, 1963, NARA 104-10302-10019; *Daily Summary,*

November 29, 1963, NARA 104-10302-10022. Nonetheless, some authors—not unreasonably—have speculated that the cache was actually planted by the CIA. But evidence provided by Rodríguez Lahera and a report by the US Army General Counsel, indisputably confirm Cuban responsibility. See "Interim Report by US Military on Venezuelan Arms Cache," December 23, 1963, NARA 198-10004-10089 and "Debriefing of Defector from Cuban Intelligence," n.d., NARA 104-10247-10389.

53. Helms, *Look Over My Shoulder,* p. 227.
54. Herbert Matthews, interview with Fidel Castro, Butler Library, Columbia University.
55. Ibid.
56. Tad Szulc, interview with Ramiro Valdés, CHC.
57. Richard Mahoney, *Sons and Brothers* (New York: Arcade Publishing, 1999), p. 286.
58. "Subject: Tepedino, Carlos," September 22, 1965, NARA 104-10183-10410. I appreciate the help of archivist Mary Kay Schmidt at the National Archives, who helped me locate this document. Tepedino took a second CIA polygraph exam on January 5, 1966. Report dated January 19, 1966, NARA 104-10183-10271.
59. Church Committee, Book V—"The Investigation of the Assassination of President John F. Kennedy: Performance of the Intelligence Agencies," pp 78-79.

CHAPTER 10: GREAT MINDS

1. Ted Shackley, CC testimony, August 19, 1975; Harold Swenson, CC testimony, May 10, 1976.
2. Richard Helms, *A Look Over My Shoulder* (New York: Random House, 2003), p. 231.
3. "Contact Plan for Dainold Meeting with AMLASH," NARA 104-10215-10365.
4. Ibid.
5. Helms, *Look Over My Shoulder,* p. 231.
6. Author interview with David Laux; Evan Thomas, *The Very Best Men* (New York: Simon & Schuster, 1995), p. 302.
7. Author interview with Rolando Cubela; IGR.
8. Memo for the Record, November 13, 1963, NARA 104-10215-10364; Nestor Sanchez, CC testimony, July 29, 1975; IGR; Rolando Cubela, HSCA testimony, August 28, 1978.
9. IGR; Sanchez, CC testimony.
10. IGR; letter to Robert Blakey with attachment, NARA 104-10400-10090.
11. Interview with Sam Halpern by Dr. Mary McAuliffe, January 15, 1988, NARA 104-10324-10003; Scott Breckinridge, CC testimony, June 2, 1975; Thomas, *The Very Best Men,* pp. 333-334.
12. Joseph Burkholder Smith, *Portrait of a Cold Warrior* (New York: Ballantine Books, 1976), pp. 377-378; Thomas, p. 303.
13. "Entire AMLASH Group Insecure," June 23, 11965, NARA 104-10216-10403; "Victor Dominador Esponosa," June 12, 1965, NARA 157-10004-10240; Castro University Speech, FBIS, March 14, 1966.
14. Operational AMLASH/AMOT, July 29, 1969, NARA 104-10216-10027; "Operational lead/Cuba," May 20, 1980, NARA104-10216-10003.
15. IGR.
16. "Castro on US Subversion and Hurricane," FBIS, October 31, 1963.
17. Ibid; "Presento Fidel Las Pruebas de un Siniestro Complot de la CIA," *Bohemia,* November 8, 1963.
18. "Presento Fidel Las Pruebas ..."
19. Ibid.

20. "Participacion Directa de la CIA en Ataques a Cuba," *Bohemia,* November 8, 1963; Juan Antonio Rodríguez Menier, *Cuba Por Dentro* (Miami, Ediciones Universal, 1993).

21. "Fidel Castro's Growing Military Power," CIA, December 13, 1963, FRUS, Cuba, vol. 11, Supplement 728.

22. Ibid.; "Millon y Medio de Hombres al Servicio Militar Obligatorio: Texto Completo del Proyecto de Ley," *Bohemia,* November 15, 1963; WAVE 7356, NARA 104-10308-10017. *Daily Summary,* December 9, 1963, NARA 104-10302-10019.

23. "Fidel Castro's Growing Military Power."

24. Regarding Cubela's position in regime: Nestor Sanchez, CC testimony, July 29, 1975; "Mr. Weatherby," CC testimony, August 11, 1975.

25. "AMWHIP meeting," New York, NARA 104-10295-10154. IGR.

26. "Plans for AMLASH contact," November 19, 1963, NARA 104-10215-10360;

27. Ibid.; Sanchez, CC testimony.

28. Ibid.

29. Sam Halpern, CC testimony, June 18, 1975.

30. Contact Report, November 25, 1963, NARA 104-10215-10227; author interview with Nestor Sanchez.

31. Contact Report.

32. *Miami Herald,* November 19, 1963.

33. Ibid.; Statement of Fact, November 12, 1963, NARA 104-10307-10008.; McCone calendar, NARA 104-10306-1000; "Suggestions for Additional Administration Statements on Cuba," FRUS, Cuba, vol. 11, Supplement 723.

34. Sanchez, CC testimony; author interview with Rolando Cubela; Cubela HSCA interview, August 28, 1978.

35. Cubela HSCA interview.

36. IGR.

37. Ibid.

38. Jean Daniel, "When Castro Heard the News," *New Republic,* December 7, 1963; author interview with Jean Daniel.

39. Ibid.

40. Author interview with Aspillaga.

41. Tad Szulc, interview with Fidel Castro, January 28, 1984, CHC.

42. Jean Daniel, "Unofficial Envoy: An Historic Report from Two Capitals," *New Republic,* December 14, 1963.

43. Author interview with Jean Daniel.

44. James Reston, "Kennedy and His Critics on Cuba," *New York Times,* April 21, 1963; regarding White House Staff: author interview with Jean Daniel.

45. Box 40, Chrono, James Donovan papers, HA; H. Keith Melton and Robert Wallace, *Spycraft* (New York, Dutton, 2008), numerous citations; Gertrude Samuels, "How Metadiplomacy Works," *New York Times Magazine,* April 13, 1963.

46. Richard Helms memo to McGeorge Bundy, August 27, 1963, NARA 104-10310-10244; memo from Helms to McCone, June 5, 1963, FRUS, Cuba, vol. 11, Supplement 685

47. Daniel, "Unofficial Envoy"; John Nolan, "Notes of April, 1963 visit to Cuba and meetings with Castro."

48. Daniel, "Unofficial Envoy."

49. Author interview with Daniel.

50. Herbert Matthews papers, Box 27, Butler Library, Columbia University.

51. FRUS Cuba, vol. 11, p. 780.

52. "The Situation and Prospects in Cuba," NIE, June 14, 1963, FRUS vol. 11, Supplement 687.

53. Matthews interview with Fidel Castro.
54. Graham Greene, "Return to Cuba," *New Republic,* November 2, 1963.
55. Arthur Schlesinger letter to Tad Szulc, March 3, 1986, Szulc collection, CHC.
56. Castro's Fourth Anniversary Speech, FBIS, January 3, 1963.
57. Juan Antonio Rodríguez Menier, *Inside the Cuban Interior Ministry* (Washington, DC: Jamestown Foundation, 1994).
58. Robert Dallek, *An Unfinished Life* (Boston: Little, Brown, 2003), p. 664.
59. Ted Sorensen, *Counselor: A Life at the Edge of History* (New York: HarperCollins, 2008), p. 352; interview with Sam Halpern by Mary McAuliffe.
60. Inigo Thomas, "A Night in Havana," *George* (October 1999); Fidel Castro and Ignacio Ramonet, *Fidel Castro: My Life* (New York: Scribner, 2006), p. 591.
61. Daniel, "When Castro Heard the News."
62. Daniel, "Unofficial Envoy"; author interview with Daniel.

CHAPTER 11: CONSPIRACY OF SILENCE

1. Gus Russo and Stephen Molton, *Brothers in Arms: The Kennedys, the Castros, and the Politics of Murder* (New York: Bloomsbury USA, 2008), p. 457.
2. Fidel Castro and Ignacio Ramonet, *Fidel Castro: My Life* (New York: Scribner, 2006), p. 289; Fidel Castro, HSCA interview, April 3, 1978; regarding the essay: HSCA report on Lee Harvey Oswald's trip to Mexico City, NARA 180-10110-10484.
3. Castro, HSCA interview.
4. G. Robert Blakey and Richard N. Billings, *The Plot to Kill the President* (New York: Times Books, 1981), p. 148.
5. HSCA report on Oswald.
6. Ibid.; NARA 180-10117-10098.
7. Alexander Haig with Charles McCarry, *Inner Circles: How America Changed the World* (New York: Warner Books, 1992), pp. 115-116.
8. Max Holland, *The Kennedy Assassination Tapes* (New York: Knopf, 2004), p. 424-426.
9. Richard Helms, HSCA testimony, September 22, 1978; Richard Helms, Warren Commission testimony, May 14, 1964.
10. Maria Teresa Proenza, HSCA testimony, August 28, 1978, NARA 180-10115-10106; Juan Antonio Rodríguez Menier, *Inside the Cuban Interior Ministry* (Washington, DC: Jamestown Foundation, 1994), p. 42.
11. Re Calderon not a CIA asset—CIA letter to Robert Blakey, HSCA, February 15, 1979, NARA 104-10079-10040.
12. Albert H. Newman, *The Assassination of John F. Kennedy,* (New York, Clarkson N. Potter, 1970), p. 27.
13. Vincent Bugliosi, *Reclaiming History* (New York: Norton, 2007), p. 770.
14. Ibid., pp. 765 and 771.
15. *Warren Commission Report,* September 24, 1964 (reprinted, St. Martin's Press), p. 414.
16. Bugliosi, *Reclaiming History,* p. 783.
17. Ibid., p. 785.
18. Oswald Address Book, Warren Commission Exhibit 18, p. 47, NARA.
19. "Respuesta al Cuestionario del Comite Selecto sobre Asesinato de la Camara del Congreso de los Estados Unidos a Luisa Calderon," NARA 180-10105-10341; Cable from Mexico City, December 3, 1963, NARA 104-10213-10367.
20. Bugliosi, *Reclaiming History,* pp. 1282, 1294.
21. Memo for the Record, STEEL-1, NARA 104-10308-10197.

22. Jorge Masetti, *In the Pirate's Den* (San Francisco: Encounter Books, 2002), pp. 126-127, 109.

AFTERWORD

1. "Political Action Operation in Cuba, the Proenza Case," NARA 104-10145-10381. NARA 104-10276-10049, 104-10052-10096, 104-10079-10291, and 103-10074-10303.
2. Political Action Operation in Cuba.
3. Ibid.
4. CIA report, "The Following List of Personnel were Stationed in Mexico City," NARA 104-10307-10067; John Scelso, CC testimony, May 7, 1976; David R. McLean, Western Hemisphere Division, 1946-1965, NARA 104-19391-10001; "Request for Project Renewal," NARA 1104-10052-10208; Manuel Vega Perez, July 31, 1963, NARA 104-10276-10045; Cable Mexico City to Director, July 11, 1963, NARA 104-10276-10049.
5. Political Action Operation in Cuba.
6. Ibid.
7. Ibid; Teresa Proenza, "Homage to Diego Rivera," *Mainstream,* March 1958.
8. Maria Teresa Proenza, HSCA interview, NARA 180-10115-10106; Miguel Barroso, *Un asunto sensible* (New York: Random House Mondadori, 2010).
9. Vincent Bugliosi, *Reclaiming History* (New York: Norton, 2007), p. 1050; David A. Phillips, *The Night Watch* (New York: Athenaeum, 1977), p. 133.
10. Ted Shackley, *Spymaster: My Life in the CIA* (Dulles, VA: Potomac Books, 2005), p. 18.
11. Philip Agee, *Inside the Company* (New York: Penguin, 1975), p. 532.
12. S. D. Breckinridge Memo for the Record, September 20, 1978, NARA 104-10322-10138; General Escalante on Kennedy Assassination, FBIS, December 28, 1993; Bugliosi, *Reclaiming History,* pp. 1200-1201.
13. John Earl Haynes, Harvey Klehr, and Alexander Vasiliev, *Spies* (New Haven, CT: Yale University Press, 2009), p. 541.
14. Dom Bonafede, "Castro's Spy Network Reaches Deep in U.S.," *Miami Herald,* September 8, 1963.
15. Bill Gertz, *Enemies: How America's Foes Steal Our Vital Secrets—and How We Let it Happen* (New York: Crown Forum, 2006), p. 216; Scott W. Carmichael, *True Believer* (Annapolis, MD: Naval Institute Press, 2007), pp. 29, 157-158.
16. Juan Tamayo, "US Now has Zero Tolerance for Cuban Spies," *Miami Herald,* June 14, 2009.
17. Carmichael, *True Believer,* pp. 16-18.
18. Author interview with Miguel Mir.
19. Ibid.

INDEX